THE ART OF

PAINTING & DRAWING

WHSMITH

EXCLUSIVE · BOOKS ·

This edition produced 1992 exclusively for
W H Smith Ltd by Book Connections
Limited, 47 Norfolk Street, Cambridge
CB1 2LE.

Based on *Be Creative*.
© Fabbri Publishing Ltd
1990, 1991
All rights reserved.

A CIP catalogue record for this book is
available from the British Library.

Cover design and production in association
with Book Connections Limited, 47 Norfolk
Street, Cambridge CB1 2LE.

Printed and bound in Italy.

ISBN 0 906782 90 2.

CHRISTMAS 1992.
from Peter Ann,
Molly + James .

Thank you for such a lovely
book .

mum , Jean .

THE ART OF

PAINTING & DRAWING

CONTENTS

Section 2 – Drawing

INTRODUCTION

All of us have creative ability, but few of us find out how to make the most of it – many of us do not even realise that we have it. This book is your starting point in discovering your hidden talents and learning how to express yourself creatively. As you work your way through it you will be systematically building up your own store of knowledge and expertise. From the very first lesson you will have the satisfaction of producing your own works of art while you find out about the terms, techniques and materials you need.

The Art of Painting & Drawing is a project-based guide divided into two main sections, the first for painting and the second for drawing. You may start with either, but you would be wise to follow the order within the section you choose. The painting section starts with watercolour, and then progresses to oils. Section 2, drawing, is mainly concerned with pencil; it also includes colour pencils, conté crayon, pen and ink, pastels, oil pastels and pen and gouache. The book is arranged as a series of interconnected lessons, each complete in itself but referring to others.

As you follow each lesson you will be working on a project in which you will put into effect what you learn as you learn it. There is a main theme for each lesson; that is clearly explained with plenty of full-colour illustrations to make techniques and terms clear. Reference is made to paintings and drawings – some of them by well-known artists – that demonstrate the main theme of the lesson. Then the project is presented, along with clearly explained and fully illustrated step-by-step instructions for you to follow. As you go, plenty of practical advice is offered in the form of tips, and cross-referencing helps you to make full use of what you have already learned or points the way to aspects you will be studying later. As you work your way through the lessons, you will also learn something of the history of art; some historical background is given for many of the techniques.

You will find out about brush techniques by painting a sunset scene, about glazing by depicting a copper kettle, about round and elliptical shapes by drawing a tennis ball and shuttlecock. You will discover that there are some techniques that make painting and drawing much easier than you thought – learning how to use masking fluid is one example; as you do that you will be working on a flower painting. The strength of the approach is that you will never feel that you are a beginner, for you will have something to show for your efforts as soon as you start. Begin today on the route to artistic achievement, a route to lifelong enjoyment and satisfaction.

SECTION 1

Painting

STARTING WITH WATERCOLOUR

Watercolour is the ideal medium for any painter, whether beginner or highly skilled. In the watercolour painting, *left,* by Turner some deceptively simple techniques have been used to capture the moment of sunrise over Venice. The luminosity of the paint — and the skill of the artist — combine to produce the magical effect of a dawn sky. Yet if you examine the painting carefully, you will see that it consists mostly of colour washes and simple brush techniques, which we shall be teaching you in our first few painting lessons. It is not the techniques themselves, but the way they are used that produces a great painting.

Painting with watercolour is easy — and it's fun too! Even a beginner can produce something that's satisfying to look at in this breathtakingly beautiful medium. Whatever your style or personality, you can express it in watercolours — so get out your palette and start painting with us.

The landscape painting, *below,* which is our painting project for our first lesson, uses just basic washes with a few minimal brush strokes. Even though it is designed for the absolute beginner to paint, it nevertheless suggests the haunting quality of high, empty moorlands. After practising the techniques in this lesson you will find you can easily paint this landscape.

All you need to get started are a few paints, a brush, some paper and plenty of water.

Before you start on the lesson, try playing around with some watercolours — just splodging the colour on to the paper, dripping one colour into another and tilting the paper so that the colours run into each other. Even working in this unstructured way you will create some lovely effects.

To show you just how easy watercolour painting is we are going to start you off with a few simple exercises so that you can master the basic techniques. We also give you some essential guidance on choosing and stretching paper, and tips on buying and mixing paint, and caring for brushes.Then you will be ready to produce your first painting. And when you have followed our step-by-step instructions carefully you will find, because of the nature of watercolour, that you have produced a painting that you can treasure because it is uniquely your own.

STRETCHING PAPER

When paper is wet it stretches, but unfortunately it does not stretch equally in every direction. This means that the paper will wrinkle. Stretching the paper before you start work avoids this problem.

1 Cut four strips of gummed paper longer than the sides of the paper to be stretched.

2 Wet the paper with a sponge, or immerse it in water if it is small enough.

3 Using a clean cloth, or the side of your hand, and working from the centre, smooth the paper on to the board.

4 Dampen the gummed paper and use it to stick the four sides of the paper to the board.

Leave the paper to dry naturally. Don't worry if it looks wrinkled when wet — it will dry out flat.

PAPER AS SUPPORT

The surface on which you paint is known as the support. With watercolour, this is paper — which is fortunate as paper is cheap, easy to obtain, and light and convenient to carry around.

In watercolour, the support plays a vital part in the painting, affecting the way the surface holds the paint, the way the paint responds, and the ease with which the brush moves over the surface. So it contributes in several ways to the overall look of the final painting.

Watercolour is transparent. Painters familiar with other media sometimes find it difficult to come to terms with this quality. It means that the paper (if white) is always the lightest part of the painting. This is quite different from oil painting, in which the support is usually completely obliterated. In watercolour, a white flower will be the white of the paper — in an oil painting, it will be depicted with white paint. Because of the transparent nature of watercolour, you are always aware of the support. So the choice of paper is very important.

Paper is graded by weight, expressed as pounds per ream (480 or 500 sheets) or gram per square metre (gsm or gm). The weight of paper is important because the heavier the paper, the more readily it will accept water — light papers tend to distort and wrinkle. As a rough guide, a light paper is about 70 pounds (150gsm); a heavy paper 140 pounds (285gsm). The heaviest papers have a special quality that makes them pleasing to work with, but they are also the most expensive.

Right side, wrong side

Most paper has a right and wrong side. The right side has a more even surface and is often sized (sealed with a glue-type substance which gives it a tougher, less absorbent surface). The most expensive papers have the manufacturer's name embedded in the paper — you can read the name from the right side, whereas on the wrong side it will be back to front.

Sheets or pads

Watercolour paper is sold by the sheet or in pads. Pads come in a range of sizes and may be spiral bound or 'perfect bound' like a paperback book. Some pads are glued all the way round making stretching unnecessary.

TYPES OF PAPER

The surface of watercolour paper is an important element in the finished painting. Papers are grouped into three broad categories.

Rough This paper has a highly textured surface — 'tooth' — which is achieved by very light rolling in the manufacturing process. The recesses in the surface hold the paint, leaving the raised areas either uncovered or only lightly covered, and this gives the painted areas a lively sparkle. This brilliant, textured effect is ideal for certain subjects — light on water for example — and for a loose, expressionistic painting style, although it is not perhaps the best paper for beginners to use.

Hot Pressed (HP) This is the smoothest type of paper. The fine, untextured surface is achieved by running the paper through hot rollers which 'iron' it. It is suitable for small-scale work, and detailed paintings such as botanical illustrations. The smoothest HP papers don't hold washes well, so it is best to avoid them.

NOT or Cold-Pressed This paper is NOT hot pressed during manufacture. It is run through cold rollers which press the surface smooth. It is a good paper to start with as it has enough 'tooth', without having too much texture.

There are two qualities of watercolour paint. The best, and most expensive, is artists' colour. Students' colour is cheaper because the paints are made from cheaper pigments and synthetic equivalents. Artists' paints are made using the best pigments and they are intense and saturated with colour. This means that they are easier to use, go further, and last longer than students' colour.

Watercolour is supplied in tubes or pans (either full or half pans). The paint in tubes is softer than in pans, so tubes are ideal for making up large washes. However, pans are easier to handle and the colours are immediately accessible. Remember to replace caps on tubes and close boxes of pans to prevent the paints drying up.

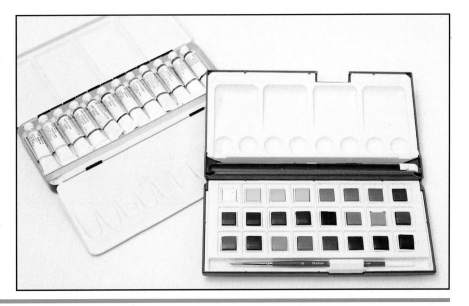

CARING FOR YOUR BRUSHES

Brushes are made from different materials — sable, blended hairs (ox, squirrel and sable) and synthetics. Sizes range from tiny 000s to 1in (25mm) wash brushes and they are also made in different shapes: rounds; flats which are chisel shaped; brights which are also flat but shorter; filberts which are flat but rounded at the end. You can also buy all kinds of exotic brushes — fans, domed flat wash brushes and big soft mop brushes.

Care of brushes
Your brushes are a vital and fairly costly part of your equipment. Follow a few important rules and they will last longer and be pleasant to work with.

1 Always clean your brushes after use by rinsing them carefully in clean water.

2 Dry them by shaking them with a flick of the wrist. This should bring them back into shape. If not, shape them with your fingers.

3 Store them, hair end up, in a pot. If you put them away in a box make sure they are perfectly dry first. If you are carrying them around, roll them in paper or material and bind the roll with an elastic band. The important thing is to protect the brush head.

4 *Never* leave brushes standing in water, resting on their hair.

Above, left to right
1 Winsor & Newton 'Artists' Sable - size 7
2 Rowney 'Kolinsky Sable' - size 9
3 Winsor & Newton 'School of Art' Sable - size 12
4 Daler 'Dalon' - size 5
5 Daler 'Dalon' - size 10
6 Daler 'Dalon' - size 16
7 Winsor & Newton 'Sceptre' - size 7
8 Winsor & Newton 'Sceptre' - size 12
9 Winsor & Newton 'Cotman' - size 12
10 Winsor & Newton 'Cotman' - size 16

MIXING PAINT

When painting with watercolours, you always mix the paint in a dish first. To begin with, use paint in pans. You will also need two jars of clean water, one for mixing paint, one for cleaning your brush, plus several mixing dishes.

Transfer some water to a shallow mixing dish by dipping your brush in the water jar, taking the brush to the dish and tapping it gently so the water is dropped. Repeat this two or three times. Now dip the brush in the water jar and tap it on the side of the jar to remove surplus water. Work the brush over the top of the pan — the paint will dissolve and be picked up by the brush. Transfer the paint-loaded brush to the dish and work the brush in the water so that the paint is transferred. Continue transferring paint to the dish until the mixture is as dark as you want it. Test the mixture on a scrap of paper. If it is too dark, add more water — too pale, add more paint. Simple!

A FLAT WASH

This is the basic technique of watercolour painting. It is quite simple, but good watercolour painting requires speed and a sure hand. To achieve these you need knowledge, patience and lots of practice. Make sure you have several sheets of paper ready to practise on — you can turn each sheet over and use the reverse side when the first side is dry. The object of this exercise is to lay the flattest, smoothest film of colour you can. It will probably be a bit uneven the first time, but you will soon get the knack.

YOU WILL NEED:
A large brush, say a size 10 or larger; a pan of paint (any colour will do, but a dark colour such as blue or green will show best); a jar of water; a sheet of stretched paper; a mixing dish.

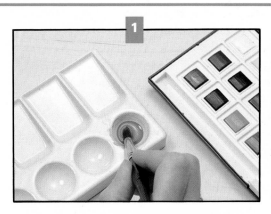

1 Mix a wash of colour. Make sure you have plenty, as you don't want to have to mix up more paint halfway through. If you do, the paint you have put on the paper will dry and you will get a hard edge in the middle of your wash.

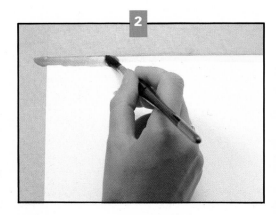

2 Load the brush with dilute paint from the dish. Hold the board so that it tilts towards you and, starting at the top of the paper, take the brush from one side to the other, drawing the paint on with a steady hand.

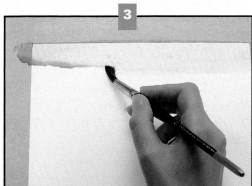

3 The paint will run down and collect at the bottom of the band of colour. Bring the brush back in the other direction, picking up the stream of paint from the strip above as you go. Repeat this, reloading the brush with paint as you go, until the paper is completely covered.

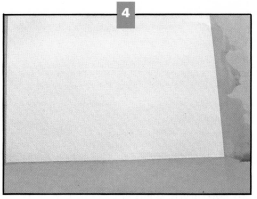

4 Leave the wash to dry naturally and examine the result carefully. Have another go — repeat until you are able to produce a flat, even film of colour each time.

WET-IN-WET

For this exercise you need to use two colour washes (yellow and blue) mixed in separate dishes. First wet the paper all over with clean water, using a brush or sponge. It should be damp, but not running with water. Now fill a brush with your yellow wash and put splodges of colour over the paper while it is still wet. Wash your brush and fill it with the blue colour

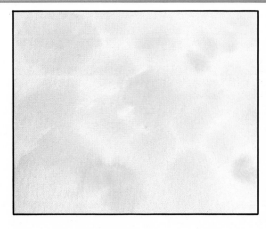

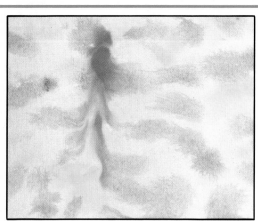

mix. While the paper and yellow paint are still wet, put dabs of blue in the white parts of the paper. Leave to dry. When

this is dry, you will find that the colours have merged together to give a hazy effect.

A MOORLAND SCENE

Now you know how to stretch paper, mix a wash and lay a wash, you are ready for your first painting project. This is a very simple moorland scene, *right*. The white of the paper is the whitest you can get — here we use it for the moorland track and the palest part of the sky. We use a pale blue wash for the sky and a series of green washes for the moors. We suggest you copy this project carefully, following the instructions as closely as possible.

1 First draw the outlines of the painting lightly in pencil as shown. If you wish you can enlarge the above drawing on a photocopier until you reach the desired size, then trace the outlines on to your watercolour paper.
Using a size 10 brush, cover the sky area with clean water so that it is damp all over.

M A T E R I A L S

size 10 and size 6 brushes
half pans of cobalt blue and sap green
2 pots of water
mixing dishes or palette
stretched watercolour paper
tissues or sponge
pencil and eraser

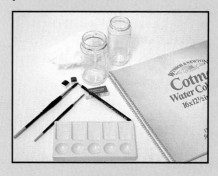

2 Mix up a pale wash of cobalt blue in a mixing dish. Lay a blue wash over the top of the sky area only, so that the colour gradually fades to white at the horizon.

3 While the wash is still wet, take a piece of tissue and blot unevenly over the blue area to create a cloud effect. Leave to dry.

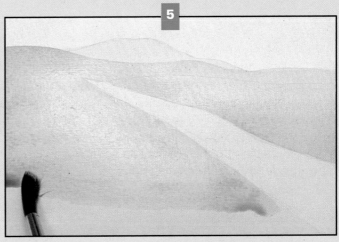

4 Clean your brush. Using the same brush, cover the area of the moorlands with clean water so that it is just damp. Leave the area of the track dry. Mix up a pale wash of sap green and lay a flat wash of green over the whole moorland area. Leave to dry.

5 Add a little more paint to your green wash to make it darker. Leaving the furthest mountain pale, lay the darker wash over the rest of the moorland area. Leave to dry. If you wish to hasten the drying process, you can use a hairdryer to speed things up.

Don't be surprised if your finished picture doesn't look exactly the same as ours. Your painting will be affected by the amount of water in your wash, the way you move your brush, the time you take, the temperature of the room and how quickly the paint dries. Try not to concentrate too much on the technique. Just get the feel of the brush, the paper and the paint, and don't worry about the finished picture. Even though it doesn't look like ours, it will look like a moorland landscape. And we know that you'll be pleased with it.

6 Add a little more paint to your green wash to make it darker still. Lay a wash of this darker colour over the part of the moorland behind the track. Leave to dry.

7 Using the smaller, size 6 brush and the dark green colour mix, lightly brush in the fence posts. Finally, with the brush almost dry, touch in the fine details of the railings and grass.

TONES AND WASHES

Many classic watercolour paintings are composed almost entirely of washes of different hues and tones. In this lesson we explain the difference between hue and tone, and demonstrate various techniques for creating tonal washes. We then show you how to apply these techniques in our step by step painting of a harvest scene, using only three colours.

On pages 3–8 you learned how to lay a flat wash, and also saw, in the moorland painting project, how overlaying washes creates darker tones. In this lesson we look at other ways of creating tones with washes, but first it is important to clarify exactly what we mean by tone.

Each one of the multitude of colours that we see around us everyday is composed of two elements — its hue (that is, whether it is red, blue, green or yellow, and so on) and its tone (that is, how dark or light the hue is). If we take grey as an example of a neutral hue, we find that when it is very dark it is almost black, and when very light it is almost white. Other colours have a similar tonal range.

When you are painting a naturalistic scene, getting the right tone of the colours you see is vital. If you need to lighten a dark colour to achieve a lighter tone, all you need to do is to add more water to the pigment. If you are using a light colour and want to darken it, you may need to add a dark colour to it. However, it is important to know what is the right colour to add, as using the wrong colour will change the hue. This is all part of the science of colour, which will be looked at in more detail in a later lesson.

Another way to darken tone is to overlay washes. On the next page you will find a variety of exercises for creating tones.

The 'Landscape with river and cattle', *above*, is by John Sell Cotman (1782-1842), one of the finest English watercolourists and a member of the Norwich school of landscape painting. The painting consists almost entirely of washes, and demonstrates how tones can be varied either by overlaying washes or by mixing colours.

Our 'Harvest Fields' painting project for this lesson, *left,* also shows in a much simpler way how to vary tones by overlaying washes and mixing colours. In this painting only three colours have been used.

TONES OF GREY

The tonal scale *below* shows seven tones of grey — but the tonal range could be much greater.

BUILDING TONE BY OVERLAYING WASHES

1

2

3

4

This exercise demonstrates how to darken the tone of a light colour by overlaying flat washes.

1 Mix up a pale wash of raw siena in a mixing dish. Draw a large rectangle on your sheet of paper and lay a flat wash over the whole area. Leave to dry.

2 Using the same colour wash, and starting a quarter of the way down, lay another wash over the first. Leave to dry.

3 Add a small amount of paint to the mix in the dish to darken the tone. Starting halfway down, lay another wash. Leave to dry.

4 Add a little more paint to the mix to darken the tone again. Lay a final band of colour and leave to dry. You now have four distinct tones.

CREATING TONE BY DILUTING PAINT

1

2

3

4

In this exercise we move from a dark tone to a light, and each band of paint is laid separately.

1 Mix up a thick, sticky wash of yellow ochre in a large mixing dish. Lay a thick, broad band of colour over the top quarter of your paper and leave to dry.

2 Dilute the paint mix with a few brushfuls of water. Lay another band of colour beneath the first and leave to dry.

3 Dilute the mix again and lay a third band of colour. Leave to dry.

4 Add more water to give a very pale wash. Lay a last pale band of colour.

LAYING A GRADED WASH ON DRY PAPER

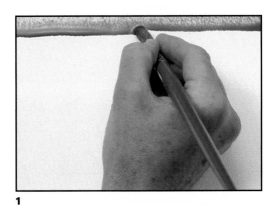

1

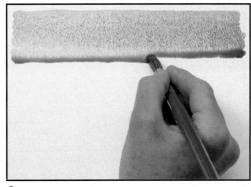

2

3

You need to work fairly quickly to achieve a good result in this exercise.
1 Mix up a dark wash of cobalt blue in a mixing dish. With a size 12 brush, lay several bands of this dark wash across the top of your paper.
2 Add 4 or 5 brushfuls of water to the mixing dish and lay several more bands of colour.
3 Dip the brush in clean water and continue to paint over the rest of the paper, gradually tapering off the colour.

GRADED WASH ON WET PAPER

1

2

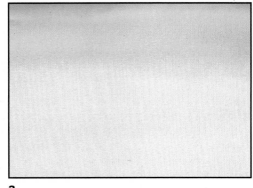

3

This is a slightly different technique.
1 Using a clean brush and clean water, wet the paper all over as if laying a wash. It should be damp but not sodden. Mix up a dark wash of sap green and lay a broad band of colour across the top third of the paper.
2 Dilute the mix by adding water, and continue laying the wash over the middle third of the paper.
3 Dilute the colour mix by adding more water, and carry on with the wash to the bottom of the paper. Leave to dry.

TONAL RANGE OF COLOURS

The tonal scales *below* in ultramarine and vermilion show a range of nine tones in these colours, and also demonstrate the delicacy and subtlety of watercolours, especially when used in light tones. When starting to paint, it is helpful to limit yourself to a restricted number of tones — say three, four or five. In this way you can train your eye to see in terms of tone — which is essential for any successful painting or drawing. Half close your eyes to see tonal values more clearly.

HARVEST FIELDS

Our step-by-step painting of harvest fields, *right*, is designed to use some of the tonal techniques you have just learned. The sky is painted with a graded wash and the rest with flat and overlaid washes. Although the painting shows a range of tones and hues, only three colours have been used.

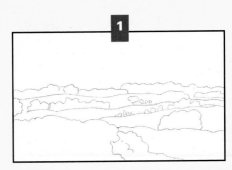

1 Draw up the outline of the painting lightly on stretched paper as shown, using a 2B pencil — our original painting was about 8 x 5in (21 x 13cm). You can either draw the outline freehand, or enlarge ours on a photocopier and trace it.

MATERIALS

watercolour paper
2 brushes, size 12 and size 6
student watercolours in cobalt blue, raw siena and burnt umber
saucer for mixing
water jar
tissues
2B pencil and eraser

2 Using a size 12 brush, mix up a wash of cobalt blue in a mixing dish. Starting at the top of your picture area, lay a graded wash for the sky. As you move down the paper, add more water to the brush so that the sky pales at the horizon. Leave to dry.

3 Mix a fairly pale wash of 2 parts cobalt blue and 1 part burnt umber. Using the size 6 brush, lay a flat wash of this colour mix over the most distant hills and the first line of trees. Leave to dry.

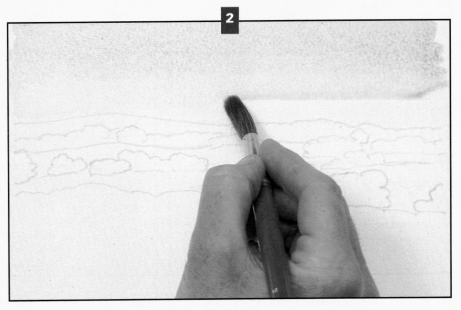

4 Using the same colour mix, overlay a wash on the distant line of trees (this will result in a darker tone). Leave to dry.

5 Mix up a pale wash of raw siena with just a touch of burnt umber. Use this to lay a flat wash over the whole of the harvest fields area (just paint right over the drawn clumps of trees, as shown). Leave to dry.

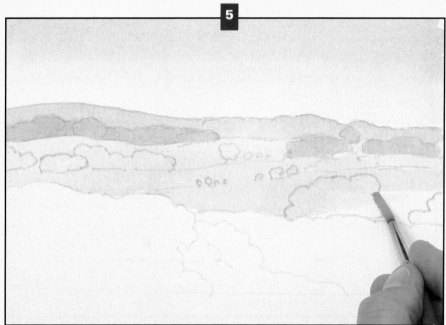

6 Mix up a richer, darker colour made up of burnt umber with a touch of raw siena. Lay a wash of this colour mix all over the foreground fields. Leave to dry.

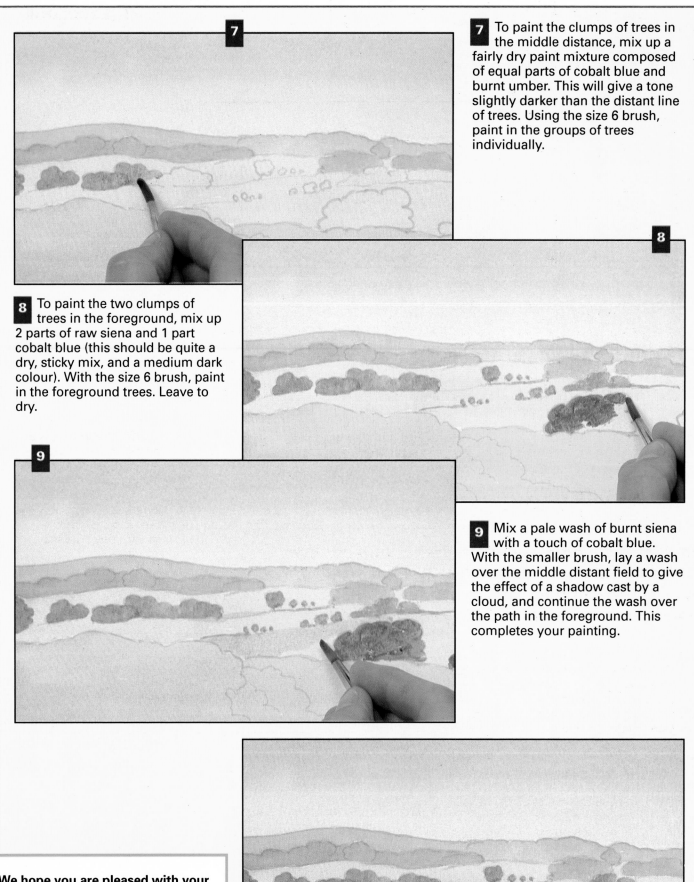

7 To paint the clumps of trees in the middle distance, mix up a fairly dry paint mixture composed of equal parts of cobalt blue and burnt umber. This will give a tone slightly darker than the distant line of trees. Using the size 6 brush, paint in the groups of trees individually.

8 To paint the two clumps of trees in the foreground, mix up 2 parts of raw siena and 1 part cobalt blue (this should be quite a dry, sticky mix, and a medium dark colour). With the size 6 brush, paint in the foreground trees. Leave to dry.

9 Mix a pale wash of burnt siena with a touch of cobalt blue. With the smaller brush, lay a wash over the middle distant field to give the effect of a shadow cast by a cloud, and continue the wash over the path in the foreground. This completes your painting.

We hope you are pleased with your finished painting. While painting it, you have laid a graded wash (step 2) to lighten tone, and overlaid a wash (step 4) to give a darker tone. You have also seen how mixing colours in different proportions varies hue and tone.

BRUSH TECHNIQUES

Now that you have some experience and confidence in laying flat and graded washes, we move on in this lesson to look at some of the many ways you can use the brush to express texture and describe detail.

Though many classic watercolour paintings are composed entirely of washes, the use of brush techniques offers the watercolourist a much wider range of expression and detail.

Brush marks can express texture, create mood and even reveal the feelings of the painter in some cases. On the following pages you will find a range of exercises to practise, demonstrating how the way the brush is held and moved over the paper can give rise to many different effects.

The secret of these brush techniques lies in the movement used. Some are made with a movement of the wrist, some from the elbow, and big, expansive brush strokes may be made by moving the whole arm from the shoulder. Some marks are made with a movement that glides over the paper, others by stabbing at the paper with the brush.

You can invent your own effects by experimenting with different types of brush, different strokes and different textures of paper. Keep all your efforts — you may need to refer to them in the future when you are looking for a particular effect for a particular painting.

A combination of washes and brush strokes gives this painting of the village of Dittisham in Devon, *left*, a fresh, lively quality. The exuberant brushwork of the painter, Paul Riley, seems to tell us something about the artist himself.

Also composed of washes and brush strokes, our project for this lesson, *below*, has a tranquil quality quite different from the painting above. The peaceful evening scene is created by quiet, muted colours and understated, meticulous brushwork.

ROUND BRUSH TECHNIQUES

It's good experience (and good fun too) to practise the brush techniques shown here. Use a round-ended, size 10 brush and Prussian blue for the techniques on this page.

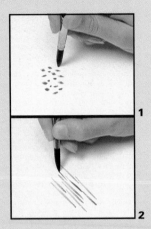

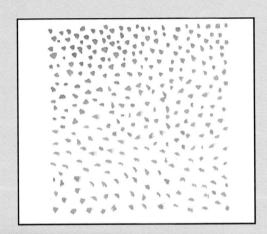

1 Hold the brush almost vertically and make small dabbing marks with the tip of the brush, moving the hand from the wrist.

2 Holding the brush vertically, make short, sweeping parallel lines with the end of the brush, moving the arm from the elbow.

3 Holding the brush at 45°, make broader, sweeping strokes, varying the direction of movement.

4 With the brush held at 45°, make thick, stabbing strokes, pushing the brush right down on to the paper.

5 Using slightly lighter stabbing dabs, make brush marks with 'tails' all over the paper.

6 Push the loaded brush head right down and rotate it (it's easier to do this using both hands). Repeat to make 'splodges'.

FLAT BRUSH TECHNIQUES

We used a size 9 flat-ended brush and Hooker's green for the techniques below. Take your time with these to get the feel of them, and keep all your work for future reference.

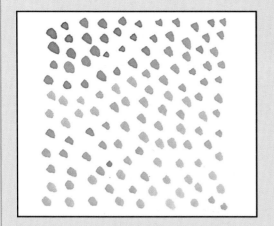

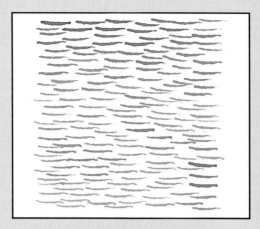

1 With the brush held at 45°, make small dots with the corner of the brush, moving the hand from the elbow.

2 Holding the brush vertically, make dabbing marks with the end of the brush, moving the hand from the wrist.

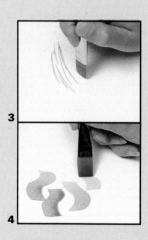

3 With the brush held vertically, make curved strokes, moving the hand from the elbow and varying the stroke direction.

4 Holding the brush at 45°, make a pattern of short, broad, wavy lines, keeping the wrist loose.

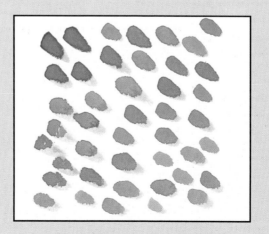

5 Holding the brush at 45°, make broad, short, straight strokes in a loose chequerboard pattern.

6 Using the side of the brush head and gentle pressure, make stabbing marks on the paper.

A SUNSET SCENE

M A T E R I A L S

watercolour tubes: yellow ochre,
sap green, burnt umber, cobalt blue,
Payne's gray and cadmium red
size 10 and 6 brushes
mixing palette
jars of water
watercolour paper
HB pencil
tissues

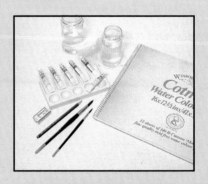

This tranquil sunset scene is achieved by a combination of soft, muted washes and some simple brush techniques. Take your time with this painting, and don't forget to let it dry thoroughly between steps when instructed.

1

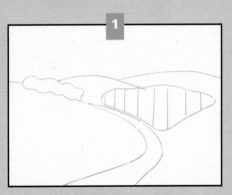

2

1 Lightly sketch the outline of the painting as shown, using an HB pencil.

2 Mix up a pale wash of cobalt blue. Also mix up a pale wash of cadmium red. Using a clean size 10 brush and clean water, dampen the sky area, leaving a few random patches dry. Fill the brush with the blue wash and brush colour unevenly over the top of the sky area. Leave to dry slightly.

3 While the paper is still slightly damp, fill the (clean) brush with cadmium red and lay colour unevenly over the lower part of the sky. The colours will blend together to resemble the evening sky. Leave to dry.

3

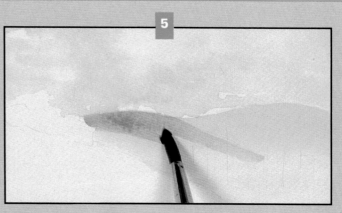

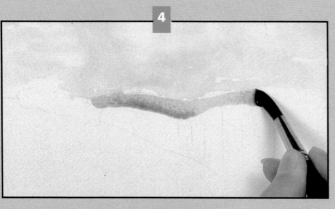

4 Mix up a pale wash of Payne's gray and add a touch of burnt umber. Also mix a watery wash of equal parts sap green and yellow ochre to have ready. Clean your brush and lay a flat wash of the Payne's gray wash over the far distant hills. Leave to dry.

5 Add a little more burnt umber to the Payne's gray to produce a darker hue, then lay this colour over the middle distant hills.

6 Before the grey wash has dried, lay the sap green and yellow ochre wash over the righthand and lefthand fields (the colours will merge where they join).

7 Mix Payne's gray with a touch of sap green to produce a dark grey-green colour and, before the fields are dry, lay a wash over the horizon of the lefthand fields to represent a clump of trees. This wash forms the shadows cast by the trees. Leave to dry.

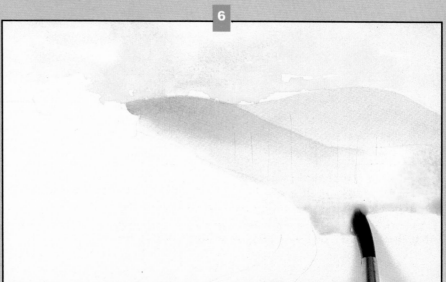

8 Using the size 6 brush, lay another Payne's gray and sap green wash over the shadow, and lay a wash of the same colour over the fields on the right to indicate the large copse.

9 Thicken up the grey-green wash with a little more Payne's gray, then brush in vertical lines for tree trunks using the size 6 brush. Dry the brush and brush from side to side over the trunks to give a branch effect. Leave to dry.

10 Add a little more Payne's gray to the wash and paint in the vertical tree trunks again, indicating a few more dry brush branches at the same time.

11 Add some Payne's gray to the cobalt blue wash, making it fairly pale, then use the size 6 brush to lay a wash over the stream area. Leave to dry slightly, then add touches of very pale cadmium red to the upper part of the stream to indicate reflections of the setting sun. Leave to dry.

12 Using the same wash as in step 7 (Payne's gray with a touch of green) and the size 6 brush, lay a narrow band of colour down the side of the stream to indicate the bank of the stream. Let it blend into the stream at the water's edge.

13 While the paint is still wet, use a clean, dry brush and flick the colour upwards to indicate reeds and grasses on the bank. Leave to dry.

To make sure that your painting has the same delicate touch as our sunset scene, use pale colours and an almost dry brush when adding the brush detail. Your final painting may not look exactly like ours, but it will be nonetheless pleasing.

STIPPLING AND SPATTERING

So far we have been applying paint only with a paintbrush. But exciting effects can be achieved by applying paint with items such as sponges and household brushes, or by flicking the paint over the paper. We show you a selection of these techniques and use some of them in our project.

Rough or rich textures, or interesting special effects, can all be achieved by applying paint with a variety of aids. If you 'print' on the colour by dabbing the paint on with a piece of natural sponge you achieve a coarse, mottled texture, and if you use a piece of synthetic sponge, which has much smaller holes, you will get a lighter, finer texture. You can use almost any household brush you can think of — toothbrush, nailbrush, or decorator's brush — to apply colour, and each will give a distinct texture. It's worth experimenting to try and invent your own textural effects.

Another technique that will give a lively quality to your painting is spattering. This involves loading a paintbrush with colour and flicking the brush with your finger over the paper. The paint will fall in a mass of irregular spots — over your painting and probably over you and the surrounding area as well. So you may find it advisable to wear an overall and mask the areas of painting you don't want to spatter with a tissue.

You can spatter over wet paper or dry — each will give a different effect. Or you can spatter paint over a wash of a different colour, or spatter many colours, giving an effect similar to the pointilliste technique.

It's a good idea to try out all these techniques on scrap paper first of all, so that you get the idea of how to control the paint without wasting expensive paper. Stippling and spattering are often used in landscape painting to suggest rough textures or foreground detail, and are an effective means of suggesting weathered stone buildings, or mountains, rocks, a pebbly beach, waves or dappled sunlight.

They are exciting techniques to use because the effect produced is always fairly unpredictable — and can never be exactly reproduced.

The painting of seas breaking over rocks (*top*) shows some of the exciting and sophisticated effects that can be achieved by stippling and spattering paint. Our painting project for this lesson (*inset*) is a slightly simplified version that uses stippling and spattering to create the rough texture of the rocks. Only three colours are used in this painting — the variety of contrast and texture comes from the skilful way the colours are mixed and applied.

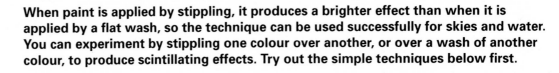

Below: Stippling with a one-inch decorator's brush, a hard nailbrush, a synthetic sponge and a natural sponge.

When paint is applied by stippling, it produces a brighter effect than when it is applied by a flat wash, so the technique can be used successfully for skies and water. You can experiment by stippling one colour over another, or over a wash of another colour, to produce scintillating effects. Try out the simple techniques below first.

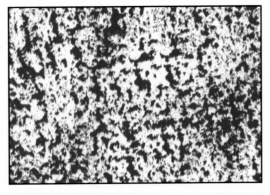

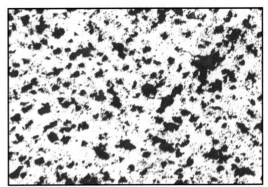

1 Mix ultramarine paint with a little water on a palette. Dip the tip of the decorator's brush in this and, holding it upright, dab it up and down on the paper.

2 Dip the tip of a hard nailbrush in water and dry off a little with a tissue. Work the tip of the brush into the paint and dab it over the paper, as in **1**.

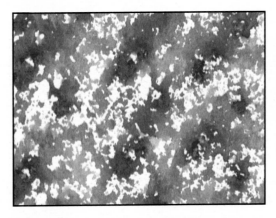

3 Dampen a piece of synthetic sponge with water. Dip it in a wash of ultramarine and dab the sponge up and down over the paper.

4 Slightly dampen a piece of natural sponge. Dip it in the paint and dab the sponge over the paper. This gives a more open textural effect.

SPATTERING ON WET AND DRY

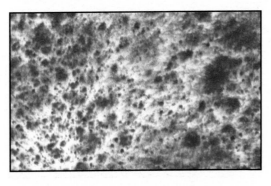

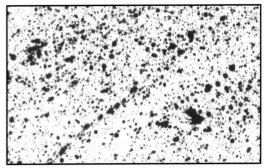

1 Dampen a piece of paper. Mix a thick wash of paint and, using a size 8 flat, hog-hair brush, flick the paint off the brush with your left index finger so that it spatters over the paper. The paint will spread as it dries.
2 Repeat the technique over dry paper. This produces a lighter effect.

A ROCKY TEXTURE

Our step-by-step painting project on the following pages uses a combination of stippling and spattering to build up the rough, complicated texture of rock surfaces. The exercise below is designed to give you some practice in the technique before you embark on the project itself.

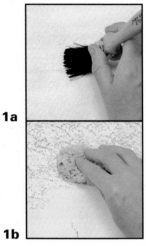

1a

1b

1 Using a thick wash of yellow ochre and the decorator's brush, lay colour all over the area, working from top to bottom, bottom to top, and then top to bottom again (**a**). Leave to dry. Dab all over with a natural sponge dipped in yellow ochre (**b**).

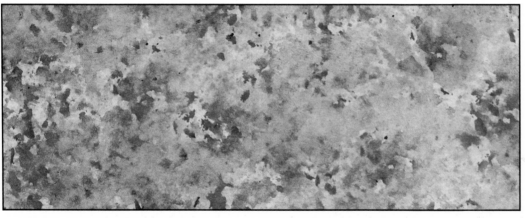

2

2 When the first stage is dry, dab all over with a sponge dipped in a thick wash of ultramarine. Leave to dry.

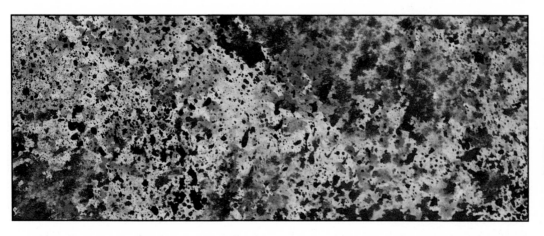

3

3 Mix up some Payne's grey to a thick, sticky wash consistency. Using a flat hog-hair brush, spatter the colour over the area by flicking the loaded brush against your left index finger.

A ROCKY SHORE

M A T E R I A L S

stretched watercolour paper
student colour tubes of ultramarine,
yellow ochre and Payne's grey
Dalon filbert-shaped brush size 8
filbert-shaped hog-hair brush size 8
small natural sponge
mixing dish or saucer
tissues
water jar
B pencil and eraser

This atmospheric painting of a rocky shore shows you how dramatic effects can be achieved with stippling and spattering techniques using only three colours. The variations of hue and tone are made by varying the density of the colours and mixing them in different proportions.

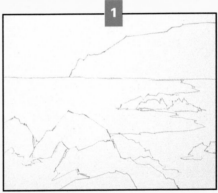

1 Draw up the outlines of the painting in pencil as shown.

2 Put separate dabs of ultramarine, yellow ochre and Payne's grey on a mixing dish. Using clean water and the Dalon brush, wet the sky area. Starting at the top of the sky area, apply the three colours separately, letting the colours run into each other, and paling off (use more water) towards the horizon. Leave to dry.

3 Mix ultramarine and yellow ochre together in the mixing dish so that they are not quite fully blended. Use this to outline the headland, then fill in using broad sweeps of the brush so that the different hues in the mix show.

4 Mix up a medium strength wash of ultramarine and yellow ochre with a touch of Payne's grey. Lay this over the sea area, starting at the horizon and leaving a white line of surf around the bottom of the headland. Let the colour run out (by adding more water and using an almost dry brush) towards the shore, so that the colour of the sea lightens. Leave to dry.

5 Mix a pale wash of yellow ochre and lay this on with the brush unevenly all over the beach and rocks area, leaving patches of sand and the highlights on the foreground rocks white. Leave to dry.

6 Mix a wash of Payne's grey and yellow ochre and use this to paint the contours of the foreground rocks.

7 While the wash is still wet, dip a sponge into a mix of equal parts of Payne's grey, ultramarine and yellow ochre and dab this over the foreground rocks to give a stippled effect. Leave to dry.

8 Mask the upper part of the painting with a piece of tissue, cut to fit round the foreground rocks. Spatter the three colours separately over the rocks, using the hog-hair brush. Don't worry if a little colour spatters on to the sea. You can clean it off carefully, using the cleaned brush just slightly damp. Leave to dry.

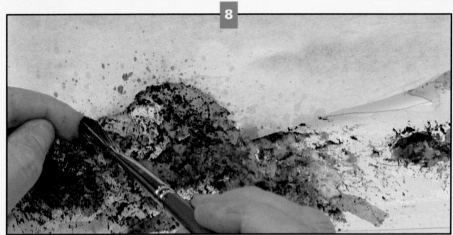

9 Using the Dalon brush and a mix of Payne's grey with a touch of yellow ochre, paint round the outlines of the rocks to give them definition. Leave to dry.

While you are painting this picture, just enjoy using the techniques and don't worry too much about the finished result. You are learning all the time how particular effects in watercolour are created.

USING MASKING FLUID

Masking is an exciting technique that enables you to paint sweeping background washes right over foreground details, yet subsequently paint in the details on white, unmarked paper. We introduce you to the technique and show you how to apply it to painting a colourful still life with flowers.

A flower painting, like the one shown *left* by Lillian Delevoryas, is typical of the kind of painting that can benefit from the masking technique. The flower shapes, vase and table can be masked out while the background colour is painted over the whole area. When dry, the masking material is stripped off, leaving white spaces where the rest of the composition can be painted in. This is exactly the technique that is used *above* in our still life project for this lesson.

I f you are painting a picture containing a mass of small, light objects set against a dark background, masking out the pale areas can save you the time and trouble of having to paint a background wash painstakingly around them. Instead, you paint straight over them — then remove the masking material revealing white paper where the pale objects will go.

A rubbery substance

One of the most popular ways of masking areas of the paper that you wish to keep white is by using masking fluid. This is a runny mixture of rubber latex and ammonia which is sold in small bottles by artist's suppliers. It can be diluted with water, and is either white or pale yellow, which makes it easier to see on white paper. When it is applied to paper it dries quickly, forming a rubbery substance. You can then paint over it, and when the paint is completely dry, the masking fluid and covering paint can be rubbed off with the fingers revealing white, unmarked paper underneath. This technique is demonstrated overleaf.

Masking fluid is usually supplied in 75ml bottles and can be applied either with a paintbrush or a pen (**1**). Masking fluid dries very quickly, and if you allow it to dry on your brush the brush will probably be ruined.

To protect your brush, pour a little liquid soap into a small container. Dip your brush into the liquid soap, then wipe the tip of the brush with a tissue. Dip the brush into the bottle of masking fluid (shake it well first) and paint the fluid on to your painting as required. The liquid soap left on the brush will stop masking fluid collecting and drying around the ferrule.

You can continue to paint with the masking fluid for about 60 seconds. Then dip your brush in a large jar of clean water and agitate it vigorously to clean it. Dry it with a tissue and bring the brush to a point. Then dip in the liquid soap again, and continue as before.

You can practise using masking fluid by drawing a simple flower shape on a piece of watercolour paper (**2**). Paint the shape with masking fluid as described above and leave to dry (**3**). The fluid dries in about 5 to 10 minutes, but you can use a hairdryer to speed this up. When dry, touch it lightly with your fingers. It will feel tacky and rubbery even when fully dry.

Now paint all over the paper with a coloured wash (**4**). Just paint straight over the masked area as if it were plain paper. Leave to dry.

Now, using two or three (clean) fingers, rub off the masking fluid. The covering paint will come away with it, leaving a white area in the shape masked out (**5**).

This can now be painted with the flower colour (**6**).

1
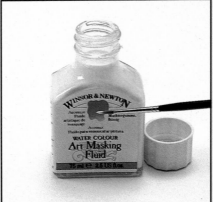

2

3

4

5

6

HELPFUL HINT

• The results will be unsatisfactory if you simply blob the masking fluid on to the paper and hope for the best. Apply it as if you were drawing with it. Shape your marks as you go, or follow light pencil lines. You can continue using the fluid to enlarge treated areas even after the first application has dried. And you can always rub dry fluid off and start again if you make a mistake.

• Interesting results can be achieved using a brush and pen in conjunction.

• Manufacturers recommend that you do not leave masking fluid on the paper for more than a day or so. Preferably remove it as soon as the paint is dry.

• Avoid using soft, absorbent or blotting papers as they will come away with the dry fluid when you rub it off. If you are unsure, test the paper first.

STILL LIFE WITH FLOWERS

To the inexperienced artist it might appear that the flower painting *right* involves an enormous amount of meticulous work painting in the background behind the bouquet of flowers. But the skilled use of masking fluid makes this unnecessary.

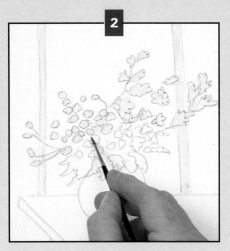

1 Draw up the outlines of the flowers and vase using a 3B pencil. Also outline some of the leaves and draw the outlines of the window and table.

2 Using a size 1 brush, put masking fluid all over the flowers, the window frame and the vase. Follow the procedure described on page 28 to protect your brush from the masking fluid. Leave to dry. This will take about 5 to 10 minutes (but you can use a hairdryer to hurry things along).

MATERIALS

NOT acid-free watercolour paper
3B pencil
eraser
3 brushes, size 1, 6 and 11
bottle of masking fluid
liquid soap
tissues
water and water jar
palette
student watercolours in cobalt blue, viridian, yellow ochre, cadmium red, cadmium yellow, alizarin crimson, burnt umber and raw umber

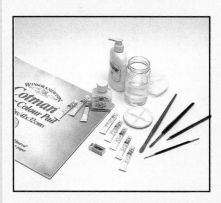

3 Now you are ready to put a wash of colour all over the lefthand window area. Mix up quite a strong wash of cobalt blue and, using a size 11 brush, paint broad strokes of colour down the page from the top of the window to the bottom, painting right over the masked bits. Don't try to lay an even wash — uneven brush strokes give texture to the painting.

4 Dilute the wash and mix in a little viridian. With the size 11 brush, apply this colour to the righthand part of the window by starting at the bottom and taking the colour upwards in broad sweeps. Don't try to cover the area completely — streaks of white will give sparkle to the window.

5 For the wall area on the left, mix alizarin crimson with cobalt blue to give a soft mauve colour. Apply this with the large brush in broad sweeps down the page, blending in a touch of yellow ochre towards the bottom. Leave to dry.

6 For the table, use a fairly dry mix of yellow ochre and burnt umber. To show the texture of the wood, paint on this colour in broad horizontal strokes, taking it straight across the table and vase in unbroken lines. Mix in a little more yellow ochre as you go, and leave streaks of white to give shine. Paint in the shadow with burnt umber.

7 Using the smaller size 6 brush and raw umber, paint the edge of the table with a single brush-stroke (you can turn the page to make this easier). Don't worry if there are patches of white at the table edge — they will give sparkle. Using a mix of cobalt blue and burnt umber, paint in the table leg. Leave to dry.

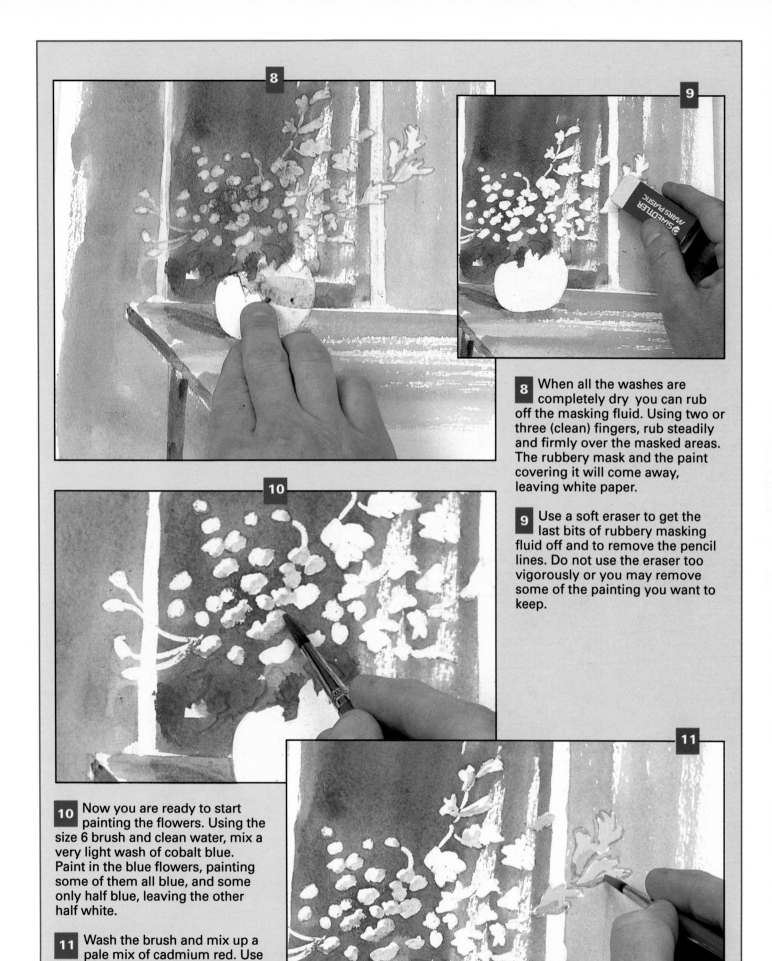

8 When all the washes are completely dry you can rub off the masking fluid. Using two or three (clean) fingers, rub steadily and firmly over the masked areas. The rubbery mask and the paint covering it will come away, leaving white paper.

9 Use a soft eraser to get the last bits of rubbery masking fluid off and to remove the pencil lines. Do not use the eraser too vigorously or you may remove some of the painting you want to keep.

10 Now you are ready to start painting the flowers. Using the size 6 brush and clean water, mix a very light wash of cobalt blue. Paint in the blue flowers, painting some of them all blue, and some only half blue, leaving the other half white.

11 Wash the brush and mix up a pale mix of cadmium red. Use this to paint in the red flowers. Paint a slightly darker wash at the base of each flower to indicate shadows.

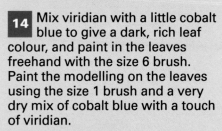

12 Mix up cadmium yellow, and paint in the yellow flowers and the centres of the daisies. Indicate the petals of the daisies with flicks of light cobalt blue, applied with the size 1 brush.

13 To model the light and shade on the vase, first go over the vase with clean water so that it is just damp. Mix up alizarin crimson with a little cobalt blue and paint in the shaded part of the vase with this colour using the size 6 brush. Dilute the wash until it is very pale, and use this to paint the rest of the vase.

14 Mix viridian with a little cobalt blue to give a dark, rich leaf colour, and paint in the leaves freehand with the size 6 brush. Paint the modelling on the leaves using the size 1 brush and a very dry mix of cobalt blue with a touch of viridian.

15 To complete your painting, use a light mix of yellow ochre with a touch of viridian to paint in the flower stems.

Now that you have finished your still life with flowers, you will understand the advantages of using masking fluid. Your painting looks as if you painstakingly filled in the background around all the blooms — but in fact you simply painted straight over them.

WET-IN-WET

Watercolour is a marvellous medium for portraying mist and mystery by painting wet-in-wet. We introduce you to the intricacies of wet-in-wet, and show you how to paint a luminous scene of Westminster at dusk.

We touched on painting wet-in-wet on pages 3–8. In this lesson we are going to look at the technique in greater depth. The essence of painting wet-in-wet is that the paper is wetted before the colour is applied. When several colours are applied adjacent to each other on wet paper, the colours will blend and merge to create misty effects.

The final effect produced by this technique is fairly unpredictable, and it is only by constant practice that you will learn how to get good results. The outcome is affected by how much water is put on the paper first, and by how thick or thin the colour washes are. You will also find that watercolours always dry out paler than they looked when wet — here again, experience will help you judge how dark your colours should be.

You will find as you use the wet-in-wet technique that it demands you work quickly and think on your feet. The essence of a successful painting done like this is a feeling of freshness and spontaneity. Because it produces blurred outlines, the technique lends itself to scenes of rain or mist, or the haze characteristic of dawn and dusk.

Practice run

Our painting project in this lesson uses the wet-in-wet technique for a dusk scene, and in order to give you plenty of practice before you start, we have based our exercises on the following pages on the colours you will be using in the project. The exercises show you a range of possibilities, including how not to do it. There are often valuable lessons to be learned from doing something the wrong way first!

J.M.W. Turner's painting of Windsor Castle, *top*, demonstrates the marvellously evocative effects to be achieved in watercolour by using the wet-in-wet technique. Buildings in the misty distance, and sunlight, are wonderful subjects for this technique — and we tackle both of them in our painting project, *above*.

On these two pages we are giving you a range of exercises to do to get you accustomed to the wet-in-wet technique. We are using some of the colours used in the step-by-step painting project to give you a pre-run with them before you do the painting.

The first set of exercises is designed to help you paint the setting sunlight in the project. By carrying out these exercises you will see how the colours behave on wetted paper, and how far you can control the process with your brush. You will also discover some of the pitfalls before you start on your project painting.

The trial areas to be painted are all about 10cm square, so you can get several on one sheet of paper. You will need a size 7 brush, watercolour paper, a palette, some kitchen tissue and the colours used in the project.

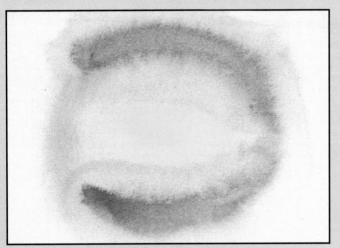

1 Wet the paper lightly all over, dabbing the water on with a piece of kitchen tissue. Mix up light washes of cadmium yellow, vermilion and cobalt blue. Using a swirling motion of the brush, lay a circle of cadmium yellow in the centre of the area, and touch in a little vermilion around it. Then surround the whole area with cobalt blue blending the colours where they meet with the brush.

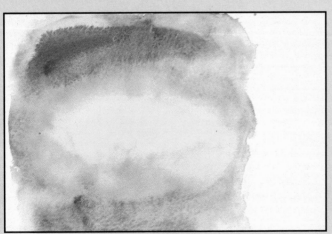

2 Now use a darker mix of colours on wetter paper. Dip the clean brush in clean water and cover the whole surface of the paper with water so that it is quite wet. Lay on the colours as before and observe the effect. You will see that the colours are much less controllable, and may be so wet that 'tide marks' form, as they have here.

3 Now wet the paper as you did in **2**, and use a light colour mix as in **1**. This produces a pale, misty effect where the colours have blended together almost imperceptibly where they meet. This is the effect to aim for in the project.

4 For this trial we are going to use very wet paper and a very dark colour mix. Cover the paper with plenty of clean water, and then swirl on very dark mixes of cadmium yellow, vermilion and cobalt blue. The result will be interesting! You will find that the colours 'run wild' and are almost impossible to control.

In the second set of trial exercises we are going to re-wet the paper and paint in a tower shape. Many people are surprised by the idea of putting water over dried watercolour paints, but if this is done correctly you will not disturb the underlying paint. Make sure your first set of exercises are quite dry before embarking on the exercises on this page.

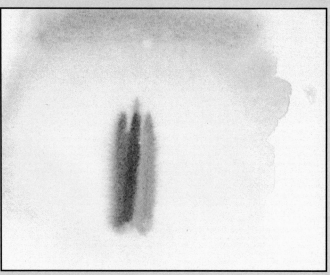

7

5

5 Using your painting from **1**, lay water lightly over the central area, using a wetted tissue as in **1**. Take care to dab lightly — if you scrub or rub at the painting you may disturb the paint. Mix a light wash of cobalt blue, burnt umber and alizarin crimson and, using the brush fairly dry, paint in a tower shape with quick, light brush strokes on the wetted background.

7 Using the painting from **3**, go over the central area with a brush dipped in clean water so that it is moderately but not over-wet. Using a medium mixture of the building colours, paint in the tower shape with light strokes. You will find you have greater control than in the previous trial.

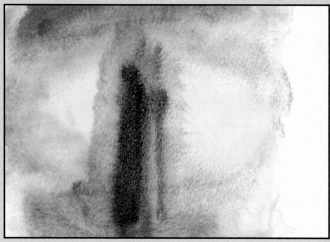

8

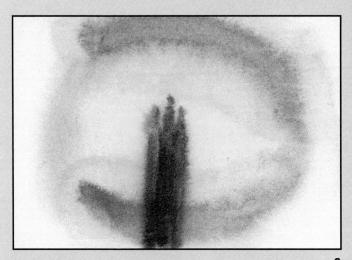

6

6 Using painting **2**, cover the central area with clean water, using a brush, so that it is quite wet. Mix up a thick mix of the colours used in **5**, and paint in the tower shape. You will find that the brush strokes run together more than they did in **5**.

8 Using painting **4**, over-wet the paper and use a very dark, thick mix to paint the tower. You will find the paint is fairly uncontrollable and the tower colour will run and spread into the surrounding area.

You can repeat these exercises a number of times until you feel confident that you know from experience just how wet the paper should be — and how thick the colour mix — to achieve the effects you want. But remember that watercolour is essentially an unpredictable medium, and that is part of its charm.

WESTMINSTER AT DUSK

Our step-by-step painting project this lesson uses the wet-in-wet technique to portray the Houses of Parliament at dusk. The essence of this technique is spontaneity, so you will find you need to think quickly and improvise as you go along.

M A T E R I A L S

Winsor & Newton artist's watercolour NOT paper, 140lb/300gsm
pencil
masking fluid
liquid soap
brushes size 1, 7 and 12
tissues
palette, water jar and water
watercolour tubes: cobalt blue, vermilion, cadmium yellow, alizarin crimson, burnt umber

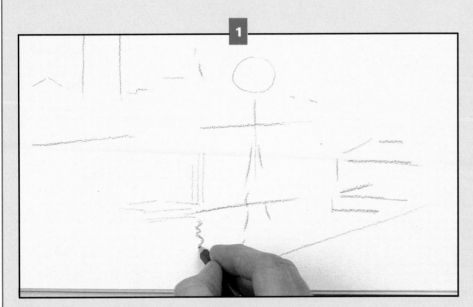

1 Draw a few guidelines in pencil on your paper to indicate the position of the main forms, such as the tower, the globe of the street lamp and the jetty and pier.

2 In the finished painting the globe of the street lamp will be the lightest, and brightest, object. To preserve it while you do the rest of the painting, paint over the globe with masking fluid using a size 1 brush. (See page 28 for how to use masking fluid.)

3 To paint the sky and the water, mix up separate washes of cadmium yellow and cobalt blue so that they are ready to hand. Wet the paper all over with clean water, using the size 12 brush (if you tilt the paper so that the water catches the light, you will be able to see any dry spots). Working quickly, lay a free wash (moving the brush in any direction) of cadmium yellow over the yellow sky area and its reflection in the river.

4 While the paper is still wet, lay cobalt blue around the yellow in the sky area, blending it in with the yellow. Add a little alizarin crimson to the blue wash on the palette to darken it and paint this over the river round the reflection.

5 Working quickly while the paper is still wet, paint the clouds on the lefthand side of the sky with a darker mix of cobalt blue, taking the colour over the yellow.

6 Continuing with the darker blue, paint the reflections of the clouds in the river, again taking the colour over the reflected yellow light.
Leave until thoroughly dry.

7 To paint the Houses of Parliament, prepare a mix of cobalt blue and alizarin crimson in equal proportions. In order to give the buildings a misty outline, the central part of the painting is wetted again, using clean water and a size 12 brush. Paint in the buildings freehand, adding more blue to the mix as the buildings fade into the distance. Use a darker mix to touch in the darker side of the tower, its reflection in the water, and other details.

8 For the foreground objects, use a thick, sticky mix of cobalt blue, burnt umber and a little alizarin crimson. With a size 7 brush, paint in the landing stage, jetty and near bank.

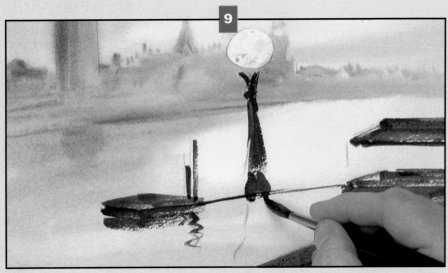

9 Make the mix even darker by adding a little more alizarin crimson. Using the size 1 brush, paint in the lamp standard. Leave to dry.

10 Rub off the masking fluid from the globe of the lamp. Using the same dark mix as before, and the size 1 brush, paint in the final foreground details of the metal railings and the reflections in the water.

11 Using a mix of cadmium yellow, vermilion and a touch of burnt umber, paint in the metalwork round the globe with the size 1 brush.

In this project you have combined techniques learned in earlier lessons with wet-in-wet to paint an atmospheric evening scene, with the street lamp casting a luminous glow over the river and the misty, distant outlines of the Houses of Parliament.

REFLECTIONS IN WATER

Water is always a fascinating subject to paint, but it's not always easy to make reflections in water look convincing. We explain how reflections work, and give you a range of exercises that demonstrate the various degrees of distortion that movement in the water causes.

W e have already painted reflections in water in our project for the previous lesson (Westminster at dusk), but it is useful to look at exactly what happens when an image is reflected in still or moving water.

The first thing to remember is that reflections always appear directly under the object they relate to, and go straight down into the water (this is quite different from the way shadows behave). If the water is completely still, you will see an almost perfect inverted mirror image of the scene above. Slight movement will distort the image slightly, and the greater the degree of movement in the water, the greater the distortion and dislocation of the image. In very choppy water the image may disappear altogether.

When reflections are broken up by movement in the water, this has the effect of elongating the image. In very ruffled water the reflected image of trees and tall buildings may appear to be several times the length of the actual objects.

On the dark side
Another thing to note when you are painting is that the reflection will often appear slightly darker than its related object. This is particularly so if the water is muddy or full of algae. However, there are exceptions to this — if the water is particularly clear and the day very bright the reflection may be the same colour or even lighter. As with so much in painting there is nothing to beat personal observation — make a point of going out to look at reflections and note for yourself how dark or light they are.

Above: This watercolour painting of a 'Landscape with bridge over a stream' by John Clayton Adams (1840-1906) successfully captures the freshness of the scene and the feeling of movement in the stream. Not surprisingly, watercolour is far and away the best medium for painting water — its transparent nature matches that of water itself. But water in the landscape is rarely completely still, and this means that the reflections in it are constantly on the move — which makes them difficult to paint. One way of coping with this is to take a photograph of the scene, which will show you the reflected images frozen at one instant in time. Our painting project for this lesson, *top*, and the exercises overleaf are designed to give you practice and develop your confidence in painting reflections in water.

To help you to paint reflections in water we have devised a series of exercises showing how the reflection of a post set in a lake changes according to the degree of movement of the water. Even though these exercises appear very simple, they will give you confidence when tackling reflections in your own paintings.

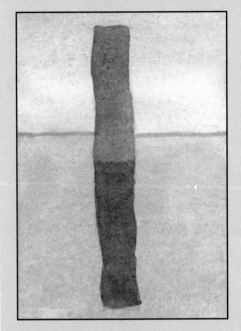

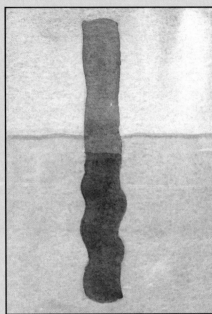

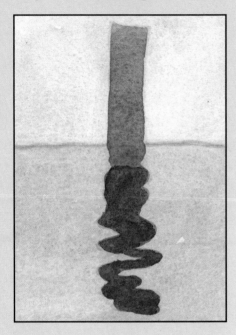

1 Still water on a calm day. Draw the outlines in pencil. Paint the sky and sea in shades of cobalt blue and the post in burnt umber (with the reflection in a darker tone).

2 A calm day with a faint breeze and slightly undulating water. The undulations show in the outline of the reflection.

3 A light breeze is giving a gentle ripple to the surface of the water. The reflection is very wobbly and showing signs of breaking up.

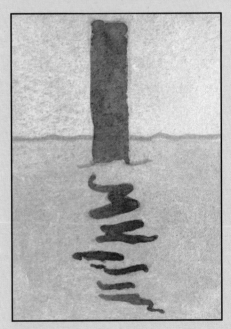

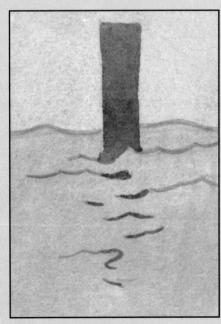

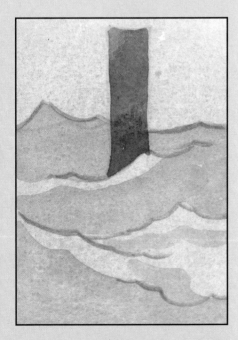

4 The surface of the water is ruffled quite strongly by wind or a current. The reflection is broken up and indicated by agitated lines.

5 The water is whipped up by wind into waves, and the reflected image is disappearing in the movement of the water.

6 A stormy day. A strong wind is producing such large waves that the reflection has broken up and disappeared altogether. The swell of a large boat passing would produce a similar effect.

The difference in reflections in still and choppy water is shown dramatically in these photographs. Still water, *below*, gives an almost perfect mirror image, while in ruffled water, *left*, the image becomes impressionistic.

7 Using cobalt blue, burnt umber and vermilion (you can work out the mixes by testing them on a piece of scrap paper) paint the above exercise showing a mirror image in completely flat water. The only thing different about the inverted image is that the colours are a little darker.

8 As a final exercise, paint the above scene which shows the reflections breaking up in rippling water. You will see that you have to adopt an impressionistic style to make these images look convincing. Paint all these exercises in your sketchbook, if possible, and keep them for future reference.

CANAL IN AMSTERDAM

Our painting project of a canal scene is designed to give you practice in painting reflections and to show you how they are affected by water gently rippled by a breeze.

MATERIALS

Artist's watercolour NOT paper, 140lb/300gsm
HB pencil
watercolours in cobalt blue, burnt umber, vermilion, cadmium yellow
water jar and water
brushes size 12, 7 and 1
palette

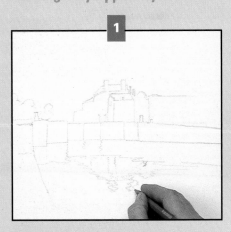

1 Draw the outlines of the scene on your watercolour paper in pencil, including the outlines of the reflections in the water.

2 Mix up a good quantity of cobalt blue for the sky. Using a size 12 brush lay the colour on dry paper, starting at the top with strong colour and adding water to pale off towards the horizon. Leave patches of white for clouds. Take care to paint right up to the outline of the buildings so that no white gaps remain.

3 To paint the lock and gates use a size 7 brush and a fairly thick dark mix of cobalt blue and vermilion. Don't get the mix too wet — you need it quite dry to

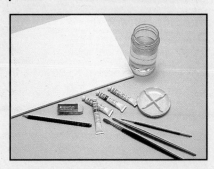

give you control as you brush it on (it's a good idea to test colour mixes on a piece of scrap paper before using them). Paint in the lock, using a dry brush effect, and add a touch of burnt umber to darken the mix for the lock gates. Add more blue to the mix and brush in the righthand bank.

4 Paint in the reflections of the lock and bank, using similar mixes to those you used for the objects themselves, but adding a little more cobalt blue to darken them. The reflections are painted with wobbly outlines to indicate ripples in the water.

5 Paint in the canal bank on the left using the size 12 brush and a light mix of vermilion and cobalt blue. Add more blue to the mix for the foreground, to indicate shadow.

6 For the buildings use the size 7 brush and a moderately dry mix of vermilion with small additions of cadmium yellow and cobalt blue. Add a touch of burnt umber to the mix to paint the righthand wall.

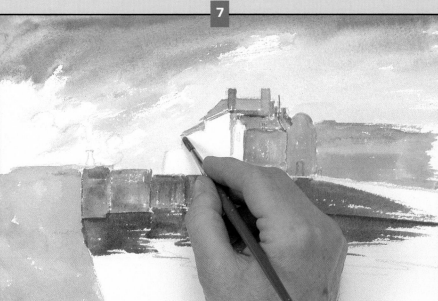

7 Paint the brightly lit roofs catching the sun with a fairly dry mix of vermilion and cadmium yellow.

8 Paint in the reflections of the buildings using the size 7 brush and the same colour mixes you used for the buildings, darkened with a touch of cobalt blue. Leave to dry.

9 Mix up a fairly wet wash of cobalt blue and lay this over the remaining canal area with the size 12 brush (leave the reflection of the sunlit side of the building white). While the wash is still wet, add more blue to the mix and paint brush strokes of the darker colour across the foreground to indicate ripples.

10 Paint in the distant trees on the lefthand bank with the size 7 brush and a mix of cobalt blue with a touch of burnt umber.

11 To add the details to the building (windows, doors, eaves and chimney pots) use the size 1 brush and a fairly dry, greyish mix of cobalt blue and vermilion. Don't overdo the detail or you risk losing the freshness of the painting.

12 Finally, brush in the sunlit canal bank on the right with a light mix of vermilion, cadmium yellow and a touch of cobalt blue.

Your canal painting should have a fresh, lively quality suggesting a day of bright sunshine, with gently moving reflections in water rippled by a light breeze.

COLOUR MIXING

The colours used in a painting have a profound effect on its appeal. Bright or drab, warm or cool, colour sends its own message quite separately from the forms depicted. We look at the essential nature of colour and show you how you can mix many different colours from just a few.

We have already looked briefly at colour on pages 9–14 and seen that colour is composed of hue (blue, red, etc.) and tone (how light or dark the hue is). Colour also has a third property — saturation, or intensity.

Some colours can be thought of as cool or warm. This is a subjective response, but experiments have shown that most people (and even animals) respond to colours in the same way. Colours in the range of mauve, blue, blue-green and green are seen as cool, while others in the range of red, through orange to yellow are seen as warm colours.

'Local' colour is the term used by painters to denote what is thought of as the natural colour of an object. So the local colour of a grape may be dark purple, and that of a porcelain bowl white. But this local colour will be changed by shadows or reflected light, or if the surface of the object reflects other colours or is bathed in coloured light.

Mixing to match

When you want to match a colour you have to consider three things — what hue it is, how dark or light it is, and how saturated, or intense, it is.

To match any particular hue you need to

know what pigments to mix (or discover them by experimenting) to achieve that hue. You can make things easier for yourself by constructing your own colour chart (similar to the one shown overleaf) based on the colours in your palette. This will give you a ready reference to a wide range of hues.

To make a colour lighter, it is normally enough just to add water. Darker tones can be achieved (as we saw on pages 9–14) by adding more colour, or overlaying colour. Sometimes different pigments have to be added to darken the tone, and we give you help with this on the following page.

We shall return to colour theory in later lessons; see pages 51–6 and 129–134 for more detail.

There is much to be learnt about the use of colour from this watercolour painting 'Summer table', *above*, by Annie Williams. You can see how the local colour of the 'brown' floor is altered by sunlight and by the reflections of the table and chairs, and how the 'white' parts of the tablecloth are changed by shade and shadows. It is very important when you are painting to paint the actual colours that you *see* — not the ones you *think* are there. Our still life project for this lesson, *far left*, is designed to give you practice in this and in mixing colours.

The exercises on this page are designed to familiarise you with a range of colour mixes.

VARYING TONE

It's simple to lighten the tone of dark pigments such as cobalt blue, ultramarine, viridian, alizarin crimson and burnt umber by just adding water (see example *below*).

To darken the tone of medium pigments such as raw sienna and vermilion, you need to add small amounts of two other pigments (see example *below*).

Light pigments such as cadmium yellow also need the addition of small amounts of two other pigments to make them really dark (see example *below*).

A light brown (burnt umber mixed with a moderate amount of water).

A medium brown (burnt umber mixed with a little less water).

A dark brown (burnt umber mixed with very little water).

A light red (vermilion mixed with a moderate amount of water).

A medium red (vermilion mixed with a little less water).

A dark red (vermilion mixed with a little burnt umber and viridian).

A light yellow (cadmium yellow with a moderate amount of water).

A medium yellow (cadmium yellow mixed with a little less water).

A dark yellow (cadmium yellow with a little burnt umber and viridian).

COLOUR MIXES

It's a useful exercise to paint a colour chart of all the colour mixes you can get from a palette of seven basic pigments. In the chart (*right*) we have used the seven pigments used in our painting project for this lesson.

First draw up the chart in pencil, making each box about 2.5cm square. Then paint the righthand boxes, from the top, with the pure pigments cadmium yellow, raw sienna, vermilion, alizarin crimson, cobalt blue, viridian and burnt umber.

Paint in each square, using a mix of the pure pigments above and to the right of each square. Mix the colours in equal proportions, keeping the mix quite thick. Your completed chart should look like ours.

Repeat this exercise on another sheet of paper, this time mixing a third of the top pigment with two thirds of the righthand pigment. Finally, paint a third chart, mixing two thirds of the top pigment with one third of the righthand pigment. Keep your completed colour charts for reference.

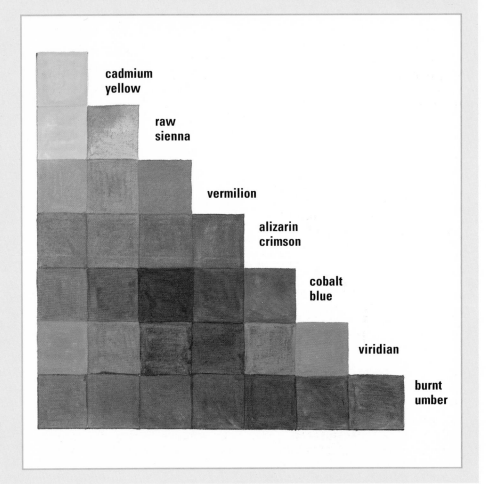

cadmium yellow

raw sienna

vermilion

alizarin crimson

cobalt blue

viridian

burnt umber

A BOWL OF FRUIT

M A T E R I A L S

artist's watercolour NOT paper,
140/300gsm
HB pencil and eraser
brushes size 1, 7 and 12
palette
water and water jar
watercolours: cadmium yellow, raw
sienna, vermilion, alizarin crimson,
cobalt blue, viridian, burnt umber
tissues
scalpel or razor blade

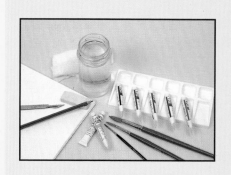

The seven pigments in our colour chart have been mixed in a great variety of ways to produce all the different hues and tones in this colourful and vibrant still life.

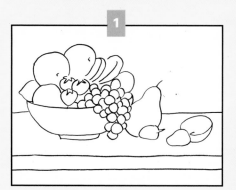

1 Draw up the outlines of the objects lightly in pencil to give a clear indication of their shape.

2 Use a size 12 brush to lay the background wash, and tilt the board slightly. Mix a wash of alizarin crimson and, starting at the top of the paper, lay a pale wash on dry paper. Add a little cadmium yellow about halfway down (mixing the colours on the paper) and a touch of cobalt blue where the background reaches the table.

3 Paint the table top with a thick wash of raw sienna using the size 12 brush. Use long, sweeping horizontal brush strokes to give vitality to the table surface. Paint the side of the table with raw sienna darkened with a little burnt umber.

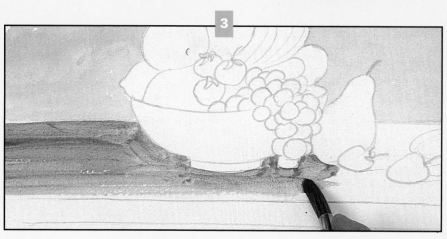

4 Paint underneath the table using the same sweeping strokes and a mix of cobalt blue, alizarin crimson and a touch of burnt umber. Leave to dry.

5 Paint the grapes with a size 7 brush using a mix of cobalt blue and alizarin crimson, adding an occasional touch of vermilion to give a warmer effect. At this stage the fruit are painted fairly flat — moulding and highlights will be added later.

6 To paint the oranges mix vermilion with cadmium yellow to give a rich, intense colour (it's a good idea to test all colour mixes on scrap paper before using them). Paint the oranges with a thick colour mix and, while the paint is still wet, lift off some colour with a dry, clean brush to give the sheen on the fruit.

7 Paint the pear with a thick, sticky mix of raw sienna and viridian. Add a touch of cobalt blue to the mix and paint in the darker tones wet-in-wet.

8 Paint the bananas with a light, fairly dry mix of raw sienna with a touch of vermilion. Add more raw sienna to darken the mix and paint in the darker tones when the light colour is almost dry.

9 Paint the lemons with a light mix of cadmium yellow. Give them form in the same way as the oranges, by lifting off the highlights with a clean dry brush. The darker side of the fruit is painted wet-in-wet with a richer, darker mix of cadmium yellow (note that the light is coming from the lefthand side).

10 The shaded part of the bowl is painted with a pale mix of cobalt blue with a touch of alizarin crimson. Don't forget to paint the bit of the bowl showing behind the grapes on the right-hand side.

11 Paint the strawberries vermilion and, while still wet, paint the shaded sides with alizarin crimson.

12 The peaches are painted with a mix of raw sienna and vermilion, with a darker mix of the same colours applied wet for the shaded areas. Use the same mix with a touch of cobalt blue to paint in the small patch of peach showing under the grapes in the centre. Paint the cut side of the lemon cadmium yellow with a hint of viridian, and the outside of the lemon cadmium yellow with a touch of raw sienna.

13 Use a fairly dry, rich mix of raw sienna with a touch of burnt umber and paint in the shadows on the table with the size 7 brush. This will help to give the objects form and solidity.

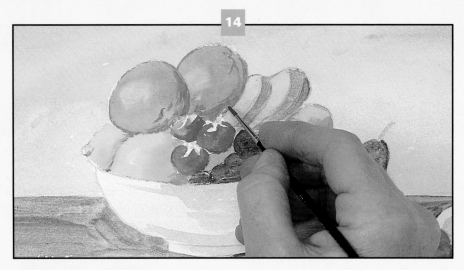

14 We now come to the crucial stage of adding shading to each fruit individually to establish its form. All this detail work is done with a size 1 brush and a fairly dry colour mix, and it takes time! We give you the colour mixes (see box below) to use for each type of fruit (remember too that each piece of fruit will cast a shadow that may appear on the fruit on its right). Leave to dry.

Oranges: raw sienna, cadmium yellow and vermilion. **Lemons:** cadmium yellow with a touch of vermilion. **Peaches:** vermilion and raw sienna with a touch of burnt umber. **Centre (partly hidden) peach:** burnt umber with vermilion. **Strawberries:** alizarin crimson with a touch of burnt umber. **Grapes:** cobalt blue, alizarin crimson and a little burnt umber. **Inside and righthand edge of bowl:** cobalt blue and alizarin crimson.

15 To give the final touch to the grapes the bloom is lifted off. Using the size 1 brush loaded with clean water, rub each grape to soften the paint, and dab off the colour with a tissue to give the effect of bloom.

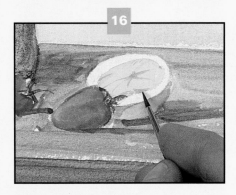

17 Scratch out the white pips of the strawberries using a scalpel or razor blade. Touch in the tiny shadows round the pip indentations with a mix of vermilion, alizarin crimson and cadmium yellow. Finally paint the stalk holes of the oranges with alizarin crimson and raw sienna.

16 Paint the stalks of the strawberries with a dark mix of viridian and raw sienna. Use the same mix to paint the shadow on the lefthand side of the pear. Paint the segments of the lemon with a mix of viridian and cadmium yellow.

When you have worked through this lesson you should feel much more confident about mixing colours. Remember to keep a note of all your colour mixes for future reference.

ATMOSPHERE, LIGHT AND COLOUR

Left: This painting of a moorland scene by Henry Sutton Palmer (1854-1933) exhibits clearly the effect of atmosphere on colours. The strong colours and tones of the foreground give way to medium tones in the middle distance, and these in turn pale to an almost monochromatic haze in the far distance. The effect of yellow light from the afternoon sun is also seen in the foreground. Where the sun catches the tops of the trees their colour changes from mid green to yellow, while the shaded areas are dark green.

Anyone who has ever noticed how the setting sun alters an evening scene has already observed that the colours of a landscape are not constant but are modified by factors such as light, distance and weather. In this lesson we show you how to portray these colour changes in your paintings.

You have learned that it is important to paint the colours that you actually see, not the colours that you may believe to be there. No painter can afford to make assumptions about colour. You may think you know that the leaves of a tree are green, but what you have to ask yourself is, 'Am I seeing green?' The natural, or 'local', colour of an object may be changed by the amount and quality of light falling on it and, in outdoor scenes, by the atmosphere.

Atmosphere
The air is full of water vapour and tiny particles of dust which act like a series of transparent screens, blurring colours and outlines. The result of this is that the further away things are, the hazier they appear. Another result is that colours lose

their sharpness and clarity as they get further away from the observer, and distant objects appear lighter in tone. The far distance may be seen as a bluish haze. This phenomenon is called 'aerial perspective'.

Light
Light will also change the perceived colour of an object. White light will change the lit and shaded surfaces of an object to a lighter and darker tone of the same colour. But coloured light will actually change the colour of the object where it illuminates it. The lit surface will take on much of the colour of the light source, and will be quite a different colour from the shaded surface.

Above: Our painting project for this lesson is designed (together with the exercises overleaf) to give you plenty of practice in painting the colour changes caused by atmosphere and light. It shows a fishing village on the Greek island of Lemnos, and is clearly divided into foreground, middle distance and far distance. The scene is lit by the yellow light of late afternoon sun, and the colours of the lit surfaces of the rocks are modified accordingly, while the shaded surfaces take on a bluish tinge.

HOW ATMOSPHERE AND LIGHT AFFECT COLOUR

The exercises on this page will help you to understand how atmosphere and light affect colour. Draw up the outlines first in pencil. Then paint in the colours in the order given.

Atmosphere

The effect of the atmosphere on colour is most easily seen on a misty day. The mist (which is water vapour suspended in the air) blurs outlines, reduces tonal contrasts and renders the whole scene pale and virtually monochromatic. Exercise **1** shows a scene on a bright, clear day with the sun overhead. Objects are clearly defined and brightly coloured. The same scene on a misty day (exercise **2**) shows everything blurred and colours reduced to a few pale tones.

Similar effects can be observed in any distant landscape. When the light is overhead, or the sky is overcast, features more than half a mile or so distant will usually be seen as lighter in tone than features in the foreground. There will also be less contrast between their light and shaded surfaces, and colours will tend to take on a bluish hue (exercise **3**).

Light

Under white light, such as light from the midday sun, from an overcast sky or a white fluorescent lamp, the lit and shaded surfaces of an object will be tones of the same colour (exercise **4**). When the light source is coloured as, for instance, at sunset and sunrise

1 *A bright day* Sky: cobalt blue. Trees, lit surfaces: raw sienna with a little cadmium red; shaded surfaces: burnt umber. Grass, lit areas: viridian, raw sienna, a little cobalt blue; shadow: add more cobalt blue.

when sunlight is usually a warm yellow, the lit and shaded surfaces of an object will not only be different tones but also different colours.

The lit surfaces will contain much of the colour of the light source, while the shaded surfaces, as a rule, will not. Exercise **5** shows a green box lit by the warm yellow light of the setting sun. The

2 *A misty day* Background wash: pale cobalt blue with a little alizarin crimson. Use same colours, stronger tone, for foreground wash and background tree. Add a little cadmium red to the mix for the foreground tree.

3 *Rooftop vista* Foreground roof: raw sienna with a little cadmium red. Tiles: burnt umber with a little cadmium red. Other roofs: cobalt blue and alizarin crimson. Walls, lit surfaces: cadmium yellow and cadmium red (with a little alizarin crimson in foreground building); shaded surfaces: alizarin crimson and cobalt blue. Distant church: pale cobalt blue with a touch of alizarin crimson.

lit surfaces are consequently golden green, while the shaded surface is a cool, dark green, almost turquoise, that complements the colour of the lit surface — a phenomenon often seen under these conditions.

Exercise **6** shows a brown box lit by yellow light. The lit surface is golden brown while the shaded surface is a cool dark brown.

4 *Green box lit by white light* Box: light, medium and dark mixes of viridian green. Background: cobalt blue. Table: raw sienna and burnt umber (add more burnt umber for the shadow).

5 *Green box, yellow light* Background and table as 4. Box, lit side: cadmium yellow with a touch of viridian; top: viridian with a little cadmium yellow; shaded side: viridian with a little cobalt blue.

6 *Brown box lit by yellow light* Background and table as 4. Box, lit side: raw sienna with a little cadmium red; top: raw sienna and cadmium red; shaded side: burnt umber.

GREEK FISHING VILLAGE

The painting project for this lesson shows a fishing village on the Greek island of Lemnos, *right*, bathed in late afternoon sunshine. You can see how the yellow light of the setting sun modifies the bright blue of the sky, which turns to a pale turquoise towards the horizon, and these colours are reflected in the sea. The lit surfaces of the central rock and the other rocks are a warm yellow, while their shaded surfaces contain a complementary bluish tinge.

1 Draw the outlines of the painting on the watercolour paper using an HB pencil.

M A T E R I A L S

90lb watercolour NOT paper, 14 x 10in
HB pencil and eraser
size 12, 7 and 2 brushes
student watercolours in cadmium yellow, cadmium red, alizarin crimson, cobalt blue, raw sienna, burnt umber and viridian
palette
water jar and water
tissues

2 To paint the sky, mix up a medium tone of cobalt blue in one section of the palette and, in another section, mix cobalt blue with viridian to make turquoise blue. Tilt the painting surface slightly, so that the paint runs downwards and, using a size 12 brush, lay a blue wash, starting at the top of the paper. Work quickly and, as you move downwards, blend in (on the paper) the turquoise colour towards the horizon. Paint carefully round the top of the rocks, and lift off any excess paint with a dry brush. Use a tissue to dab off colour to give a pale translucent sky.

3 To paint the lit surfaces of the rocks in the middle distance, mix a medium tone of raw sienna with a little cadmium red. Using a size 7 brush, paint the lefthand rocks first, adding a touch more red to the last one. Paint the central rock a more intense colour (by making the colour mix stronger). Introduce a touch of viridian to the righthand side, to make it a fraction darker.

4 Paint the distant island with a pale wash of alizarin crimson with a little cadmium red, and the distant mountains with a pale wash of cobalt blue with a little alizarin crimson. Note that the tones of these distant features get paler and paler as they recede. Paint the nearer righthand mountains with a pale wash of cobalt blue.

5 Make up a rich mix of cobalt blue for the sea. Using the size 7 brush, paint in the sea, starting at the horizon. Lay the colour on with generous left to right brush strokes, using a dragging stroke to leave patches of white to give sparkle. Introduce some viridian towards the centre, to mirror the viridian hue in the sky. Finish off with a fairly dry brush, or dab off excess colour with tissue. Leave to dry.

6 Using the size 7 brush, paint the sandy shore in the righthand foreground with a mix of cobalt blue, alizarin crimson and a little cadmium yellow. Paint the righthand foreground rock with a mix of raw sienna with a touch of cadmium red and cobalt blue. Paint the middle foreground rock with a mix of raw sienna and cadmium red, and for the lefthand rock add more cadmium red to the mix.

7 To paint the shaded surfaces of the middle distance rocks, make up a fairly dry mix of cobalt blue with alizarin crimson to give a complementary colour to the lit surfaces. Use a fairly dry size 7 brush to paint in the shading, as this will give greater control. Darken the colour for the central rock. Use a paler mix for the distant island, and for the distant mountains use a light tone of pure cobalt blue.

8 Now introduce shading across the foreground. Use a mix of cobalt blue and burnt umber for the beach shadows, and a mix of cobalt blue, alizarin crimson and a touch of burnt umber for the foreground rocks. Leave to dry.

9 As most of the buildings are white, we only need to paint their shaded surfaces. To do this use the size 7 brush, almost dry, and a medium tone mix of pure cobalt blue. Use the same mix to paint the shaded area on the righthand side of the picture.

10 Two of the buildings are colour-washed. Use a medium tone cobalt blue for the blue building, and a pale tone of pure alizarin crimson for the pink building.

11 To add the final touches, paint the beach on the far shore pale alizarin crimson with a touch of cobalt blue. Paint the castle on the top of the hill alizarin crimson with a touch of cadmium red; the shading for the castle is cobalt blue with a touch of alizarin crimson. Use the size 2 brush to touch in some detailing of doors, windows and roofs on the buildings, using a mix of cobalt blue, burnt umber and a touch of viridian. Don't overdo the detailing — just suggest enough to characterise the buildings.

You should by now be feeling confident enough to be able to mix your colours to match the ones on the page. Remember to test colour mixes on a piece of scrap paper before using them in your painting.

WAX RESIST

One of the challenges of watercolour is how to depict natural features such as rocks and water without overworking the painting. Here we show you how to use the wax resist method to portray subtle textures.

On pages 27–32 you learned how to use masking fluid to save areas of the paper that you wish to keep white while working unhampered on the rest of the painting. In this lesson we take the same basic principle — the fact that wax repels water — and use it to create subtle and exciting textural effects in a technique called wax resist.

Wax resist is a method of creating areas of broken colour by rubbing or drawing with a white wax candle, wax crayon or an oil pastel and then overpainting with colour. The wax adheres unevenly to the paper, catching on the raised tooth and leaving the indents untouched. When a wash of colour is applied, the wax repels the paint, causing it to coagulate in droplets. The result is an attractive broken, grainy pattern that can be used to suggest all kinds of textures and special effects. The technique works best on a rough or textured paper.

When the paint is dry you can leave the wax in place as part of the finished painting. Or you can remove it by laying a sheet of absorbent paper over the area and pressing with a cool iron until the paper has absorbed all the melted wax.

The power of suggestion

The beauty of watercolour is its freshness and immediacy — its power to suggest without overstatement. Using a subtle hint of wax resist you can convey, simply and economically, the powerful forces of nature: a gushing waterfall, waves crashing against the shore, the grandeur of a rainswept mountain. Closer to home, you can also use it to imitate textures and surface effects such as tree bark, sand, rocks and stone, the sparkle of light on water and glass, or more linear effects such as the mortar between bricks, the tips of feathers, hair, grass, and the highlights on fruit and flower petals.

Top: This detail from a painting by Charles Knight entitled 'Church ruins' is a good example of a subject that can benefit from the wax resist technique. The grainy texture of ancient weathered stone, as seen on the ruined arch, can be easily rendered by drawing on the paper with a white wax candle or crayon before starting to paint.

Our project for this lesson, *above*, uses wax resist to good effect to depict water falling from the bowls of a fountain and foaming in the pool below.

There are many instances when the use of wax resist can be helpful in achieving a successful effect in your painting. We give you some examples here, together with examples of using coloured oil pastels and even petroleum jelly. The advantage of using coloured pastel is that the colour becomes part of the completed painting. Try painting these examples to get used to the technique before embarking on the painting project for this lesson. Under each example we have told you what resist medium to use, and the watercolours to use for the rest of the painting. In all cases, the wax or pastel is put on the paper first, and then painted over with the watercolours. As you paint these exercises, make a note of any difficulties you meet, and how you got round them. And keep your paintings and notes carefully for future reference.

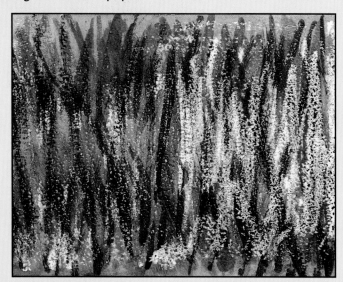

1 Window *Glass:* white candle; *frame:* black oil pastel; *plant pot:* brown oil pastel; *plant:* coloured oil pastels; wash over with raw sienna, burnt sienna and Payne's grey wet-in-wet, letting the colours mix together on the paper.

2 Grapes Draw the outlines first lightly in pencil. *Highlights:* white candle; *fruit:* shades of burnt sienna, alizarin crimson and Paynes's grey; *stalks:* a touch of pale sap green.

3 Long grass White candle, using tip to make broad vertical strokes. Wash over with sap green and let dry. Use viridian, Prussian blue and raw sienna to make vertical stripes. Finally do the same with Payne's grey to give definition.

4 Tree bark Use side of a short piece of white candle to make vertical strokes on rough surfaced paper to give texture. Paint over with raw sienna, burnt umber and Payne's grey wet-in-wet.

5 Water Zigzag strokes down the paper with tip of wax candle. Paint over using short horizontal strokes in raw sienna and ultramarine, letting the colours run into each other on dry paper.

6 Wet pavements, reflecting coloured lights. White candle, plus red, yellow and pink oil pastels for the reflected lights. Wash over with ultramarine, Payne's grey and raw sienna, wet-in-wet.

7 Flowers Draw the yellow and orange markings on the flowers with oil pastels. Paint the flowers in various shades of red, using cadmium red, alizarin crimson and magenta. Leave to dry. Paint the background by dabbing on viridian and sap green, leaving patches of white. Finally, add touches of Payne's grey to the centre of the flowers.

8 Clouds Using cotton wool lightly smeared with petroleum jelly, dab over the cloud area, dabbing more heavily at the top. Use the tip of a wax candle to define the area more clearly. Wash over wet-in-wet with Payne's grey and ultramarine.

A ROMAN FOUNTAIN

Broken, grainy effects such as the sparkle of water falling in a fountain, and the weathered surface of ancient stone buildings, are surprisingly easy to portray with the magical help of the classic technique known as wax resist.

1 Lightly draw up the main outlines of the picture with an HB pencil.

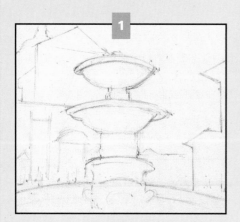

2 Using the blunt end of a piece of white candle, draw freehand the fall of the water from the fountain. Bear down quite hard on the paper so that the wax sticks firmly to the surface tooth. Put some wax strokes in the pool of the fountain to indicate spray, and some more strokes on the buildings to give the effect of pitted stone. (Refer to the final painting if you are in doubt where to put your wax strokes.)

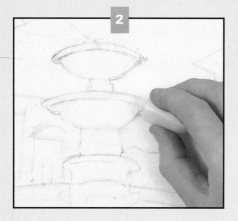

3 Using a size 10 flat sable brush, wet the sky area with clean water. Mix a large wash of ultramarine and cerulean blue on the palette and lay in the sky, starting at the top. Use a fairly intense colour at the top, and as you move down the sky area gradually reduce the colour by adding more water to the mix (you can also dab the paint off the painting with a tissue if you wish).

MATERIALS

acid-free watercolour paper 190gsm
white wax candle
flat sable brush size 10
watercolours: ultramarine, cerulean blue, raw sienna, burnt sienna, Payne's grey
palette
water jar and water
HB pencil and eraser
tissues

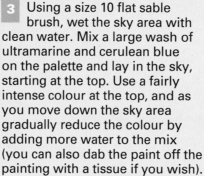

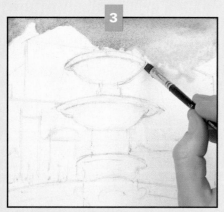

HELPFUL HINT

As you lay your washes on the painting you may find bits of wax where you don't want them. Have a scalpel handy so that you can carefully scrape these bits of wax off the paper.

4 Put dabs of raw sienna, burnt sienna and ultramarine on the palette and mix them together loosely so that the colours are not completely blended. Paint the buildings behind the fountain on the left with this mix — as you put it on you will still be able to see the separate colours. This gives the effect of light and shade on old weathered stone more effectively than a wash of just one colour.

5 To paint the building on the right of the fountain, use burnt sienna and Payne's grey separately, letting the colours run into each other on the paper. Use the straight edge of the brush for the edge of the building.

6 For the shadow on the building on the extreme right, use a mix of Payne's grey and ultramarine. Introduce a touch of burnt sienna to the lower part of the building, letting the colours run into each other.

7 Mix a thick, sticky wash of ultramarine and burnt sienna and use this to paint the shaded areas of the fountain, the shadows in the water, and the dark rim of the fountain pool.

8 Paint the other coloured areas of the bowls and pedestal of the fountain with a mix of raw sienna, burnt sienna and Payne's grey.

9 To paint the bright, sunlit areas on the fountain, use a mix of raw sienna and burnt sienna.

10 The water in the fountain pool is painted with a mix of cerulean blue and ultramarine.

11 Mix together raw sienna and Payne's grey and use this to paint round the sides of the pool, and to add touches to the water in the pool.

12 To add architectural features to the buildings use a pale Payne's grey. Touch in the tops of roofs, window and door outlines and other detailing. Dab the colour off the brush with tissue if necessary, to give a very light touch of pale colour.

In the completed picture you can see how well the grainy pattern of the waxed areas conveys the effect of water cascading down the fountain and sparkling on the surface of the pool.

PAINTING TREES

Landscapes and trees are favourite subjects for all watercolour artists, especially beginners. But making trees and foliage look convincing can be quite a challenge. Here we show you how to capture the essential textures of a tree with some simple and effective techniques.

Watercolour lends itself perfectly to outdoor scenes as its fluidity and translucency help convey the shifting patterns caused by light and atmosphere. It is these effects on trees and their foliage that you are aiming to paint rather than the precise shape of every branch, twig and leaf. Although a tree is a complex structure with an intricate surface, you can only hint at its details. But this needn't make it look any less effective — simplification often leads to the most satisfying results.

Try to paint outdoors from life whenever you can rather than from a photo, so that you get used to the changes caused by breezes, clouds and the movement of the sun. This may mean you have to work quickly but your painting will look more immediate and natural.

The main parts of a tree in leaf are, of course, its trunk and foliage. While the trunk forms part of the basic structure, the foliage screens most of the branches and twigs so you will have to concentrate on conveying its general texture and the changing patterns caused by light. Look at your chosen tree with half-closed eyes to establish where the broad areas of shade are in relation to the highlighted parts.

Foliage tends to hang in clumps — each one made up of hundreds of leaves which create a freckly texture. If you treat the clumps separately, you will notice that they are different not only in size and shape but also in the distribution of light and shade. So try to avoid giving every clump of foliage the same importance — or you will create a series of blobs that don't look as if they belong together on one tree!

On the following pages we show you a simple method for painting a tree. You'll find that having a system gives better results than a hit-and-miss approach, and once you have grasped the basics you'll soon be able to develop your own more elaborate methods.

Above: In this painting, entitled 'By the river in northern Greece', Lucy Willis successfully captures the freshness of summer foliage lit by the sun. Close examination of the picture reveals the simplicity of her technique: a transparent wash of light green is overlaid with small strokes and dabs of darker greens, while tiny flecks of white paper are left bare to give a sense of air and light. Our painting project, *left,* shows you how to use similar techniques to produce a pleasing impression of parkland trees in full leaf.

The best preparation for painting trees is to go out and about and look at them! Carry your sketchbook with you whenever possible and sketch the outlines of as many different trees as you can. Your sketchbook is an invaluable source of reference when you come to do a painting.

Different varieties of trees have different outlines and textural qualities, and it is important to become aware of these if the trees in your paintings are not to look all the same. We give you some tips here on how to go about painting trees successfully.

1

First sketch the outline of the tree roughly in pencil, **1**.

2

Then draw in the silhouettes of the main leaf clumps, **2** and **3**.

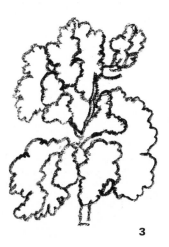

3

4

Paint the main lit areas of the foliage first, matching your green to the brightest part of the tree, **4**. Paint the trunk and main branches without any modelling.

5

Paint the shaded areas last, **5**, including the shaded sides of the main clumps of foliage. Add modelling to the shaded side of the trunk.

6

Shape of the canopy
To get the shape of an individual tree right, look carefully at the shape of the canopy of leaves, and its height and spread in relation to the trunk — it is often bigger than you think, **6**. 'Lollipop' trees are usually the result of making the canopy too small.

7

To give foliage a lacy, airy feeling, leave small gaps of white when painting the canopy, **7**. Note how often there are large gaps between clumps of foliage through which the branches can be glimpsed.

Trunks and branches

Tree trunks don't shoot out of the ground like telegraph poles — you can often see the roots beginning to spread out at the base of the trunk, **10**. The trunk will require some modelling — note how one side may be darker than the other, and the foliage may cast shadows across it. Let the light and dark tones blend where they meet — the soft edge will give the trunk a rounded appearance.

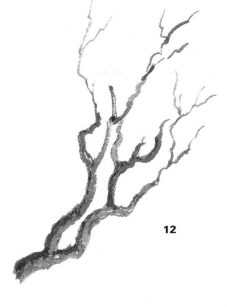

To get the feathery effect of foliage use light, dabbing strokes using dryish paint, **8**. Make the strokes looser and lighter at the outer edges.

For twigs and branches, brush control is important, **12**. Use a dry mix and paint them thinly and delicately — if they are too thick they will look clumsy. Branches are thickest where they leave the trunk, and become thinner and lighter as they grow outwards. Start at the trunk and work outwards, following the shape with your brush and gradually taking the pressure off the brush, finally flicking it lightly off the paper for the fine twigs at the end.

For trunks seen close up, you need to indicate the texture of the bark, **11**. First paint the rounded form with blended washes and leave to dry. Then use the tip of a small brush to 'draw' the gnarled and pitted texture of the bark.

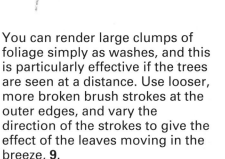

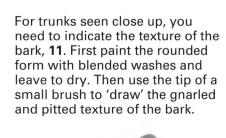

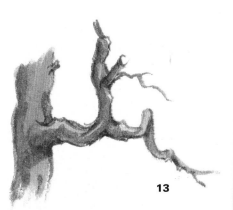

You can render large clumps of foliage simply as washes, and this is particularly effective if the trees are seen at a distance. Use looser, more broken brush strokes at the outer edges, and vary the direction of the strokes to give the effect of the leaves moving in the breeze, **9**.

Branches not only spread out at the sides of the tree. They also grow towards you, when they appear foreshortened, **13**. This helps to make the tree look three-dimensional.

A PARKLAND SCENE

Our step-by-step painting of a parkland scene demonstrates how to paint summer trees using simple washes and brushstrokes to convey an overall impression of clumps of foliage. All the foliage greens are mixed from blues and yellows, which gives a more lifelike result than greens used straight from the tube.

M A T E R I A L S

stretched **NOT** surface watercolour paper
watercolour tubes: cadmium yellow, cadmium red, alizarin crimson, cobalt blue, raw sienna, burnt umber, viridian
round brushes, sizes 12, 7 and 2
water jar and water
HB pencil and eraser
mixing dish or saucer

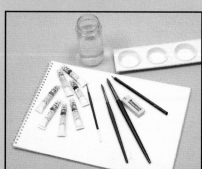

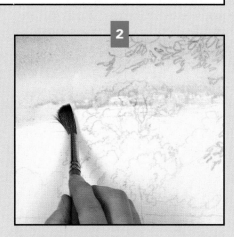

1 Make an outline drawing of the scene in pencil as shown. Using a size 12 brush, cover the sky area with clean water to dampen it.

2 Mix a large pool of cobalt blue in your palette. Use a well-loaded size 12 brush to apply a graduated wash in broad sweeps across the sky area. Make the wash darkest at the top, becoming lighter towards the bottom to give the effect of the sky receding towards the horizon. Don't worry about spreading the wash over the trees, as a lot of the blue will be picked up by the greens of the foliage later.

3 Using a mixture of raw sienna and viridian and a size 7 brush, paint those areas of the tree foliage which are illuminated by the warm afternoon sunlight. Use the paint more thickly now, for making clean, controlled brushstrokes. Introduce variety into the greens by varying the density of the colours and by mixing them in different proportions.

4 Paint the light-struck areas of the overhanging branch in the righthand foreground with a mixture of viridian and a touch of raw sienna. Use broad, loose strokes to suggest, rather than define, the foliage: too much detail will spoil the balance of the painting by drawing attention away from the central tree, which is the focal point of the picture. Returning to the main tree, paint the darker, cooler areas of the foliage with a mix of viridian and cobalt blue. Use deft, light strokes — and remember to leave some gaps, or 'holes for the birds to fly through', in the foliage. This prevents the tree from looking like a cardboard cut-out.

5 Using the same mixture of viridian and cobalt blue, paint the darker foliage on the righthand overhanging branch with loose strokes. Mix cobalt blue, alizarin crimson and a touch of raw umber to create a subtle greyish brown. Using the point of a size 2 brush, indicate a few branches with light, deft strokes. Keep the branches very thin, otherwise they will look clumsy. Paint the tree trunk with the same mixture, then indicate the shadow on the upper trunk.

6 Because they are so far away, the trees in the distance appear hazy and bluish in tone. Paint them loosely with a dilute mixture of cobalt blue and a touch of viridian.

7 Mix viridian and cadmium yellow together in the mixing dish so that they are not quite fully blended. Use this to paint the foreground grass with broad sweeps of a size 7 brush. The different hues in the mix indicate the play of light and shadow on the grass.

8 Paint the shadow in the immediate foreground with a mix of viridian and cobalt blue. Add more blue to the mix to paint the shadow cast by the tree. Use a fairly dry mix so that you can control the wavering lines of the shadows, which indicate the undulations in the grass.

9 The overhanging spray of foliage from a tree outside the picture is a device often used by artists to provide a natural 'frame' through which the spectator views the scene beyond. Paint the lighter leaves of the foliage first, using a mixture of raw sienna and viridian.

10 Paint the leaves in shade with a mixture of cobalt blue and viridian. Use the point of the brush and make small, light flicks and dabs to give movement to the foliage. With a mix of burnt umber and raw sienna, dash in a few delicate twigs with the lightest of touches.

11 The broad outlines of the painting are now complete and all that remains is to enrich the textures and tones in the central tree to bring the picture more into focus. Using a mixture of viridian and cobalt blue, indicate some individual sprays of leaves with the point of a size 2 brush.

You will have learnt quite a few 'tricks of the trade' for portraying trees by painting our parkland scene, and these should prove helpful when you start on your own paintings of trees 'from life'.

FOREGROUND AND DISTANCE

One of the most exciting aspects of painting a landscape is being able to create the illusion of vast space and depth on a small piece of paper. In this lesson we show you how to vary colour, tone and definition to give the impression of earth and sky stretching back into the far distance.

Beginner painters often find difficulty in conveying a sense of depth in their landscapes. So we are devoting this lesson to the techniques you can use to portray a feeling of distance.

To find out about linear perspective see pages 191–4. This is the classic device for showing how objects become smaller as they recede towards the horizon. Here we take a look at how atmospheric perspective affects colour, tone and definition. Atmospheric (or aerial) perspective is the term used to describe the effect that atmosphere has on colour and form. If you study the landscape you will notice how bright, warm colours fade to cool and hazy tones in the distance, while light objects become darker. Contrasts between tones also diminish towards the horizon.

The reason for this is that the atmosphere is full of tiny drops of moisture and dust particles. This atmospheric haze cloaks the distant landscape in a series of bluish veils, and the further you can see, the more 'veils' you have to look through. Just as colour is partly obscured by the haze, so detail diminishes and edges are blurred in the distance.

Because watercolour is so delicate and transparent, it is ideally suited to capturing the effects of atmosphere on the landscape. The most effective way to paint a distant landscape is to work progressively from the furthest distance to the foreground. Start off in a 'whisper' with pale, bluish tones and soft, wet-in-wet effects. Then 'raise your voice' with slightly stronger colours and a little more detail in the middle ground. Finally, end with a 'shout' of stronger tones and crisper detail in the foreground.

In 'Morning, city and lake of Como' *above* Thomas Rowbotham (1823-1875) has painted a breathtaking view of the Italian city of Como with the lake and mountains beyond. Notice how the composition is divided into three distinct planes going back into space — the strong, dark foreground, the brightly lit middle ground, and the hazy, blue-grey mountains in the background. Detail and contrast are strongest in the foreground, becoming blurred and less distinct as the eye travels into the distance. This device not only encourages the eye to move through the picture, creating the illusion of depth, but also adds an air of mystery to the scene which captures the viewer's attention.

In this watercolour landscape, 'Bridge at Kippenross', *above*, Edward Goodwin uses atmospheric perspective and the overlapping shapes of hills and trees to create a strong sense of space and depth. The painting divides naturally into foreground, middle ground and background (as shown diagrammatically *right*) and you can see quite clearly how the painting changes as the eye travels from the foreground into the distance.

To achieve a sense of receding space when you are painting your own landscapes, remember to divide the picture into three distinct planes — foreground, middle ground and background, and alter your treatment in each plane. If you study the painting *above*, you will see the following changes in the planes as your eye travels back through them.

This has the effect of making the trees, bridge and figure in the foreground seem close at hand. The trees jutting into the picture create a natural 'frame' through which we view the scene beyond, while the overlapping trees create a sense of depth by emphasising the three visual planes of foreground, middle ground and background.

cooler. Contrasts of texture and tone are less marked and outlines less distinct.

cloaked in a bluish haze, and all textural detail is lost. This makes the background appear to fade away as it recedes.

Note too that the nearer clouds are darker in tone than those in the distance. As in the landscape, this contrast between strong and weak tones creates a feeling of receding space.

FOREGROUND

The colours in the foreground are strong and warm, and detail and texture are clearly defined.

MIDDLE GROUND

In the middle distance you can see that colours become progressively more muted and

BACKGROUND

In the far distance the colours become paler and the tones weaker. The trees and hills are

ACROSS THE LAGOON

Our painting project for this lesson takes us to Venice for a view of San Maggiore, looking out over the lagoon from the Doge's Palace on a grey misty morning. The scene is constructed from a series of simple tonal washes and gives a powerful impression of atmosphere and distance.

1 Draw the outlines of the painting lightly in pencil as shown. Notice how the composition creates a feeling of depth: the horizon line is positioned high up to give emphasis to the receding stretch of water. Also, the three foreground poles break the frame of the picture, so they appear very close to us. By bringing the foreground images forward, the distant buildings recede by comparison.

MATERIALS

200lb/400 gsm artist's watercolour NOT paper
round brushes, size 1, 2, 4, 7, 18
watercolours: cobalt blue, ultramarine, Payne's grey, ivory black, sepia, chrome yellow
masking fluid
gum arabic
deep-welled mixing palette or 2 small jars
HB pencil
eraser

2 With a size 2 brush and masking fluid, make tiny dots and strokes to represent the sunlight sparkling on the water. Make the strokes small and closely spaced in the distance, becoming bigger and more spread out towards the foreground. Leave the masking fluid to dry for about 5 minutes. Clean your brush in water immediately after use to prevent the fluid drying on the bristles. (See page 28 for how to use masking fluid.)

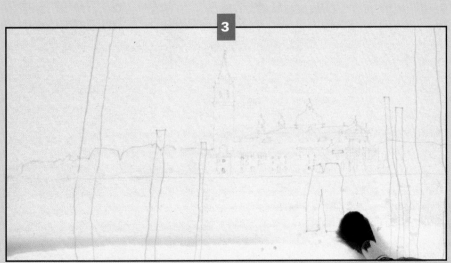

3 Make sure the masking fluid is completely dry. Mix up a pale wash of cobalt blue and, using a size 18 brush, paint a flat wash of colour over the whole painting, sweeping right over the masked-out areas. Make sure you mix plenty of paint so that you don't run out halfway through. Leave to dry.

4 Using a size 4 brush, paint the silhouette of the distant buildings with a pale wash of Payne's grey, ivory black and a touch of chrome yellow. Paint right over the shapes of the poles as these will be painted darker anyway. Leave to dry.

5 Apply a second wash over the darker parts of the buildings, indicating the shapes of roofs, pillars, windows and so on. Leave to dry and then use a size 1 brush to paint the darker, finer details such as the windows.

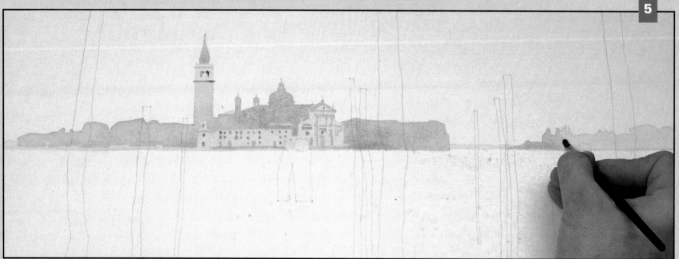

6 Mix up a large quantity of a pale wash of cobalt blue, Payne's grey and a touch of chrome yellow and apply this colour over the whole of the water area using a well-loaded size 18 brush. Here you can see where the wash is repelled by the masking fluid. Leave the wash to dry.

7 Add more cobalt blue, ultramarine and chrome yellow to the wash to darken it slightly and give it a greener hue. Starting just below the line of the buildings, so as to leave a narrow band of pale tone representing light on the water, use a size 18 brush to sweep in a wash of this colour with loose strokes. Leave to dry.

8 Starting with the distant water, use a size 4 brush and the same colour mix to jot in small, closely-spaced strokes to represent the ripples on the water's surface. As you reach the middle, change to a size 7 brush and make the strokes slightly bigger. Use a size 18 brush for the waves in the immediate foreground, which are bigger and more widely spaced. Use both the flat and the tip of the brush to give variety to the shapes. Leave to dry.

9 Intensify the colour of the wash by adding more pigment to the mixture. Paint more waves and ripples on top of the ones you have just painted, this time using a size 4 brush throughout, to give more definition to the shapes. As before, make the waves larger and more widely spaced as you move towards the foreground. Vary the angles of your strokes to indicate the choppiness of the water.

10 Intensify the colour again for the final stage of painting the water. Add a few dark passages to give variety and indicate the play of light on the surface.

11

11 When the painting is completely dry, remove the masking fluid by rubbing gently with the tip of your (clean) finger. The mask will come away from the paper as rubbery crumbs, revealing the white paper underneath. The white patches will give an impression of light shimmering on the water.

12

12 Now you are ready to paint the poles sticking up out of the water. Mix a wash of Payne's grey and sepia, and add a few drops of gum arabic. (Gum arabic can be bought in art shops and intensifies the colour slightly, as well as giving the paint more texture.) Using a size 4 brush, start with the furthest poles, darkening the wash with more sepia as you move forward to the foreground.

In the final painting you can see how a very convincing feeling of depth has been created. The dark tones in the foreground appear to come forward, pushing the paler tones, by contrast, back into the far distance.

PAINTING CLOUDS

Few of us can fail to be inspired by the beauty of cloud effects — delicate wisps of cirrus cloud, billowing towers of cumulus cloud on a windy day, or the magic of a cloudy sky at sunset. In this lesson we show you how to harness the special qualities of watercolour to make your skies more convincing and so add to your enjoyment of landscape and seascape.

The first thing you'll discover when you set out to paint a sky is that you have to work quickly. Clouds will be constantly shifting and changing due to the wind and the shadows cast by the sun. Since speed is crucial, and you are dealing with a phenomenon based on water and light effects, watercolour is the perfect medium for painting cloudy skies.

Cloud studies

Take every opportunity to observe cloud patterns, and make-on-the-spot sketches as often as you can. The English landscape artist John Constable (1776-1837) made hundreds of sketches of skies, in both oil and watercolour. On the back of each he noted the date, time of day, wind direction, and type of weather — a valuable source for all his full-scale paintings.

Happy accidents

For the beginner, complex and ever-changing cloud formations can be a daunting subject. The trick is not to be too literal in your approach, and always be ready to capitalise on those 'happy accidents' that often occur in watercolour — for example, a too-wet wash may suggest the perfect way to paint rain clouds, or you could soak up the colour with a damp sponge or a tissue to create pale, wispy cloud effects.

When you paint skies outdoors, try to simplify the shape and number of clouds — attempting to paint everything that you see will only lead to confusion. By selecting the principal shapes and tones, you will find your painting will have more strength because it is clear and uncluttered.

Cloud shapes can change rapidly and each new effect will seem to be better than the last. It is tempting to try to catch each one, and this can lead to disaster, as pushing the paint around too much is the surest way to destroy the soft, vaporous quality of the clouds. To avoid overworking the paint, plan the sequence of washes you are going to use and apply them quickly and decisively.

With practice you will begin to experience that combination of skill and luck which makes watercolour such an exciting and enjoyable medium to use.

Above: In this painting entitled 'Somerset Levels', Lucy Willis gives an exciting impression of the vastness of the sky. Clouds directly in front of the sun are particularly attractive, as the backlighting gives them luminous white edges. As in our project painting of a windmill, *below*, it is the contrast between the strong tones of the sky and clouds and the brilliant white of the paper that gives the sky its radiance.

CLOUD FORMATIONS

To paint clouds convincingly, you need a working knowledge of the various cloud types and their individual structure and characteristics. Clouds divide into three main types: cirrus, a thin, wispy high cloud; cumulus, with dark bases and white cauliflower-like tops; and nimbus, a dark, vaporous rain cloud. In between these are variations such as cumulonimbus, or 'anvil' clouds. Often you will find a mixture of different cloud types, which present a fascinating panorama of shapes and colours.

1 Cumulus clouds

Heaped cumulus cloud in a blue sky recalls balmy summer days and sea breezes. Cumulus cloud formation is well defined, with distinct areas of light and shadow. Paint around the cloud shapes, using a dry brush to create ragged edges. Leaving bare white paper for the lightest parts of the clouds, indicate the shadows with a dilute mixture of cobalt blue and a little burnt umber, keeping the paint quite dry. As the clouds approach the horizon, they become smaller and are greyed by the intervening atmosphere.

2 Cirrus clouds

Cirrus clouds, high in the sky, are fine and vaporous, forming delicate, feathery plumes where they are blown by the wind. Use cobalt blue to paint the sky with upward sweeping strokes, leaving narrow white shapes with ragged edges for the clouds. Lay in a pale wash of blue over the misty distant clouds.

2

1

3 Storm clouds

Storm clouds give you plenty of scope for creative interpretation. First apply a graded wash of cobalt blue for the sky, working around the shapes of the clouds. Then paint the edges of the clouds that are tinged with the light of the setting sun with a mix of cadmium yellow and a small touch of cadmium red. Leave to dry, then paint the dark clouds with loose mixtures of cobalt blue, raw umber and a little alizarin crimson. Work wet-in-wet for the bulky clouds, then paint the wispy clouds with dryish paint and a bristle brush, letting your brushstrokes follow the sweep of the windblown clouds. Use fairly strong colour, remembering that it will dry lighter.

3

4 Evening clouds

A cloudy sky in late evening is particularly striking. Where the sun is lower than the clouds, the undersides of the clouds are brilliantly lit while their tops are in shadow. First paint the background sky colours, leaving a circle of white paper for the sun's centre. Use cobalt blue for the blue sky, graduating it into a very pale wash of cadmium red and finally cadmium yellow around the sun. Depict the high, white clouds by lifting out some of the colour with a clean, dry brush. Leave to dry, then paint the clouds using the drybrush technique to give them a ragged, vaporous appearance. Use cadmium yellow and cadmium red for the golden clouds, and cobalt blue with a little alizarin crimson for the darker clouds.

5 Rain clouds

Threatening nimbus clouds give you the opportunity to really let go and flood your colours wet-in-wet to create an impression of mist and rain. Wet the paper with clean water and apply loose, separate washes of cobalt blue with burnt umber and a little alizarin crimson. Allow the washes to bleed together where they meet, tilting the paper to make the paint flow in the direction you want it to go. Use a heavy grade paper — at least 140lb/280gsm — for this technique, so that it doesn't buckle as you paint.

4

5

6 Cloud perspective

Think of the sky not as a vertical backdrop to the landscape but as a huge dome stretching overhead towards the horizon. As this simplified diagram shows, the rules of diminishing perspective apply, with the clouds nearest to you appearing larger and more clearly defined than those further away. As they recede towards the horizon, clouds overlap each other and appear smaller, flatter and closer together.

6

WINDMILL WITH CLOUDS

This atmospheric scene gives a wonderful impression of cumulus clouds scudding across the sky, yet it is deceptively simple to paint. The secret lies in working quickly and using expressive brushstrokes that follow the form and movement of the clouds.

artist's watercolour NOT paper, 90lb/190gsm
watercolours: cobalt blue, viridian, alizarin crimson, burnt umber, cadmium red, burnt sienna
round brushes size 0, 1, 7 and 12
HB pencil and eraser
water, water jar and palette

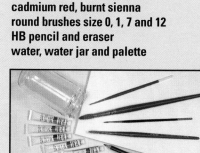

1 Draw the outline of the cliffs, windmill and buildings. Then sketch the outlines of the clouds, but do this very lightly, giving just a bare indication of their shapes. You don't want the pencil lines to show through the thin washes of paint, nor do you want them to restrict the flow of your brush marks.

2 Using a size 12 brush and a wash of cobalt blue, paint the patches of blue sky in the foreground, working quickly around the shapes of the clouds. Wipe some paint off the brush on to a piece of tissue so that the paint is fairly dry and catches on the rough texture of the paper, giving a ragged edge to the clouds.

3 Add a touch of viridian to your sky wash and lighten it with more water to paint the sky in the middle distance. This cooler, paler blue gives depth to the sky. Let the two sky colours bleed into each other where they meet to give a graduated effect.

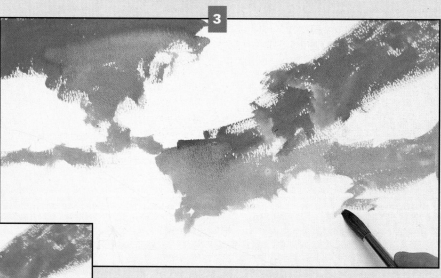

4 For the sky in the far distance, use a size 7 brush to make smaller strokes. Use the residue from the wash used in step 3, paling it down to a mere hint of colour. Again, keep the paint fairly dry so as to give ragged edges to the cloud shapes. The sky is now broadly indicated and you are ready to begin modelling the cloud forms.

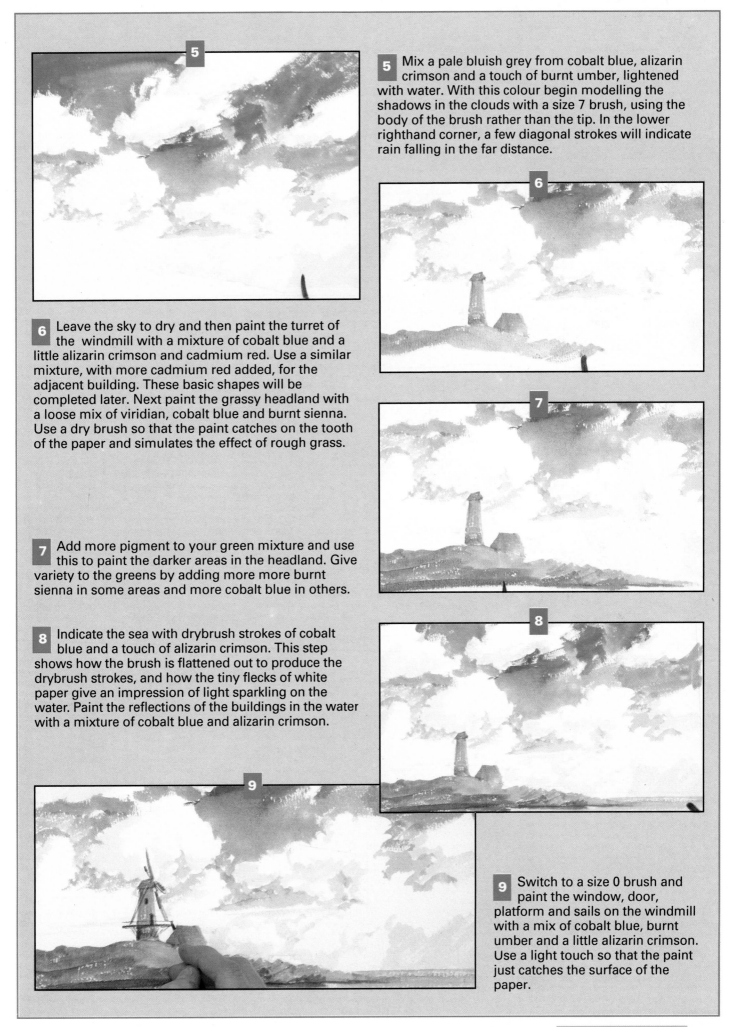

5 Mix a pale bluish grey from cobalt blue, alizarin crimson and a touch of burnt umber, lightened with water. With this colour begin modelling the shadows in the clouds with a size 7 brush, using the body of the brush rather than the tip. In the lower righthand corner, a few diagonal strokes will indicate rain falling in the far distance.

6 Leave the sky to dry and then paint the turret of the windmill with a mixture of cobalt blue and a little alizarin crimson and cadmium red. Use a similar mixture, with more cadmium red added, for the adjacent building. These basic shapes will be completed later. Next paint the grassy headland with a loose mix of viridian, cobalt blue and burnt sienna. Use a dry brush so that the paint catches on the tooth of the paper and simulates the effect of rough grass.

7 Add more pigment to your green mixture and use this to paint the darker areas in the headland. Give variety to the greens by adding more more burnt sienna in some areas and more cobalt blue in others.

8 Indicate the sea with drybrush strokes of cobalt blue and a touch of alizarin crimson. This step shows how the brush is flattened out to produce the drybrush strokes, and how the tiny flecks of white paper give an impression of light sparkling on the water. Paint the reflections of the buildings in the water with a mixture of cobalt blue and alizarin crimson.

9 Switch to a size 0 brush and paint the window, door, platform and sails on the windmill with a mix of cobalt blue, burnt umber and a little alizarin crimson. Use a light touch so that the paint just catches the surface of the paper.

10 Use a size 1 brush and various mixtures of cobalt blue, alizarin crimson and cadmium red to paint the distant rooftops and complete the modelling on the building next to the windmill. Leave to dry.

11 Returning now to the sky, mix pale washes of cobalt blue alone, cobalt blue and burnt umber, and cobalt blue and alizarin crimson to create warm and cool greys. Use these to complete the modelling of the clouds. To do this, use a size 1 brush to make tiny strokes that follow the 'bumps' in the clouds. This is quite a time-consuming process, but very satisfying as you see the clouds begin to take form as you build up the different tones of grey.

We hope you are pleased with your finished painting. With practice and experience, you will find that your speed and confidence increase: somehow the brush picks up its own rhythm and you will develop an intuitive 'feel' for the shapes and characteristics of the clouds.

PAINTING PORTRAITS

Portraits are one of the most challenging and rewarding subjects for an artist to attempt. In this lesson we describe techniques for tackling 'difficult' features such as eyes, mouths, skin and hair and show you step-by-step how to produce an accomplished watercolour portrait of a child.

When it comes to portrait painting, watercolour has a reputation for being difficult because the fluid nature of the medium is not easily controlled. This reputation is undeserved, however, and more and more artists are discovering that watercolour is a marvellous medium for portrait work: its fluidity and translucency are perfectly matched to the subject, bringing out the delicate, living qualities of skin and hair.

Luminous skin

The secret of painting portraits in watercolour is to work systematically and confidently, keeping your washes as clear and fresh as possible. Beginners often make the mistake of using the paint too thickly and overworking the skin tones, with the result that the skin appears muddy and flat. The beauty of watercolour is that delicate, transparent washes allow light to reflect off the paper beneath, creating an impression of the skin's natural luminosity. So always start with very pale, diluted colour and gradually strengthen the tones with successive washes laid one over the other.

In our project painting for this lesson we use gum arabic, a material sometimes used by watercolourists to change the characteristics of the paint (it was also used in our project painting 'Across the lagoon' on page 71). Gum arabic is the medium that binds the pigments in watercolour paints. You can also buy it in bottled form in art shops, specifically for adding to the paint. A few drops mixed into a wash enriches the colour and also increases the solubility of the paint. This means that even after a wash has dried you can re-wet it with water and make alterations, or lift out some of the colour to create pale shapes within a dark area. This is a great advantage when painting portraits, allowing you to move the paint around and correct mistakes without spoiling the freshness of your washes. Paint containing gum arabic also dries with a subtle texture which can be useful when describing textures such as hair.

Above: The freshness and delicacy of watercolour is well suited to the portrayal of children. In this portrait, 'Sarah watching television', Lucy Willis employs soft washes to bring out the bloom of the child's skin. Small flecks and patches of untouched white paper make the painting appear to vibrate with light.

Our painting project for this lesson, *above left,* also uses delicate washes, applied wet-over-dry, to create an appealing and lifelike portrait. Gum arabic is mixed with the paint to enliven the texture of the hair and skin.

Practise the watercolour exercises below for painting hair, eyes and mouths before tackling the portrait project on the following pages.

PAINTING HAIR

1 Mix yellow ochre with a touch of cadmium yellow and sepia, and apply a flat wash for the lightest tone of the hair. When dry, apply a second wash for the darker areas.

2 Darken your mixture with a little Payne's grey and sepia to paint small individual clumps of hair. Alter the strength of the washes to introduce variety.

3 Now add more Payne's grey and a little gum arabic to the mixture and paint the darkest parts of the hair. When dry, dip your brush in clear water, dab off the excess and 'draw' lines in the dark wash to create pale strands of hair.

EYES

1 Lightly sketch in the shape of the eye. Apply a pale wash of brown madder alizarin and yellow ochre to the area around the eye, leaving the eye itself untouched. When dry, add a touch of sepia to the mixture and paint the shadows in the skin.

2 Strengthen the shadows with the same mixture, darkened with a touch of cobalt blue. Paint the iris with a pale tone of sepia, leaving a tiny highlight. Use sepia and a little Payne's grey for the eyebrow. Leave to dry.

3 Strengthen the shadows around the eye with overlaid washes. Use sepia and Payne's grey to paint the eyelashes and darker parts of the iris, brown madder alizarin for the inner corner of the eye, and ivory black for the pupil. Darken the white of the eye with a very pale tone of yellow ochre and Payne's grey, leaving a small highlight at the inner corner.

MOUTH

1 Sketch the outline of the mouth. Using a light wash of brown madder alizarin and yellow ochre, cover the mouth and surrounding area, leaving the teeth and a small highlight on the upper lip untouched. When dry, apply further washes of this colour to strengthen the darker areas.

2 Redden the darks in the lips with a mix of brown madder alizarin and a little cadmium yellow. As one wash overlaps another, the various planes of the lips are defined without being overstated. Use a mix of sepia and Payne's grey to paint the inside of the mouth, working carefully around the shapes of the teeth.

3 Continue painting the lips with overlaid washes of brown madder alizarin in various strengths. Darken the colour with cobalt blue and paint the dark shadow beneath the lower lip. Strengthen the darks inside the mouth with sepia and Payne's grey. Darken the tone of the teeth with a very pale mix of yellow ochre and Payne's grey, leaving white patches for highlights.

PORTRAIT OF ALICE

Our painting project is a delightful portrait of a young child and her rocking horse, which uses the classic watercolour technique of working from light to dark, building up the forms with a series of transparent washes that capture the glowing skin tones.

1 Start with a fairly detailed drawing in pencil, defining the main areas of light and shadow as well as the outlines of the subject.

2 Mix together brown madder alizarin and cadmium orange, diluted with plenty of water to make a very pale wash. With a size 6 round brush, apply the wash all over the face except for the eyes, the teeth and the strand of hair falling over the child's forehead. Leave to dry.

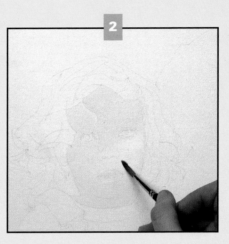

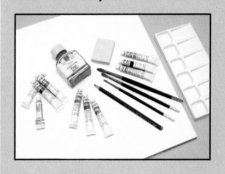
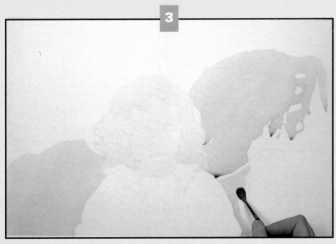

3 Using the same brush, paint the hair with an all-over wash of yellow ochre mixed with chrome yellow, again diluted to a very pale tone. Leave to dry, then fill in the shape of the rocking horse with a pale wash of Payne's grey and yellow ochre. Work carefully around the shapes of the horse's bridle, reins, etc.

4 Now mix brown madder alizarin, cadmium orange and a tiny touch of cobalt blue. Use this colour to strengthen the darker skin tones on the right side of the face, the end of the nose, the lips (leaving a highlight on the lower lip) and the neck. Work quickly and decisively so that the wash is smooth and unmarked. Leave to dry.

5 To paint the darker sections in the hair, use a basic mixture of yellow ochre, sepia, brown madder alizarin and Payne's grey. Vary the amounts of each colour used in the mixture, and add more or less water, to create a variety of browns and greys. The crown of the head, for instance, is much lighter than the hair around the lower face. Use a size 1 brush to paint the individual clumps of hair, leaving the pale underwash showing in the lightest parts.

6 Using a size 1 brush, paint the irises of the eyes with Payne's grey diluted to a fairly pale tone, leaving tiny white highlights. Paint the inside of the mouth with a mix of brown madder alizarin and a touch of cobalt blue. Add yellow ochre to this mixture and, using a size 4 brush, darken the eye sockets and the shadows on the 'wings' of the nose and the tip of the chin. Now you can see the three-dimensional form of the face beginning to emerge.

7 Use a size 1 brush and a mix of Payne's grey and ivory black to paint the pupils of the eyes. When this is dry use a slightly paler mixture to indicate the shadows cast onto the eyes by the upper lids. Leave to dry, then use brown madder alizarin and a touch of Payne's grey to strengthen the lines of the eyelids and give a subtle indication of the eyelashes.

8 At this stage it is a good idea to add a little gum arabic to your colour mixtures; this substance makes the paint more soluble when dry, so enabling you to move the paint around and make alterations if you wish to. With a mixture of yellow ochre and Payne's grey, and a touch of gum arabic picked up on your brush and mixed with the paint, strengthen the darks in the hair. Use a size 1 brush for the smaller strands and a size 4 for the larger clumps.

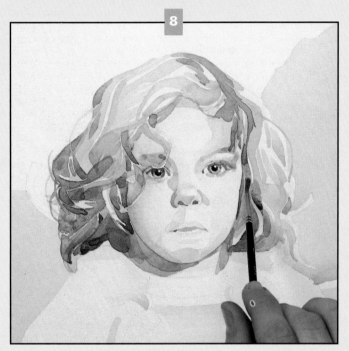

9 Continue to strengthen the darks in the skin with a mixture of brown madder alizarin, cadmium orange and a touch of cobalt blue, plus a little gum arabic. Use the same mixture, less diluted, to build up the form of the mouth. When this is dry use a size 1 brush and a pale wash of Payne's grey for the shadow on the lower teeth and the inside of the mouth.

10 Now paint the clothing and background. At this point do not add gum arabic to the paint as you will be painting flat areas of colour. Starting with the child's T-shirt, use a size 6 brush to paint the right sleeve chrome yellow, the left sleeve cadmium red, and the neck cerulean blue. Paint the brass clasps on the dungarees with yellow ochre and a touch of ivory black. Leave to dry, then paint the rocking horse as follows: mix sepia, brown madder alizarin and yellow ochre for the saddle, bridle and reins. Use a size 1 brush for this, as you must work carefully around the strands of hair. Leave to dry, then use a size 6 brush to swiftly brush in loose washes of diluted Payne's grey for the spotted pattern on the horse. Paint the mane and tail with ivory black, switching to a size 1 brush to cut in around the strands of hair. Use brown madder alizarin and cadmium red for the horse's eye and nostril, and paint the centre of the eye black, leaving a white highlight. Leave to dry.

HELPFUL HINT

Payne's grey is a useful colour which can be mixed from ultramarine and black. When you buy tubes or pans of Payne's grey, it is worth noting that the colour varies from one manufacturer to another. The Payne's grey we used here is by Winsor & Newton and is recommended because it has a strong bluish cast and works well when mixed with other colours.

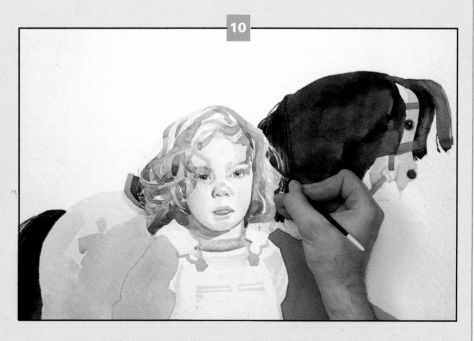

11 With a size 4 brush and a mix of cadmium yellow, cadmium orange and a touch of ivory black paint the creases on the yellow sleeve. Use a mix of cadmium red and brown madder alizarin for the creases on the red sleeve, and the same mix paler to deepen the tones on the face and the mouth. Mix cerulean and Payne's grey and paint the ribbed pattern on the neck of the T-shirt with a size 1 brush.

12 Using a size 4 brush, mix brown madder alizarin, a touch of ivory black and a drop of gum arabic and use this to paint the stripes on the dungarees. The gum arabic helps the paint to flow more easily. Vary the tones of red a little to indicate the play of light and shade on the striped pattern.

13 To finish off the painting, use a size 6 brush to apply loose washes of very pale Payne's grey with a scrubbing motion. Finally, hold the brush horizontally above the paper and flick it lightly to spatter some drops of paint to indicate the dappled pattern on the horse's flank.

Now that you have completed your first portrait painting you will realise how easy it can be when treated simply and directly. Paint what you see, have the courage of your convictions, and you will be surprised how lifelike your portraits appear.

SCRATCHING OUT AND LIFTING OFF

Scratching out and lifting off are useful techniques that enable you to continue to refine a painting after the colour has been laid on. With their help you can introduce an extra dimension to your pictures by giving them additional highlights and texture.

S cratching out (otherwise known as sgraffito) is the technique of scratching lines into dry paint, using a sharp instrument such as a knife, razor blade, scraperboard tool or even your fingernail. This exposes the colour or paper beneath, and in watercolour it is often used to create highlights or to give the texture of grass or wood.

The knife or other instrument used should be very sharp, and only light pressure is needed. It is important that the paint is completely dry, as if it is wet it may run into the line, or the paper may tear. You need to use a fairly heavy paper (at least 140lb) with a rough or NOT surface when you are going to scratch off paint.

Lifting off

Another way of creating highlights is by lifting off paint. This is done by using a cotton bud, sponge or tissue on wet paint to dab off some of the colour. In contrast to scratching out, this gives a soft, hazy impression, and is a useful way of dealing with the complex effects of a clouded sky.

The suffused, smudged effect that lifting off produces is appropriate for painting the modelling of rounded objects, such as fruit. The technique can also be helpful for correcting mistakes. With a piece of sponge or a tissue you can remove accidental blobs of paint, or take out an ill-considered area of colour.

Lifting off gives an altogether softer effect than masking, or leaving the paper free of paint. You can give the effect of different textures by using different materials to dab off the paint — a crumpled tissue will produce a different effect to a cotton bud, and harder materials such as plastic clingfilm, a rag or kitchen foil will each produce their own texture.

Note that some pigments are difficult to lift off. Prussian blue and the synthetic phthalocyanine blue can be difficult, as can strong reds. It is also important to use a paper with a non-absorbent surface, such as Bockingford, Saunders or Cotman. An absorbent paper is completely unsuitable.

Scratching out and lifting off are both techniques that can be used to give paintings added vitality. You can see in the painting of 'Boston' by Albert Goodwin, *top*, how the painter has used scratching out to good effect on the trees and foliage on the right, see detail *above*, imparting a sense of light and movement to the foreground. In our painting project for this lesson, *left*, we have also used scratching out to give surface interest and texture to the leaves and tree bark, and to give the impression of the reflections in the lake. On the following pages we give you exercises to try in both techniques.

WATER LILY POND — scratching out

Paint the reeds in the background with a loose mix of cadmium yellow, Payne's grey and viridian. Use the same colours for the water, starting at the bank in the background and gradually adding more Payne's grey around the water lily leaves. Use ultramarine in the foreground. Leave to dry. Using a razor blade, scratch vertical strokes on to the reeds, and scratch the water in the background in horizontal zig-zags down the paper to make reflections. In the foreground, scratch the water in longer horizontal strokes. Finish off by adding more colour to the lily leaves.

CLOUDS — lifting off

Lifting off is an excellent way of achieving the effect of clouds. In the exercise *below* washes of cerulean blue, Payne's grey and burnt sienna are laid wet-in-wet, and then lightly dabbed at with a crumpled tissue.

In this exercise *right* paint the clouds with a wash of raw sienna and Payne's grey. Use ultramarine for the sky beneath. With a flat wedge of tissue, dab off the cloud shapes. While still wet, paint more Payne's grey under the clouds.

ROCKS — scratching out

Paint the rocks with Payne's grey, raw umber, burnt umber and raw sienna, laid down wet-in-wet. Paint the sky with a simple wash of Payne's grey. When the paint is thoroughly dry, use the flat side of a razor blade to scratch away the highlights, giving a gritty, weatherbeaten texture.

FRUIT — lifting off

BARK — scratching out

The texture of the bark of a tree is ideally suited to the scratching technique. Here a wash of raw sienna and viridian is laid down for the background. When the paint has dried, paint the tree trunk with a wash of Payne's grey, burnt sienna and raw umber. Apply a mixture of viridian and Payne's grey in long, sweeping strokes for the grass. Leave to dry. Using the side of a razor blade, scratch away the texture of the bark. Scratch the highlights on the grass with quick, jabbing strokes, using the tip of the razor blade.

Lifting off is an excellent way of suggesting the uneven modelling of fruit. In the exercise *above* the background is painted with a wash of dilute Payne's grey. When this has dried, paint the fruit separately, using various mixes of Payne's grey and scarlet lake for the darker tones, and, for the lighter tones, mixes of cadmium yellow with a touch of scarlet lake and alizarin crimson. While the paint on each fruit is still wet use a cotton bud dipped in water to take out the highlight.

The orange *right* is painted in a similar way. Lay a graduated wash of ultramarine and Payne's grey for the background, and while this is still wet paint the fruit with a mixture of cadmium yellow, scarlet lake and viridian, letting the colours run into each other. Use a dampened cotton bud to take off the highlight.

BIRCHES BY A LAKE

For the beginner, painting the kaleidoscope of highlights and suffused lighting caused by sunlight shining through foliage may seem too much of a challenge. But with the skilled use of scratching out and lifting off you will see how easy it can be to achieve the effect of dappled light and silvery bark.

1 Draw up the outlines of the scene using a soft 3B pencil.

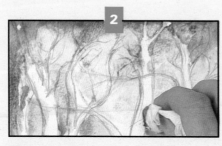

2 Using a size 8 round brush, paint the sky area with washes of ultramarine and cerulean blue, letting the colours blend on the paper and painting over the small branches. For the clouds, dab off the wet paint with crumpled tissue.

MATERIALS

watercolour paper
3B pencil
eraser
brushes: size 6 and 8
watercolours: ultramarine, cerulean blue, raw sienna, cadmium yellow, burnt sienna, Payne's grey
palette
water jar and water
tissues
cotton buds
Stanley knife blade

3 Paint in the shadows under the clouds with raw sienna while still damp.

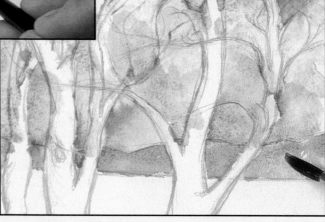

4 When the paint is thoroughly dry, mix up some cadmium yellow and, with your size 6 round brush, begin to paint in the hills. While the paint is still very wet, mix up some cerulean blue and paint the colour over the top of the cadmium yellow. The two colours will run into each other, mixing and blending and giving the paint surface a textural feeling. This technique is called a variegated wash. Leave to dry.

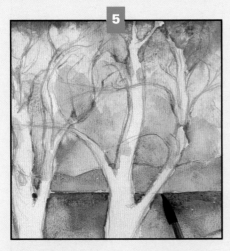

5 Using the same brush, paint the lake, using a mix of ultramarine with a touch of cadmium yellow, letting the colour run out towards the foreground.

6 In the foreground of the lake use a mix of raw sienna and ultramarine, dabbing the colour on with the brush, and letting some of the white paper show through.

7 With a mixture of raw sienna and ultramarine, paint in the foreground with your size 6 round brush. Use short, dabbing brushstrokes to suggest the textural qualities of the earth and rocks. Let your brushwork be relaxed and free. If small areas of white paper are left showing through the paint, all the better — one of the best aspects of watercolour painting are the 'happy accidents' which sometimes occur.

8 After the paint has dried (you can use a hair-dryer to speed up the process), mix up some raw sienna and add a dab of ultramarine. Dip your size 6 round brush into the paint and then, with a piece of tissue or the tips of your fingers, squeeze off the excess water from the bristles. With an almost dry brush and using rough, stabbing strokes paint in the long thin blades of grass.

9 When the paint has dried, paint the trees with an equal mixture of burnt sienna and Payne's grey. Lift the paint off the white areas with the tip of a cotton bud. If the paint is too dry, you can dip the bud into some water.

10 With a darker colour mix, paint in the shadows on the trees using a size 6 brush. Once again, spontaneity is the key word. Let the brush rest loosely in your hand and don't be afraid to make mistakes. Remember, with the lifting out technique, errors can be erased fairly easily.

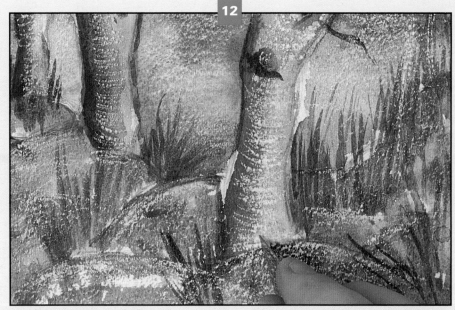

11 When the paint is completely dry, use the edge of a Stanley knife blade and, taking care not to cut yourself, gently scratch away the paint to form the reflections in the lake.

12 With the tip of the blade, scratch away the foreground to suggest the grass and the grainy texture of the trees. Try to be as subtle as possible in your use of the blade as overworking of the paper can often look unattractive.

13 Complete the painting by scratching away highlights on the grass in the immediate foreground. Use long sweeping strokes to mirror the free, slashing marks of the brushstrokes.

The technique of scratching out is well worth practising until you feel confident in using it. It is essentially an experimental technique that will add a unique textural quality to your paintings.

MIXING GREENS

Every watercolourist loves to find a picturesque scene in the countryside to paint from life. Lush green trees, grass and hedgerows all offer a tempting prospect, but in practice the multitude of greens the landscape presents may prove difficult to capture on paper. In this lesson we give you some help in reproducing nature's infinite variety.

Left: In this painting of 'The gamekeeper's rest' by Erskine Nicol many greens are called into play from the dark blue greens of the shadowed areas of the green lane to the browny greens of the path and the light, yellow greens in the sunlit patches where the sun breaks through the tree canopy. When you are learning to observe the different greens in the landscape it can be helpful to take a colour photo of the scene. Keep this in your sketchbook along with a note of the colour mixes you made on the spot. There is really no substitute for this kind of basic training exercise that you carry out for yourself.

Before you attempt to paint the myriad number of greens you will find in the landscape, you need to train your eye to see them. Do not assume that a tree, field or hillside is just 'green'. It will actually be a tapestry of hues and tones, which will change as the sun comes out or goes behind a cloud. Even the best landscape painter can only hope to suggest the ever-changing picture that lies before him.

If you look back at our lesson on 'Atmosphere, light and colour' on page 51, you will be reminded of how coloured light — yellow sunlight, for instance — actually changes the local colour of an object. So the sunlit surfaces of 'green' trees may well be yellow, while the parts that are in the deepest shade may be a very dark green, or even blue.

It is a very good exercise to simply go out into the countryside, sit down in a quiet spot, and look carefully at the panorama in front of you, section by section. Isolate patches of the scene, perhaps by using a viewfinder, and try to determine the actual colours that compose it. Then have a go at mixing paints to match the colours you see. You will find that even a very small area of landscape will yield a bewildering number of hues.

When you are trying to match any green you see in nature, ask yourself first what hue it is. Is it a yellowish green, or a bluish one? A 'green' can contain a combination of a number of pigments, and with practice you will come to recognise a range of greens and know instinctively how to mix them. The five most useful pigments for mixing greens are viridian, raw sienna, cobalt blue, burnt umber and cadmium yellow, and on this page we give you some basic recipes for mixing some of the greens you will need.

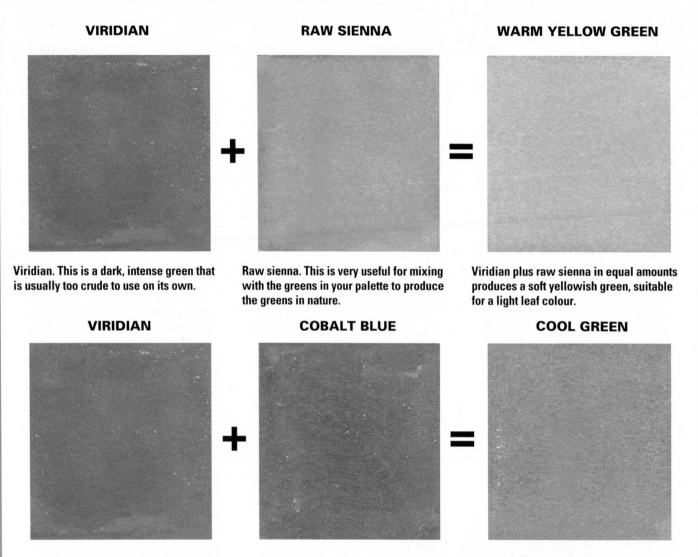

VIRIDIAN   +   **RAW SIENNA**   =   **WARM YELLOW GREEN**

Viridian. This is a dark, intense green that is usually too crude to use on its own.

Raw sienna. This is very useful for mixing with the greens in your palette to produce the greens in nature.

Viridian plus raw sienna in equal amounts produces a soft yellowish green, suitable for a light leaf colour.

VIRIDIAN   +   **COBALT BLUE**   =   **COOL GREEN**

Viridian and cobalt blue in equal amounts produce a cool, fairly dark bluish green, that you might see on a cold, grey day.

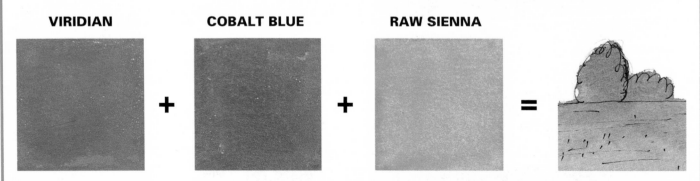

VIRIDIAN   +   **COBALT BLUE**   +   **RAW SIENNA**   =

A mix of viridian, cobalt blue and raw sienna produces a slightly warmer tone, useful on an overcast day.

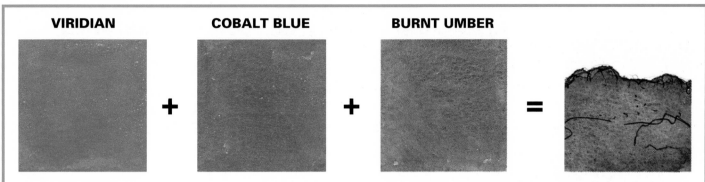

VIRIDIAN + **COBALT BLUE** + **BURNT UMBER** =

Viridian, cobalt blue and burnt umber mixed together produce a darker green — the colour of foliage at dusk.

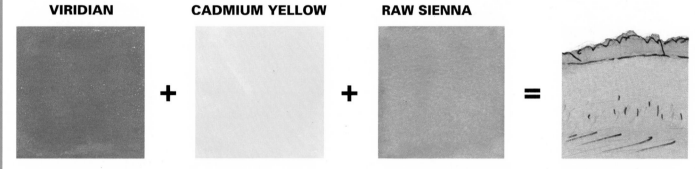

VIRIDIAN + **CADMIUM YELLOW** + **RAW SIENNA** =

Viridian, cadmium yellow and a little raw sienna produce a fresh, light green — the colour of grass in early morning sunlight.

COLOUR CHART

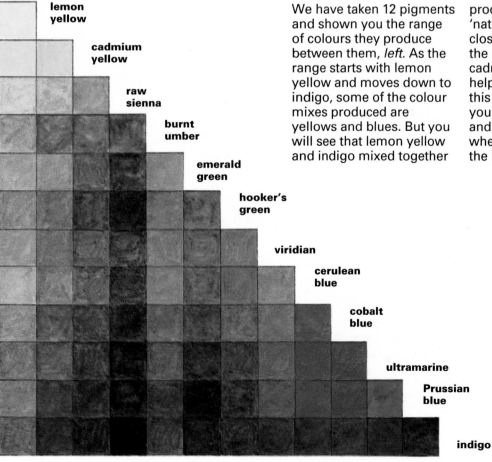

lemon yellow

cadmium yellow

raw sienna

burnt umber

emerald green

hooker's green

viridian

cerulean blue

cobalt blue

ultramarine

Prussian blue

indigo

We have taken 12 pigments and shown you the range of colours they produce between them, *left*. As the range starts with lemon yellow and moves down to indigo, some of the colour mixes produced are yellows and blues. But you will see that lemon yellow and indigo mixed together produce a very useful 'natural' green — quite close to that produced by the mix of ultramarine and cadmium yellow. It is a helpful exercise to paint this colour chart for yourself. Take it with you and use it as a mixing aide when you go out to paint in the landscape.

SHEEPDOG TRIALS

A countryside scene of sheepdog trials is the subject of our project painting for this lesson, which is designed to demonstrate how a wide range of greens can be mixed from six basic pigments.

1. Lightly sketch in the outlines of the scene with an HB pencil. Load an old brush with masking fluid and paint over the white areas of the farmer's shirt, the sheep and the light areas of the sheepdog. Leave to dry.

2. Using a size 9 flat brush, paint a pale wash of cobalt blue over the most distant hills. Mix viridian with a small amount of cobalt blue and a touch of raw sienna and, with the same brush, paint this colour over the hills in the middle distance.

MATERIALS

HB pencil
Daler 90lb/190gsm watercolour paper
masking fluid
old paintbrush
brushes: flat sizes 8 and 9; round sizes 0 and 6
watercolours: cobalt blue, viridian, raw sienna, burnt umber, alizarin crimson, cadmium red
palette
water and water jar
scalpel

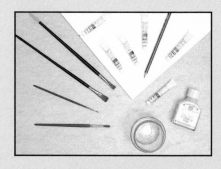

3. Use a loose mix of viridian and raw sienna in a ratio 60:40 to paint in the foreground, applying the colour across the previously masked areas with the size 8 flat brush. Indicate the path with a brushstroke of raw sienna, and leave a white patch in the left foreground to be painted later.

4. To paint the main tree clump, use a round size 6 brush and various mixes of viridian, cobalt blue and burnt umber for the different hues and tones. To get a tree effect you need to 'draw' with the brush, keeping the paint mix light and not too wet. Aim for an uneven outline around the tops of the trees.

5 With the same brush, paint the hedges in the far distance with a mix of pale cobalt blue and viridian, with the blue dominant.

6 To paint the 'hole in the sky', apply pure cobalt blue with the side of an almost dry size 8 flat brush, to give a ragged edge.

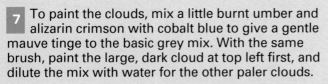

7 To paint the clouds, mix a little burnt umber and alizarin crimson with cobalt blue to give a gentle mauve tinge to the basic grey mix. With the same brush, paint the large, dark cloud at top left first, and dilute the mix with water for the other paler clouds.

8 Rub off the masking fluid with an eraser or fingertip.

9 Mix raw sienna and a tiny amount of viridian to paint the muddy area in the left foreground with a size 6 round brush. Add some cobalt blue to this mix and touch in detail on the trees.

10 Mix a little viridian with burnt umber and use this mix in varying strengths to paint the bushes and fences in the middle distance with the size 6 brush.

11 Paint the hurdle behind the farmer with a similar mix. For the dark areas on the man, the dog and the sheep, mix burnt umber and cobalt blue and paint in using the size 6 brush. Paint the shadows of the man and the animals with a mix of viridian and a small amount of burnt umber. For the farmer's shirt and hat use raw sienna and touch in a spot of pale cadmium red for his face.

12 Use the fine size 0 brush to paint in the final details, such as the braces on the farmer's shirt. Then, using the point of a scalpel blade, carefully scratch out the line of the farmer's stick.

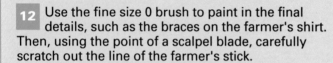

If you feel you would like more help on how to paint the trees and bushes, refer to our lesson on painting trees on page 63.

GRANULATED WASHES

One of the special techniques that watercolourists use to create atmospheric effects is granulation — mixtures of pigments that do not blend together but produce a grainy texture. We show you how to paint granulated washes and use the technique in a moonlit scene.

Granulation is an interesting textural effect obtained by combining two colours, the pigments of which reject each other and separate out to give a grainy appearance. This is caused by the different physical qualities of the pigments. The earth colours, in particular, tend to have coarse particles that separate out and 'float' above an area of flat colour giving a mottled, textured look.

Granulation is a particularly useful technique when painting sky washes, and it is ideal for capturing the moody, cloudy skies so often associated with the Lake District and the Scottish Highlands. The effect can also suggest a grainy texture — weather-beaten stonework, for instance, or sand, or newly fallen snow. More pronounced granulated effects can be achieved by sprinkling salt over a wet wash. The salt crystals absorb the paint and leave a pale, delicate pattern.

Use a high quality watercolour paper with a rough surface — you can experiment with different weights but 260lb is a good choice to begin with. First lay in a wash of one colour, and then, painting wet-in-wet, apply the second colour. In some cases a third colour may be added, too. Leave the paint to dry completely — keep the paper flat and don't be tempted to hurry along the drying process in any way as this will ruin the granulation process.

French ultramarine and burnt umber have a very pronounced tendency to granulate and you will find them a useful

colour combination. Mixed in differing proportions they can give either a cool blue-grey or a warm brown-grey atmospheric effect.

Some pigments have a tendency to granulate without adding a second colour — cerulean blue is a good example of this. On the whole, however, single colours tend to be too bright. By mixing two or three colours together you will achieve truly subtle tones, such as those predominant in the work of Sir William Russell Flint.

The painting *above left* of an industrial landscape by Charles Longbotham makes good use of the granular technique to lend interest to the grainy sky where smoke from the chimney stacks mingles with the mist of evening. Our project painting of a lakeside scene, *below*, also uses granulated washes to capture the atmosphere of a lake by moonlight.

USEFUL PIGMENTS

Some pigments have a greater tendency to granulate than others. We have chosen nine colours for you to practise with — you will probably have most of these in your palette. Note how bright these colours are before being mixed.

French ultramarine

Raw sienna

Cobalt blue

Brown madder alizarin

Venetian red

Sap green

Cobalt violet

Burnt umber

Winsor violet

Here is a selection of ten two-colour mixes, all of which have interesting granulation tendencies. Practise laying washes of each of these colour combinations yourself, and then try experimenting with other colour mixes of the nine pure colours.

This will help you learn how each of these pigments behaves in different circumstances, which in turn will allow you to use colour more skilfully and expressively. Rough surface 260lb (555gsm) paper has been used for all the exercises on these pages.

French ultramarine and Venetian red

Cobalt blue and burnt umber

Winsor violet and raw sienna

Sap green and burnt umber

French ultramarine and burnt umber

Brown madder alizarin and burnt umber

French ultramarine and raw sienna

Cobalt blue and raw sienna

Winsor violet and cobalt blue

Cobalt violet and cobalt blue

USING SALT

A variation of a granular effect — more correctly called flocculation — can be achieved by sprinkling crystals of coarse rock salt over a wet wash. When the paint is dry the salt is simply shaken off the paper. This produces some exciting textured effects that can be used to suggest flowers, mosses and lichens or falling snow. Experiment with the timing of the salt application and try using ordinary table salt for different effects.

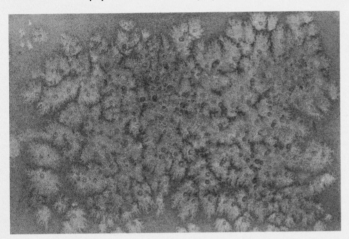

Salt crystals added to a wet wash of Venetian red.

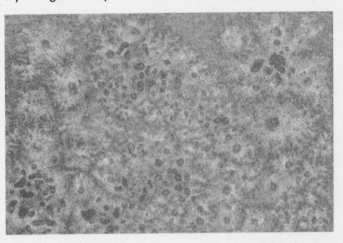

Salt crystals added to a wash of cerulean blue and cobalt blue.

The palette used for this painting of the Highlands consisted entirely of colours with pigments that encourage good granulation — French ultramarine, burnt umber, brown madder alizarin, neutral tint and raw sienna. The sky was painted with a mix of burnt umber and French ultramarine over a very light wash of Venetian red. A paper with a very rough surface was used to increase the granular effect.

LAKE BY MOONLIGHT

A quiet lake at dusk makes an evocative subject for our painting project for this lesson. The misty atmosphere of the scene is enhanced by using a series of granulated washes.

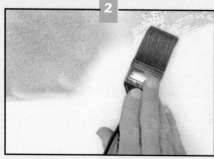

1 With the 2B pencil make a rough sketch of the composition on a separate piece of paper and keep this by you for reference. By painting straight on to unmarked paper the picture will have a loose, unstructured quality.

2 Using the wash brush lay clean water into the sky where the light area is to be. Mix equal quantities of raw sienna and Venetian red and lay this over the dry section of the sky, letting it run into the damp area.

M A T E R I A L S

artist's rough surface watercolour paper, 260lb (555gsm)
watercolours: raw sienna, Venetian red, cobalt blue, neutral tint, brown madder alizarin
brushes: 1½in flat bristle wash brush; round sable sizes 6 and 10
mixing palette
2B pencil and eraser
black fine-tipped technical pen
water jar, water and tissues
piece of paper with small circle cut out

3 Mix cobalt blue and neutral tint and lay this over the first wash. This will give a granulated effect. Leave to dry.

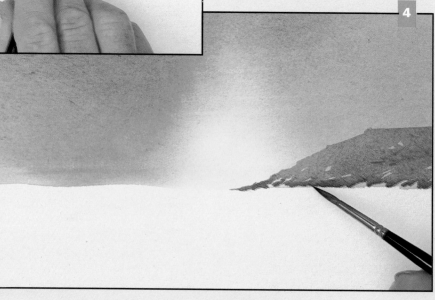

4 Paint in the righthand hill with the size 6 brush using a mix of Venetian red and neutral tint. Add a little cobalt blue to the mix for the base of the hill.

5 Now paint in the left hill, using the same colours as in Step 4 but mixed with a little more water. These paler colours will give the effect of greater distance.

6 With the wash brush lay clean water in the middle ground and in the foreground where the light is reflected. Mix Venetian red with raw sienna and using the size 8 brush, run a wash of this colour over the foreground lake.

7 Add a touch of neutral tint to the foreground, painting wet-in-wet with the size 6 brush. Leave patches of white paper to add sparkle to the water. Now leave the painting to dry.

8 Using a mix of cobalt blue and neutral tint, and the same size brush, paint in the rocky outcrop on the righthand side of the lake.

9 For the boats, use brown madder alizarin mixed with neutral tint. It is essential that the line where each boat meets the water — the water line — is horizontal. Paint the small flag on the mast of the central boat using brown madder alizarin.

10 Paint in the reflections of the boats with neutral tint, and touch them up using brown madder alizarin. With neutral tint, paint in the water on either side of the boats. Leave to dry.

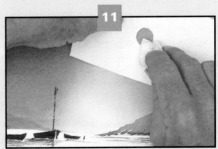

11 Place the piece of paper with the hole cut out over the sky area and with a damp tissue, 'lift out' the moon.

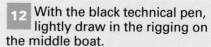

12 With the black technical pen, lightly draw in the rigging on the middle boat.

13 While the moon is still slightly damp, drop in just a touch of raw sienna with the size 6 brush.

14 Add a few touches of neutral tint suggesting shadows in the water.

To get the best effects from your granulated washes, keep the composition of your painting simple. Don't be afraid to let the sky area take up over half the overall picture, as it does here in 'Lake by moonlight'.

DAPPLED LIGHT

*The impression of
sunlight filtering
through foliage
lends a delicate,
fresh quality to a
painting,
summoning up
nostalgic
memories of
summer days. In
this lesson we
look at how to
achieve the effect
of dappled light
under a canopy of
leaves.*

Light out of doors is seldom static — it changes almost second by second as clouds feather the sun's rays while the leaves of trees and grasses stir in even the faintest breeze. Success when you are painting sunlit dappled garden scenes — whether formally composed or simply the record of a chance-come moment — depends on the ability to create an impression of variegated brightness and the transient effect of light. In this lesson we will look at ways of achieving these skills.

The patterns of dappled light are many and various, and the best way to appreciate these is to go outside with keen eyes and a sketchbook. Study different varieties of trees through the year — spring and summer foliage, for instance, will create different effects and will require quite separate palettes.

Don't forget that the time of day not only changes the position of the sun — and therefore the angle of light — but also affects the intensity of colour.

Scrutinise the many tones, colours and textures of deciduous and coniferous foliage, and observe how these are altered as they are struck by a bright ray of sunshine. You will find that the canopies of leaves act rather like a filter, screening the light, changing its colour and intensity, throwing out shadows. Some leaves become luminous, while others become translucent, allowing light to pass through diffusely. Some leaves will reflect the blue of the sky, and others may reflect clouds and surrounding foliage.

When painting leaves, a delicate touch is necessary; don't try to cover the paper completely. Patches of sky are visible even through the densest canopy of foliage, and by letting tiny specks of the white paper shine through your picture will sparkle with life.

Lucy Willis's painting of 'The garden at Cliff Cottage', *above left,* **gives a wonderful impression of a cool, airy spot under a canopy of leaves in a sunlit garden. At first glance it may seem as if the whole surface of the paper is covered with colour, but closer examination reveals innumerable small specks of white that remain unpainted. This gives a sense of light and movement to the whole scene. The painter has used thin washes of transparent colour to achieve the effect of sunlight filtering through leaves (see** *above***), and we have used the same technique in our project painting of a Brownie picnic in a sunlit garden,** *left.*

On these pages we give you some examples of a variety of effects that occur when sunlight interacts with foliage. Paint these exercises into your sketchbook first, and then try painting some examples of your own. The colours listed for the exercises given here will provide you with a useful reference, but don't feel limited — painting is all about experimenting!

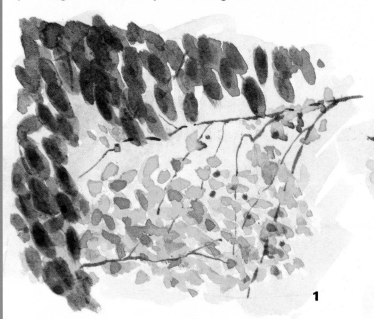

1 The sun highlighting some autumn leaves. Burnt sienna, Vandyke brown, olive green, Payne's grey and cadmium orange were used for the shaded canopy; Naples yellow, cadmium yellow and copper brown for the sunlit leaves.

2 Spring leaves in bright sunlight. The leaves were painted with Naples yellow, cadmium yellow, olive green and copper brown; burnt umber and Payne's grey were used for the tree trunk and branches.

3 A few glints of light catching some autumn leaves under a wooded canopy. Terre verte, Payne's grey, sap green, burnt umber and burnt sienna make up the darker foliage; cadmium yellow and copper brown the sunlit leaves.

4 Summer leaves glisten in the sunlight, set against a densely-shaded woodland scene. Payne's grey and terre verte were used for the shaded backdrop; Naples yellow, cadmium yellow and sap green for the light leaves.

5 Snow and ice on winter branches make them glow against a clear sky. Ultramarine was used for the sky, and Payne's grey and purple lake for the branch and ice.

6

7

7 A morning mist creates soft, luminous beams of light. The colours used here were viridian, permanent blue, Payne's grey, terre verte, sap green, chrome yellow and burnt sienna.

6 The red glow from a setting sun spreads a warm halo, silhouetting the trees against the sky. This exercise was painted with Naples yellow, cadmium yellow, bright red, brown madder alizarin and neutral tint.

8

8 Sunlight passing through summer foliage creates a green light that reflects on the tree trunk. This exercise was painted with Naples yellow, cadmium yellow, sap green, viridian and charcoal grey.

9

10

9 Leaves catching the sunlight stand out against foliage in heavy shade. The colours used here were cadmium yellow, sap green, charcoal grey, burnt umber and burnt sienna.

10 To give a realistic impression of light catching leaves, there must be a strong contrast between the lightest and the darkest leaves. For this exercise Naples yellow, cadmium yellow, sap green, terre verte and viridian have all been used.

BROWNIE PICNIC

This summer scene of a group of brownies is a pleasure both to look at and to paint. By following our step-by-step project, you will find that it is remarkably easy to convey the impression of a sun-dappled garden.

MATERIALS

artist's NOT watercolour paper
watercolours: permanent blue, Payne's grey, neutral tint, charcoal grey, Naples yellow, terre verte, burnt sienna, burnt umber, sap green, Vandyke brown, manganese blue, bright red, mauve, brown madder alizarin, chrome orange, yellow ochre, chrome yellow
brushes: round sable sizes 2, 3; round synthetic size 12; synthetic size 2 for masking fluid
HB pencil and putty eraser
mixing palette
water jar and water
masking fluid

1 With the HB pencil sketch in the main outlines of the composition.

2 With the masking brush, paint the masking fluid over the lightest leaves, the leaves in front of the house, the window frames and gable ends of the house (for how to use masking fluid, see page 28). Leave to dry. Rub over the pencil sketch lines lightly with a putty eraser to soften them.

3 Lay a pale wash of permanent blue over the sky area using the size 12 brush, carefully painting around the house. Leave the painting to dry.

4 Using terre verte mixed with plenty of water and the size 3 brush, paint in the background foliage, adding touches of manganese blue and Payne's grey wet-in-wet. Note that the light is coming from the left. Leave the painting to dry.

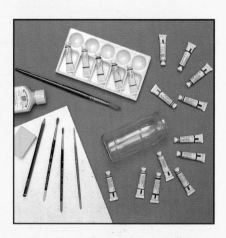

5 Mix Vandyke brown and brown madder alizarin and paint in the tree trunks, then add some shadows with Payne's grey. Build up the darker shadows on the foreground tree trunk using charcoal grey and painting wet-in-wet.

6 With a mix of chrome orange, burnt sienna and yellow ochre paint the sunlit walls of the house. Add a touch of brown madder alizarin to this mix for the chimney. For the shaded part of the roof, mix burnt umber and Payne's grey. For the right end wall mix neutral tint and burnt umber. With the size 2 brush and Payne's grey, paint the windows and then draw in the lines of the weather-boarding.

7 With a dark mix of charcoal grey and neutral tint, paint the dark righthand tree trunk. Leave to dry. Now remove the masking fluid by rubbing gently with your fingertip. Mix Naples yellow and chrome yellow and with the size 3 brush paint in the leaves, adding a little sap green to your mix for the righthand leaves. With the size 12 brush and a mix of Naples yellow and chrome yellow, paint in the grass, carefully working around the brownies. Leave your painting to dry.

8 Lay in the foreground wash with a mix of brown madder alizarin and burnt sienna. Now paint the darker leaves using sap green mixed with a little Payne's grey and charcoal grey and the size 3 brush. Add a few touches of terre verte, painting wet-in-wet. For the grass, use a mix of sap green and permanent blue and the size 12 brush. Add a few light touches of manganese blue, working wet-in-wet.

9 Use a dark mix of Payne's grey, charcoal grey and sap green and the size 3 brush for the darkest foliage on the righthand side of the painting.

10 With the size 12 brush, paint in the foreground shadows using light brushstrokes and a mix of neutral tint and permanent blue. Put in a few light touches of mauve and manganese blue. Add a few tufts of grass with a mix of sap green and Payne's grey.

11 Use a mix of burnt umber and burnt sienna and the size 3 brush for the brownie uniforms; for the girls' faces and arms use a mix of bright red, Naples yellow, chrome yellow and chrome orange.

12 The size 2 brush and a mix of Payne's grey and neutral tint are used for the brownies' hair, facial and other details. Add a few touches of manganese blue for highlights.

13 Draw in the branches with the size 2 brush and neutral tint. With Payne's grey paint in the shadows on the roof of the house, and highlight the gables and window frames with manganese blue.

Over the summer and autumn of 1890, Claude Monet made a series of paintings of the same subject at different times of the day. For further practice you might like to try this exercise yourself.

STARTING WITH OILS

If you've always wanted to try your hand at painting in oils, now is the time to start. In this lesson we introduce you to this exciting, versatile and appealing medium and offer advice on choosing paints and equipment. Plus there's a simple painting project to help you practise your new-found oil painting skills in brushwork and colour mixing.

For centuries, oils have been the most popular painting medium — and with good reason. Oil paint has a smooth, buttery consistency that is a delight to handle, and produces deep, richly saturated colours that seem to glow with an inner light.

Contrary to popular belief, oil paints are also the easiest medium for the beginner to use, because they are so flexible, responsive and versatile. Their slow drying time means that they can be freely moved around on the canvas, built up in layers, scraped off and overpainted to produce an infinite variety of textures and effects. For

example, you can apply the paint in thin layers to create a smooth, untextured surface — or you can exploit the mark-retaining qualities of oil by using it thickly to produce a textured paint surface which holds the mark of the brush.

Over the course of the lessons that follow we will introduce you to the many pleasures of painting in oils. So why not start today — take up a brush, squeeze out some paint, and have a go at this week's painting project. You may not produce a masterpiece first time, but with practice you will soon be amazed at the impressive results which you can achieve.

Gustave Courbet (1819-1877) was considered the leader of the Realist movement in 19th century French art. This painting, entitled 'Still life: apples and pomegranates', *above*, is a fine example of Courbet's use of oils to create a full and rich paint surface. The glowing colours and strongly modelled forms are built up with a variety of brushstrokes, with thick, dragged paint in some parts and smoothly blended paint in others.

111

Oil painting need not be an expensive pastime. To start off with, all you need are a few tubes of paint, three or four brushes and something to paint on. You can add extra colours, brushes and so on as your confidence in your technique grows.

CHOOSING COLOURS

Most paint manufacturers offer two grades of paint — artists' and students' (which are usually sold under a brand name). The latter are cheaper as they are made from less expensive pigments, and they are quite adequate to start off with. You can always substitute artists' quality paints once you have established your own personal palette. Another point worth noting is that students' colours are all priced the same, whereas artists' colours vary in price: they are classified in series, usually from 1 to 7, series 7 being the most expensive. The price differences reflect the expense or the rarity of the pigment used.

For the beginner it is advisable to start off with the minimum of colours, which can be added to later when you have decided which subjects you are most interested in painting. For example, if you intend painting landscapes you will need a different range of colours than if you intend painting flowers. The colours shown *right* provide a good 'starter' palette, versatile enough to see you through a wide range of subjects. Note that black is not included, the reason being that it tends to deaden other colours when mixed with them. (We shall tell you more about colour mixing later.)

Above: A suggested 'starter palette'. Clockwise from top right: cadmium red, ceruleum blue, titanium white, cadmium yellow, alizarin crimson, burnt sienna, viridian, French ultramarine, lemon yellow, raw umber.

MEDIUMS

Oil paint may be used straight from the tube, but more usually it is thinned with a medium (a combination of oil and a thinner). The most popular medium is a blend of linseed oil and turpentine or white spirit, in a ratio of 60% oil and 40% turpentine. (White spirit is actually cheaper than turpentine, has less odour and is less likely to cause the headaches which artists sometimes complain of when using turpentine.)

STARTER KIT

We show you *above* all you need to get started in oil painting: 10 tubes of colour, 2 round and 2 flat bristle brushes (a small and a medium size in each), a block of disposable palettes, linseed oil and turpentine to dilute the paint, a metal dipper to hold them (or you could use jam jars), and a canvas panel on which to paint. You will also need jars to hold white spirit for cleaning brushes, and a large supply of rags or kitchen paper for general cleaning.

PALETTES

Any smooth, non-porous surface will serve as a palette on which to prepare and mix oil paint. An old white dinner plate will do, or a piece of white formica.

Traditional wooden palettes with a thumb hole, designed for easel painting, come in various shapes and sizes, and cheaper laminated ones are also available. Before buying a palette, try out different sizes and shapes to see which feels the most comfortable.

Disposable palettes made of oil-proof paper come in handy pads; you simply tear off and throw away each sheet when you finish painting.

PAINTING SURFACES

Stretched canvas is the traditional support for oil painting, but to begin with you might want to use specially prepared canvas boards which give you an inexpensive, ready-made surface. You can also buy ready-primed and stretched canvases; these are more expensive than the boards, but have a more pleasant, springy surface. Pads of specially prepared oil paper which have a simulated canvas surface are also useful for sketching and for practising. As you gain more experience, you may wish to use rolls of canvas and stretch them yourself. This will be covered in a later lesson.

Beginners tend to buy small canvases, thinking they will be easier to cover. In fact, a larger canvas (about 60 x 90cm) will encourage a more confident approach so that you are not too bogged down with detail.

EASELS

An easel is an expensive piece of equipment and is not essential when you are starting out. You can either paint flat on a table or prop up the canvas at an angle. Oil-primed paper can be pinned to a drawing board propped up on your lap and leaning against a table.

BRUSHES

Brushes for oil painting come in a wide range of sizes, shapes and materials. Good-quality brushes cost more, but are worth the initial outlay as they hold their shape better and will last for years. It is difficult and frustrating to work with inferior brushes which will not make the kind of mark you require, shed their hairs and lose their shape very quickly.

Brushes are of two types — bristle and hair — and come in four main shapes — flats, rounds, brights and filberts. Rounds and flats are the most useful to begin with; brights and filberts can be added later, should you require them. Start with three or four hog's hair brushes in a range of sizes to suit the style and scale of your paintings.

Below, top to bottom: **Raphael sable flat brush size 8; Raphael sable round brushes size 10 and 12; Daler Bristlewhite long flats, size 2, 4 and 6; Daler Bristlewhite filberts, size 2, 4 and 6; Daler Bristlewhite rounds, size 2, 4 and 8; Daler Bristlewhite fan brushes, size 2 and 4.**

STILL LIFE WITH TOMATOES

If you have never painted with oils before, our step-by-step painting project for this lesson will make a splendid introduction. The simple shapes and vibrant colours in this group of tomatoes arranged on a cloth will give you basic practice in colour mixing and brushwork.

MATERIALS

canvas panel 14 x 10in (355 x 254mm)
oil colours: lemon yellow, cadmium yellow, alizarin crimson, cadmium red, French ultramarine, viridian, raw umber, titanium white
3 brushes: size 6 hog filbert, size 4 hog short flat, size 8 soft nylon round
disposable palette
linseed oil and turpentine
dipper or 2 small jars
pencil and eraser
rags for cleaning

1 Start by drawing the outlines of the still life, as shown. As you draw, observe carefully the size and shape of the tomatoes in relation to the picture as a whole, and note the sizes and shapes of the spaces between them. This helps you to get the shapes and proportions right.

2 When you are satisfied with your drawing, begin painting the cloth. Using a size 6 filbert brush, mix titanium white with turpentine to a thin consistency and paint the square at top left. Add some lemon yellow to the mixture for the square at top right. Mix cadmium yellow and a little viridian for the bottom right square, and finally viridian, raw umber and white for the bottom left square. Mix white and a little raw umber for the shadow underneath the tomato on the white square. Remember to keep all the paint mixes thin at this stage.

3 Clean your brush in turpentine, then mix together cadmium yellow, alizarin crimson and raw umber thinned with turpentine and use this colour to block in the shapes of the tomatoes. At this stage there is no need to attempt to paint any shadows or details, and the brushwork does not have to be perfectly smooth — this is simply an underlayer which provides a base for the colours and tones to follow. Leave the painting to dry before proceeding to the next stage: this will probably take a few hours, or you could leave it overnight and start again next day.

4 Switch to a size 4 flat brush and paint the shadows cast by the tomatoes on to the cloth with a mix of raw umber and a touch of French ultramarine. Begin to use the paint a little more thickly now, and mix it with linseed oil as well as turpentine so that it flows better. Do not paint the shadows too flatly — use small strokes and lightly blend them together so that they appear soft and natural. Make the shadows slightly darker immediately beneath the tomatoes, gradually lightening them as they move outwards.

5 Clean your brush before using it to continue building up the reds in the tomatoes. Look at the fruits constantly as you paint, and mix the paint to match the various patches of colour as you see them. For instance, paint the lighter areas with a mix of cadmium yellow, cadmium red and a touch of ultramarine; for the darker areas use cadmium yellow, alizarin crimson and a little more ultramarine. Don't worry about blending the brushstrokes smoothly at this stage.

6 Clean your brush and then use a mixture of lemon yellow and raw umber to paint the yellowish streaks in the tomatoes. Notice here how the strokes are applied at different angles, following the rounded forms of the fruits. This means the light catches the brushstrokes and adds interest.

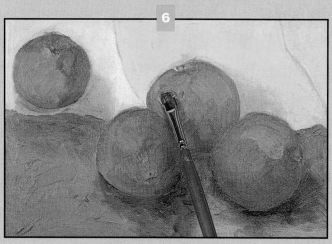

7 Now switch to a size 8 soft-haired round brush and enrich the reds in the tomatoes using a mixture of cadmium red and alizarin crimson. Use the paint a little more thickly now, again mixed with linseed oil and turpentine. Blend the colours together using feathery strokes with your soft brush.

8 Use a mixture of lemon yellow and cadmium red to brighten the upper surfaces of the tomatoes where they catch the light. Then darken the shadows on their undersides with a mixture of alizarin crimson, lemon yellow and French ultramarine. Blend the shadow tones softly into the surrounding colour so as not to create a hard edge that looks unnatural.

9 After cleaning your brush, paint the highlights on the tomatoes with a mixture of titanium white and a touch of cadmium yellow. Be careful not to overstate these or make them too white — use a delicate touch and paint them softly. You will find that some of the colour beneath is picked up by the brush and this helps to soften the highlights so that they blend in naturally. Leave the painting to dry.

10 Still using the same (clean) brush, paint the stalks on the tomatoes with a mixture of viridian, cadmium yellow and a touch of raw umber.

11 Now paint the shadows on the stalks using a mixture of cadmium yellow, viridian, ultramarine and alizarin crimson. Use the very tip of the brush and paint them carefully, keeping the shadows thin and delicate.

We hope you will be pleased with your first oil painting with its bold, bright reds in the tomatoes contrasting with the cool greens and yellows of the cloth. Note the subtlety of the composition — the three tomatoes in the foreground overlap to link them into a group, while the single tomato placed apart at the back suggests a note of spontaneity.

BRUSH TECHNIQUES

This lesson outlines some of the best-known and most useful techniques in oil painting, and explains how lively brushwork can lend vitality and expressiveness to your work.

The affinity that Van Gogh felt with nature is evident in 'Peach trees in blossom', *above left,* one of many pictures he painted in the countryside of Provence in France. Van Gogh was exhilarated by the radiantly sunlit landscape; borne along by his emotional response to the subject, he used vibrant colours and vigorous, swirling brushstrokes that invoke sensations of movement in the fields, sky and trees. His paintings were a celebration of the life-giving quality of the earth itself. In the diagram *below* we explain how Van Gogh achieved his effects in the painting with different types of brushstroke.

How is it that the style of one painter can be so different from that of another? Many elements go into creating an individual style — the way the painter sees his subject, the colours he chooses and the way he applies those colours to the canvas. Brush techniques are a crucial part of developing a personal painting style, and it is these that we are going to look at in detail in this lesson.

It is interesting to see how oil painting techniques have changed over the centuries. Early painters, such as Jan Van Eyck (c.1390-1441), applied the paint in thin layers, one over another, in a technique known as glazing, giving a very smooth finish with no visible brushmarks. Later, artists such as Titian (c.1487-1576) and Rembrandt (1606-1669), began to use a freer style in which smooth areas were combined with thick, textured paint in which the actual marks of the brush were an integral part of the picture. This technique is known as impasto.

In the 19th century, inspired by the example of the English landscape painter John Constable (1776-1837), the French Impressionists took the freedom of painting to even greater lengths by painting out of doors rather than in the studio. In their search for the ever-changing effects of light on the landscape, they adopted a broken-colour technique in which strokes and dabs of colour were laid side by side. These fragmented brushstrokes seemed themselves to quiver with light.

Today, artists can choose to paint in any style they like, and familiarity with a range of brushstrokes is vital to developing your own style. Over the page you will find plenty of ideas designed to develop your facility with the brush, and our painting project is inspired by Vincent Van Gogh, a master of expressive brushwork.

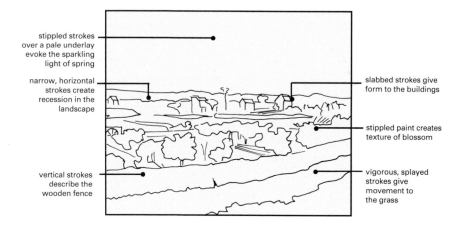

stippled strokes over a pale underlay evoke the sparkling light of spring

narrow, horizontal strokes create recession in the landscape

vertical strokes describe the wooden fence

slabbed strokes give form to the buildings

stippled paint creates texture of blossom

vigorous, splayed strokes give movement to the grass

The best way to get the feel of a brush is by actually handling it and applying paint with it, so spend some time practising the painting techniques below. You can work on any cheap paper for this exercise — wallpaper or lining paper will do, or you could use oil sketching paper.

Oil painting brushes come in a wide range of shapes and sizes, and each produces a different kind of mark. Bristle brushes are the ones most commonly used for oil painting. They hold paint well and are strong and flexible enough to cope with the consistency of the paint. Soft sable or synthetic brushes are mainly used to add fine details at the end. The most useful types of brush are shown here with a few of the natural marks they make.

Impasto
A richly textured paint surface is achieved by applying thick paint and 'sculpting' it with a brush or a painting knife. Load the brush with paint and apply it in short, heavy strokes and dabs. The brush marks help to describe form and texture.

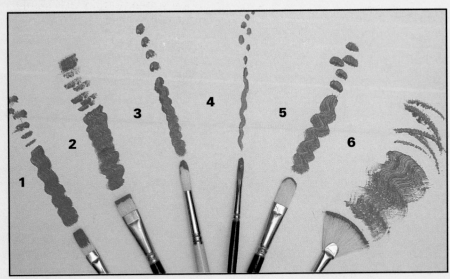

1 No 10 hog flat long This brush is for working loosely and applying paint over wide areas as the long bristles hold large amounts of thicker colour. The mark made with a flat brush can be altered by the angle at which it is held.

2 No 8 short flat hog Short-haired flat brushes are known as 'brights'. They are useful for applying short dabs of colour.

3 No 12 round hog Round bristle brushes have smooth, curved ends. They are versatile and hard-wearing, with good paint-carrying capacity.

4 No 12 round sable A soft brush for use in detailed work and for making fine strokes, as well as for glazing with thin layers of colour.

5 No 8 filbert hog A cross between a round and a flat, this brush has a long, springy head and a slightly rounded tip. It holds paint well and produces fine, rounded strokes.

6 No 12 fan blender hog This is not an essential brush but it can be useful for delicate tonal blending of colours, and for smoothing out brush strokes where an even surface is required.

Thin colour
Oil paint can be used thinly, scrubbing it on to the canvas so that the weave shows through. This results in a translucent stain, making colours appear soft and smoky.

HOW TO HOLD A BRUSH

Do not hold the brush too close to the metal ferrule as this restricts movement to the fingers and your brushmarks will be monotonous. Hold the brush where it feels naturally balanced. As you paint, the movement of your arm from the shoulder, through your elbow and wrist, should be fluid, confident and controlled.

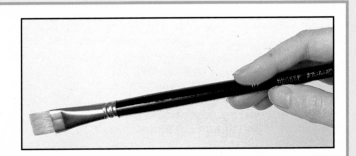

Angled strokes
Short, directional strokes, laid down with no blending or further manipulation, give energy and movement to a painting. Practise different kinds of marks, from short, stubby strokes to elegant strokes that taper and curve.

Wet-in-wet
Here, colours are applied over or into each other while they are still wet, leaving them partially mixed on the canvas. This gives the painting a soft, fluid look.

Scumbling
Scumbling means applying short, scrubby strokes of thin, dry, semi-opaque colour loosely over a dry underlayer so that the paint underneath shows through. It is useful for combining two tones to produce a subtle effect.

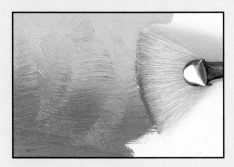

Blending
Any kind of brush can be used to blend two adjacent colours, but a fan brush is useful for a smooth effect. Brush lightly over the line where two colours meet until a smooth, melting gradation is achieved. Wipe surplus paint off the brush while working.

Dragging
Dragging is the equivalent of the watercolour technique known as 'drybrush' and is produced by working with dry colour, adding little or no medium to the paint. Load a small amount of paint on to the brush and drag it lightly over the canvas so that the paint catches on the weave and leaves a broken brushstroke. Dragging is useful because it can suggest detail with the minimum of brushwork.

Broken colour
This technique is associated with the French Impressionist painters, who showed that colours applied in small, separate strokes appear more luminous than colours physically mixed together on the palette. The paint should be fairly thick and dry so that each brushstroke retains its shape.

CLEANING YOUR BRUSHES

Brushes are one of your major investments, and if you look after them properly they will give you years of wear. Always clean your brushes after a painting session, otherwise the paint will harden on the bristles.

1 Remove excess paint with a rag, then rinse the brush in turpentine or white spirit and wipe thoroughly on a rag. Rinse with cold water, then gently rub the bristles over a block of soap. (Never use hot water — it may expand the ferrule and cause hairs to fall out.)

2 Rub the brush around gently in your palm, working up a lather. Keep rinsing and soaping until no trace of pigment appears in the lather. Rinse under running water, shake out and smooth into shape with the fingers. Leave to dry in a jar, hairs uppermost.

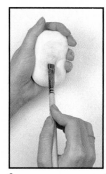

1   **2**

SUMMER CORNFIELDS

Our painting project for this lesson is a simple rural scene that provides plenty of opportunities to practise your skills with the brush. Different sizes and shapes of brush are used for a variety of marks to represent the texture of foliage, grasses, tree trunks and weathered stone.

1 Start by drawing the outlines of the composition in soft pencil, as shown.

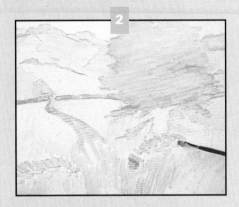

2 The stark white of the canvas can be intimidating to work on, so it is a good idea to cover the picture surface with a thin wash of colour first. Dilute the paint to a very thin consistency using turpentine, and apply it with a size 4 flat brush. Use Naples yellow for the cornfields; lemon yellow and a touch of ultramarine for the trees and foreground grass; cerulean, Vandyke brown and white to make a grey for the wall; and yellow ochre and Vandyke brown for the path. Leave to dry.

3 When the first washes are dry, paint the sky with a loose mixture of cerulean blue and white, using a size 4 flat brush. Now switch to a size 2 flat brush and paint the group of trees on the left with a mixture of viridian and ultramarine. Use fairly dry paint and make small, curved strokes to give movement to the clumps of foliage.

MATERIALS

canvas board 610 x 508mm
oil colours: ultramarine, lemon yellow, Naples yellow, cerulean blue, titanium white, yellow ochre, Vandyke brown, viridian, alizarin crimson, cadmium yellow, cadmium red
4 brushes: size 2 and 4 hog flat, size 2 and 6 hog round
palette
linseed oil
dipper or 2 small jars
pencil and eraser
turpentine for cleaning

4 Complete the tree group by painting the lighter parts with a mixture of lemon yellow and a touch of cerulean, using the same upward curving strokes. Using a size 2 round brush, add more blue and a little white to this mixture to paint the hedgerows in the distance, again using fairly stiff paint so that the marks of the brush remain. Then darken the mixture with viridian to paint the darker bases of the hedgerows.

5 Use a size 4 flat brush and a loose mixture of Naples yellow and white to paint the distant cornfields. Mix a pale bluish grey from white, cerulean blue and viridian and add a few feathery strokes of this colour here and

there, just to give variety and movement. The paint is used fairly thick and applied with loose, directional strokes that follow the rounded forms of the hills. This is quite different from applying a flat, all-over wash.

6 Using a size 2 round brush, paint the footpath with a variegated mixture of Vandyke brown, yellow ochre and white, using the paint fairly dry. Allow the brushstrokes to peter out in the foreground — this area will be painted over later. Lighten the colour with more white to paint the wall in the distance.

7 Using a size 4 flat brush, continue painting the footpath with short horizontal strokes that become smaller as the path recedes into the distance. Notice here the variations in the browns, and how the marks of the brush give texture to the path. Mix a warm yellow from yellow ochre, Naples yellow and white for the foreground cornfield. Use a size 4 flat brush and long, horizontal strokes in the distance. In the foreground use a size 2 round brush, held vertically, to make thick, stippled strokes that mimic the texture of ears of corn. The contrast between the textured foreground and the smoother background gives the effect of distance. As you paint, use your colours partially blended to give them variety, adding a hint of green (mixed from yellow ochre and cerulean) here and there to indicate shadows. Where the corn meets the footpath, use feathery strokes with your brush to knit the two colours together, so avoiding a hard, unnatural edge.

8 With a size 4 flat brush and a mixture of alizarin crimson, Vandyke brown, cerulean and white, begin painting the wall in the foreground using short, block-like strokes. For the distant wall, use a size 2 flat brush and the same mixture, darkened with more blue.

9 Continue painting the foreground wall with a size 4 flat brush, indicating the rough stones with greys and pinkish reds. Mix cerulean, Vandyke brown and a touch of white for the greys; Naples yellow, yellow ochre and alizarin crimson for the darker pinks; and the same mixture plus white for the lighter pinks. Use Vandyke brown for the cast shadows on the stones along the top of the wall.

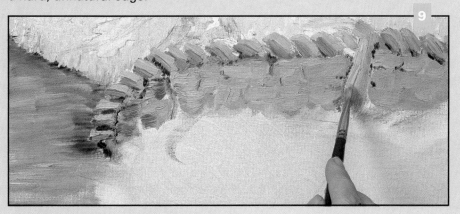

10 Use a size 4 flat brush and Vandyke brown to paint the tree trunk, using rough strokes of dryish paint. For the highlights, use a size 2 flat brush and the same pinkish mixture used on the wall in step 9 to make small, wavy strokes.

11 Start painting the tree foliage with a size 6 round brush and a mixture of lemon yellow, white and a touch of viridian. Use the paint thickly now, straight from the tube and undiluted, and stipple it on with jabbing strokes, holding the brush vertically.

12 Continue building up the crinkly texture of the foliage, painting the darker areas with the same mixture as in step 11, darkened with more viridian. Using the same brush and a mixture of cerulean and a touch of Vandyke brown, indicate the shadow cast by the tree on the corn and the footpath. Now switch to a size 2 flat brush and use the same greens used on the tree to paint the foreground grasses with long, upward strokes.

13 The painting is now almost complete, and all that remains is to soften the tones in the sky. Use a size 2 flat brush and a pale mix of cerulean blue and white to indicate the clouds with softly-blended strokes.

14 As a finishing touch, use a size 2 round brush and cadmium red to flick in a few poppies among the grasses.

By the time you have finished this landscape project, you should be familiar with most of the basic strokes and techniques used in oil painting — and should feel confident enough to tackle almost any subject.

MODELLING FORM

The still life is a subject that has fascinated artists for centuries. It's easy to set up a still life composed from everyday objects found in the home, and kitchen pots and cutlery, flowers, fruit and vegetables all make ideal subject matter. Arranged in a quiet corner, your group can remain undisturbed for as long as it takes you to paint it, and will give you unlimited scope for the study of shape, form, colour, texture and tone.

One of the techniques essential to still-life painting is the ability to model form, and this requires observation and understanding of light and shade. Without light, all objects would be seen as flat shapes. When light strikes an object, it creates a range of shadows, highlights and half-tones which our eyes use to interpret the shape and volume of that object. Thus describing three-dimensional form in paint means accurately describing the light and dark areas. These lights and darks are known as 'tones', and the word tone refers to how light or dark an area is, irrespective of its colour. For example, an apple may be red, but that red will be darker in tone on the shadow side than on the lit side.

Square-sided forms such as boxes are easy to paint as their sides show distinct changes of tone. In rounded objects, the shading is very gradual, with no sudden changes from one tone to the next, and the tones need to be carefully blended together to give a smooth gradation. The soft, pliant consistency of oil paints allows you to softly blend tones by 'knitting' them together, wet-in-wet, to achieve a subtle gradation from light to dark that creates the illusion of a curved surface.

The ability to create an illusion of solid form on a flat painting surface is an important skill for any artist. In this lesson we show you how to use the effects of light and shade to describe the solid forms of objects, and how to manipulate the paint to create gradations of tone.

Left: This detail from a painting entitled 'Cups and water biscuits II' by Lucy Willis shows how a good grasp of modelling techniques can give a convincing impression of depth and solidity to a still life. As in our 'Mediterranean still life' painting project, *above,* the careful rendering of shadows, highlights and reflections imparts the illusion of three-dimensional form to the bowl and other utensils, while the fruit seem to glow with vitality.

TONAL GRADATIONS

To understand how tonal gradations work, take a sheet of white paper and hold it to one side of a light source such as a window or a lamp. Bend the paper into a curve and observe how the tones show a gradual transition from white, nearest the light source, through to dark grey on the opposite side, which describes the smooth curve of the surface, **1**.

To make it easier to define the tonal changes, imagine the curve as a series of flat planes, each one slightly darker in tone than the one before, **2**.

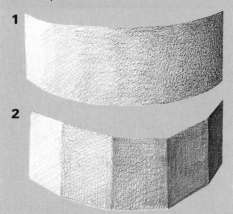

1

2

BLENDING TECHNIQUES

Because oil paint is slow to dry, it is uniquely suited to producing softly blended gradations of tone. To achieve a smooth, even finish, first lay down strips of colour or tone next to each other and blend them together wet-in-wet, as the paint is applied. Finish off with a soft brush if necessary.

A more lively effect can be achieved by allowing the brushmarks to remain visible instead of smoothing them out completely. Simply brush lightly, backwards and forwards, over the line where two colours or tones meet, dragging one colour into the other. You can use your finger instead of a brush.

LIGHTING A STILL LIFE

When painting still-life objects, consider the lighting carefully. It is best to keep the lighting simple, preferably from a single source, as this creates clearly defined lights and shadows. Generally, light

coming from slightly above and to one side of the object works best, as this gives a strong impression of form and volume (*left*). If the lighting is coming from the front, the object may appear flattened and lacking in form (*above*).

MEDITERRANEAN STILL LIFE

This colourful painting of a still life bathed in warm Mediterranean sunlight shows you how careful observation of light and shade, translated into paint with subtle blending techniques, gives form and substance to a simple composition.

1 Using a soft pencil, draw an outline of the composition on your oil sketching paper.

2 Mix up some cadmium yellow on your palette and add a small quantity of yellow ochre. Dilute the mixture with turpentine and, with a size 8 filbert brush, lay down a wash over the background. Wipe off some of the paint with a clean rag so that the canvas is lightly stained with the colour.

MATERIALS

oil sketching paper
oil colours: cadmium yellow, yellow ochre, cerulean blue, titanium white, French ultramarine, raw umber, scarlet lake, burnt sienna
3 brushes: size 4 hog flat, size 6 soft round, size 8 hog filbert
palette
turpentine or white spirit to dilute the paint
dipper or small jar
2B pencil and eraser
rags for cleaning

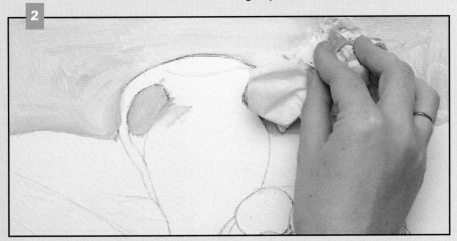

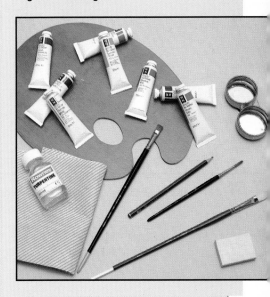

3 Mix up some cerulean blue and titanium white, and add a small quantity of French ultramarine. Clean the size 8 brush and use it to apply the paint mixture thickly over the yellow stain, but not entirely covering it. The undercoat will now shine through, causing the colours to 'vibrate' and adding visual interest to your painting. This technique was favoured by many of the French Impressionists.

4 With the same brush (cleaned) begin to paint the cloth, using a mixture of cadmium yellow with a touch of yellow ochre and titanium white. For the shadows use a mixture of raw umber and French ultramarine. Apply the paint freely, beginning with the highlights and painting the shadows wet-in-wet.

5 Paint the jug using a mixture of titanium white, scarlet lake, burnt sienna and yellow ochre. Vary the mix to match the different tones that you see. For the mid-tones add more burnt sienna and for the darker tones add a little French ultramarine. The edges of the jug need greater precision — use a size 4 flat brush for extra control.

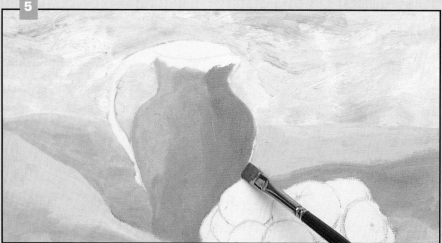

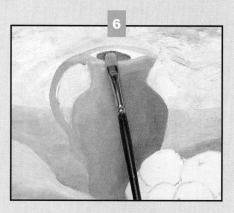

6 Using the size 8 brush and raw yellow ochre, brighten up and give the impression of texture on the jug by dragging the brush lightly across the wet surface (this technique is called scumbling). For the glazed rim of the jug, use a mixture of cadmium yellow, yellow ochre, raw umber and burnt sienna. Apply the paint freely and then, with the same wet-in-wet technique, apply raw umber for the shadow in the lip of the jug. For the lighter areas, use a mixture of yellow ochre and titanium white.

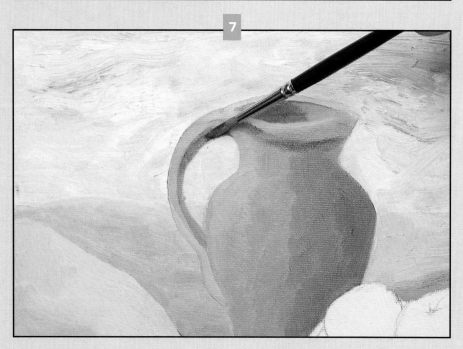

7 Now finish painting the handle of the jug with a size 6 soft round brush. Use a mixture of burnt sienna and French ultramarine for the darker areas, with a dab of titanium white for the lighter areas. Test your colour mixes on a piece of scrap paper before using them.

8 Continue modelling and refining the contours of the jug, using a mixture of burnt sienna and raw umber. Now mix up some yellow ochre with a touch of scarlet lake. With the size 8 brush, start painting the oranges. Apply the paint loosely, looking carefully at the subject all the time.

9 For the modelling of the oranges, paint the mid-tones with raw French ultramarine. For the lighter tones, use a mixture of scarlet lake and cadmium yellow. Use titanium white with a dab of cerulean blue for the highlights.

11 Paint the underside of the bowl, using a mixture of titanium white, French ultramarine and raw umber. Use the same colour combination for the inside of the bowl, adding touches of your orange mixture for the reflection of the fruit. Paint the rim of the bowl using a combination of titanium white, French ultramarine and raw umber.

10 Continue to refine the modelling of the oranges using a mixture of raw umber, French ultramarine, cadmium yellow and scarlet lake for the darker tones. Paint in the stalks of the oranges using raw French ultramarine applied with a size 6 soft brush.

12 Use a size 6 soft brush to paint in the detail on the bowl. Study the subject carefully, and look at what happens to the bowl when light hits it. Where are the shadows? Where are they hard and where are they soft? Paint the dark underside using a mixture of raw umber and burnt sienna.

13 Now it is time to begin refining the painting. Paint the highlights on the rim and top of the jug, using a mixture of titanium white and cerulean blue. For the darker tones at the base of the bowl, use French ultramarine and a touch of raw umber. Use the same mix for the base and rim of the jug. Complete the modelling of the jug using a mix of cadmium yellow and scarlet lake with plenty of titanium white. Use the size 6 soft brush to lay the colour over the underpainting.

When you have completed your Mediterranean still life, you will have some understanding of how the wet-in-wet technique can help in modelling form, so giving life and vitality to your paintings.

THE LANGUAGE OF COLOUR

The colours used in a painting will have a profound effect on the response that painting evokes. So it is important to understand the language of colour if you are to achieve the effects you want in your pictures. In this lesson we introduce you to colour theory and show you how to apply it to your work.

Colour helps us to understand what we see by giving us extra information about the things we are looking at. For example, we can recognise a tree by its shape, but its colour can tell us if it is spring, summer, autumn or winter.

However, apart from providing us with factual information, colour acts upon our feelings and emotions. Many colours have become associated with all kinds of signals or messages. For instance, red is generally perceived as hot, advancing, dangerous, loud, vulgar, and so on. Some of these messages are part of what might be called the collective unconscious, while some of them are purely subjective.

Some colours on the other hand are perceived as quiet, restful, cool, receding, etc. Obviously it is helpful to know how any particular colour is likely to be perceived before you use it in a painting. Another factor to take into account is how colours 'go together'. Some of them just don't — they create a discord. Sometimes this can be used positively in a painting, but if the painter is not aware of it he will create an effect he did not intend.

The total impact of all the colours on a canvas must also be considered. Too many bright colours used together will produce a strident effect. Similarly, too many quiet colours without any contrast will be drab.

Before any theories of colour were developed, artists learned by experience, observing the colours around them and finding out how to imitate them with coloured pigments. Painters like Titian (1487-1576), Rubens (1577-1640) and Rembrandt (1606-1669) had far fewer colours to paint with than we have now, but because they understood them so well, they could use them very skilfully. In fact, they used colour as a code, and if we understand that code their paintings become more meaningful for us.

Our painting project, entitled 'Sailing in the bay' *above left*, is an exercise in the use of only three pigments plus white. It demonstrates how skilful use of just a few pigments can produce a lively painting in many colours. The painting *below* of 'The Albanian sea' by L. Tuxen (1853-1927) uses a restricted colour range to produce a quieter effect.

Basic colour theory identifies red, blue and yellow as the primary colours of the painter's palette. These may be arranged at equal intervals around a circle with the spaces in between them filled by colours that are combinations of the primaries on either side (see **1**). This is called a colour circle, or colour wheel. It shows that when mixed together, red and yellow give orange, blue and yellow give green and blue and red give purple. Combining colours next to each other on the wheel gives less definite colours like yellow-green or orange-red, and these may be added to more complicated versions of the colour circle. It is supposed to be possible to mix colours in accordance with this arrangement and, as a basic guide, it is reasonably effective. The colour circle is too simple to account for all aspects of colour though, and it does not work properly when applied to artist's paints, because the pigments in them are not pure colours. They have undertones of other colours that show up in the mixture.

A colour circle can also tell us something about how colours relate to each other. Colours directly opposite each other are said to be 'complementary' and make each other look stronger and more lively when placed together. As you can see, orange and blue are complementary. An orange dot on a blue background is therefore more striking than an orange dot on a red one (see **2**). In fact the two orange dots appear to be slightly different colours, although they are the same.

1

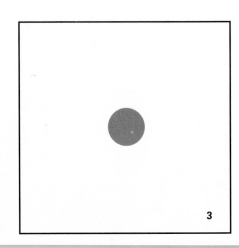

2

COMPLEMENTARY COLOURS

Complementary colours appear opposite each other on the colour circle. An understanding of the effects of complementary colours can be used to achieve dramatic effects in a painting.

The 19th century colour theorist Michel-Eugene Chevreul was the first to investigate the properties of complementary colours. He demonstrated that a strong colour such as red will show a tendency to light up its surrounding area with its opposite colour and thus affect the appearance of the colour.

He called this effect 'simultaneous contrast'.

Finding the complement
To find the complementary of any colour, take a sheet of plain white paper and paint a small dot of your chosen colour (figure **3**) on to it. Hold the paper at arm's length and stare at the colour for about 30 seconds. When you have done this, look at another piece of white paper — you will find that you will be able to see a faint after-image of the complementary colour.

3

SAILING IN THE BAY

Our project painting for this lesson demonstrates how you can use just four basic colours to maximum effect. The primary colours are represented by a strong blue, a dull yellow and a dull red, while white is used to control the tone and intensity of the colouring. A feature of the project is the special use of the complementary colours blue and orange.

M A T E R I A L S

a canvas or canvas board
3B pencil
4 tubes of student oil colour: titanium white, French ultramarine, yellow ochre and red ochre
size 6 filbert and size 2 round bristle brushes; size 1 round or flat synthetic-haired brush
palette
clean rag
linseed oil and white spirit

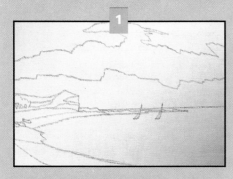

1 Use a soft 3B pencil to draw up the outlines of the composition.

2 Mix French ultramarine and titanium white to a mid-blue. Thin the paint if necessary and paint the sky at the top with long thin brushstrokes with the flat of a size 6 filbert brush. Use the edge of the brush to paint the outlines of the cloud. Work from the top left hand corner towards the right if you are right-handed.

3 Mix more white into some of the mid-blue and add a little yellow ochre to make a pale greenish-blue. Paint the sky below the clouds the same way as before.

4 Wipe the brush clean on the rag. Mix up some of the original mid-blue colour and, using the same brush, put some of this into the wet paint at the bottom of the sky, just below the cloud.

5 Wipe the brush clean again and with gentle strokes of the tip, blend the two blues together. Do not attempt a perfect blend — the effect you want is of a feathery division between them.

6 With the edge of the size 6 filbert brush, put some mid-blue along the horizon and blend it as before. You have now created

the impression of a distant layer of cloud out over the sea. Using the same mixture of blue, paint along the middle of the large cloud, mingling the darker and lighter tints together with strokes of the brush.

7 Mix a pale orange-yellow from yellow ochre and titanium white, and paint it along the edges of the cloud. Let the brushstrokes touch the blue but do not blend the colours. Keep the brush clean by wiping it on a rag after a few

strokes, then load it again with fresh paint. Here and there, touch a slightly darker tint of yellow ochre and titanium white into the clouds. Wipe the brush clean and use it soften the edges of these colours.

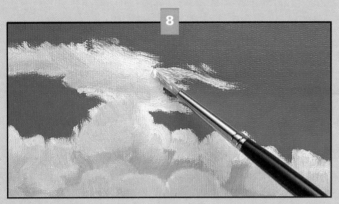

8 With a clean size 2 round bristle brush, paint titanium white along the top edges of the cloud and around the plume of cloud above it. Remember that the light is coming from the right and above, so highlights will be on surfaces facing that way. As more colour is put in place, you may wish to improve on the painting you have already done. Do so with a loaded brush, painting fresh colour into the existing wet paint without mixing them together.

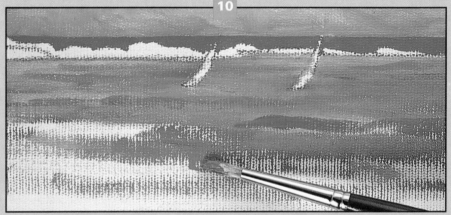

9 Mix a dull grey-green using yellow ochre, French ultramarine and titanium white. Paint in the grass on the headland and the fields behind it with tints of yellow ochre and titanium white. Paint into the green with French ultramarine to suggest shadow.

10 Paint the sea along the horizon using a deep mid-blue. Work down from this area with horizontal strokes and different tints of blue and green. Use stronger colour and more distinct brushstrokes as you approach the foreground. This has the effect of bringing it nearer.

11 Use red ochre, yellow ochre and titanium white for the cliffs and outcrops of rock. Paint them in with a small brush.

12 Mix up pale tints of pink, blue and purple-grey for the stony beach, using red ochre, French ultramarine and titanium white. Paint in these colours as shown with separate, but partly blended strokes. As more colours are added, you will need to correct colour relationships. Here, the darker field has been altered. You may also want to add details like the hedge between the two fields. Do this whilst you can reach the area without stretching over wet paint.

13 Carry on painting the beach and sea using longer brush strokes and richer colours. These will make the foreground look nearer. Use blue and green to create wave patterns curving across the sea.

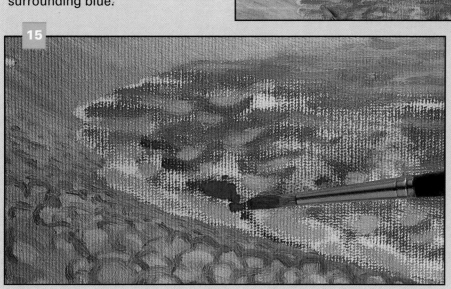

14 Further adjustments of the colour relationships are now necessary. The cliffs and rocks are made more orange to adjust their apparent distance in relation to the blue sea and sky. Some repainting of the clouds using the same colours as before is also done. Stronger, more orange tints of yellow ochre are added to increase the complementary effect with the surrounding blue.

15 Use the size 2 round brush with a strong tint of French ultramarine to outline the pebbles on the beach. Paint them smaller as they get further away and finish off with some faint dashes when they get too small to paint. Dab a few tints of yellow ochre and red ochre on to the pebbles to vary the colouring. With a strong mix of French ultramarine and titanium white, continue painting the sea.

16 Use curved brush strokes to suggest waves. The colours on the left of each wave should be darkest because the light is coming from the right. Paint the sea with tints of French ultramarine and titanium white and tints of green made from yellow ochre, French ultramarine and white. Remember to make the colours stronger in the foreground. A few orange reflections of yellow ochre and titanium white will enliven the effect.

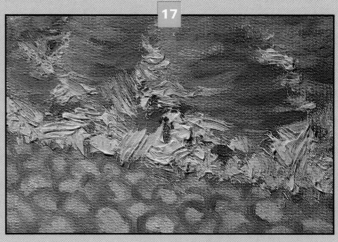

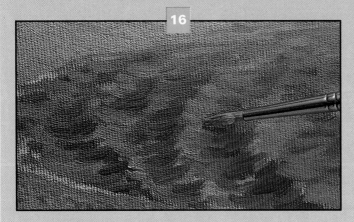

17 To paint the sea surf, load your size 6 filbert brush with titanium white and drag it over the wet paint of the sea, so that the white paint, not the brush, touches it. Clean the brush frequently and re-load with titanium white. Keep changing the direction of the brushstrokes so that the paint is drawn out in strands to represent sea spray.

18 Paint in the boats on the beach and the sails in the distance with the edge of a small flat synthetic hair brush. Some extra titanium white is brushed into the clouds on the horizon to make them more distinct, then the finished painting is left to dry. Because this painting uses oil colour you can continue working on the dry painting later on if you wish. It may be easier to make fine adjustments of colouring at that stage.

Now that you have completed the painting you can see how the skilful mixing and blending of only four colours can produce a vibrant picture composed of many colours.

BROKEN COLOUR

Broken colour is an exciting technique pioneered by the French Impressionists and still used by painters today to produce paintings full of light and a sense of movement. We introduce you to using broken colour and show you how it can bring freshness and vitality to your paintings.

In the classic, studio-based tradition of painting, painters mixed their colours on the palette before applying them to the canvas. Their aim was to paint a scene by carefully recording the gradations of light and shade that they saw, and so giving an impression of modelled forms.

The Impressionists changed all this, first by going outdoors to paint 'in the field'. Here they found that light and colours were constantly changing, and to capture these fleeting impressions they had to abandon the classic methods and adopt a new approach. As Claude Monet said, they had to 'forget what objects you have before you — a tree, a house, a field — merely think, here is a little square of blue, here an oblong of pink, here is a streak of yellow, and paint it just as it looks'.

Colour mosaic

In practice, this meant that instead of mixing colours on the palette, the Impressionists would put dabs of different unmixed colours side by side on the canvas. This technique creates a picture that close to looks rather like a mosaic of colour — but from a distance gives a picture that seems to shimmer with light.

Painters today use broken colour

technique in a variety of ways. Colours may be applied in dabs side by side; or short brushstrokes of different colours may be applied, one over the other; or more fluid strokes, or stippled strokes, may be used. On the following pages we give you some exercises in broken colour to try.

In this painting of 'The poppy field' *above left* by Alphonse Asselbergs (1839-1916) you can see how the artist has applied his various pigments to the canvas in streaks and dabs, leaving them to mix optically in the eyes of the viewer. You need to stand well back from this kind of painting to see it properly. This is an entirely different method of painting from the classic tradition, in which pigments are mixed on the palette. Our project painting for this lesson, *left*, shows a market stall full of brightly-coloured Mediterranean fruit and vegetables, painted in a free style that will serve as an introduction to painting in broken colour.

BROKEN COLOUR EFFECTS

On these pages we give you a range of exercises in broken colour to try out. Paint them in oils on an oil canvas board, and keep a note of the colours and brushstrokes you use for future reference. Remember to clean your brush between colours. When you have painted our exercises, you may like to experiment and make your own discoveries about using broken colour.

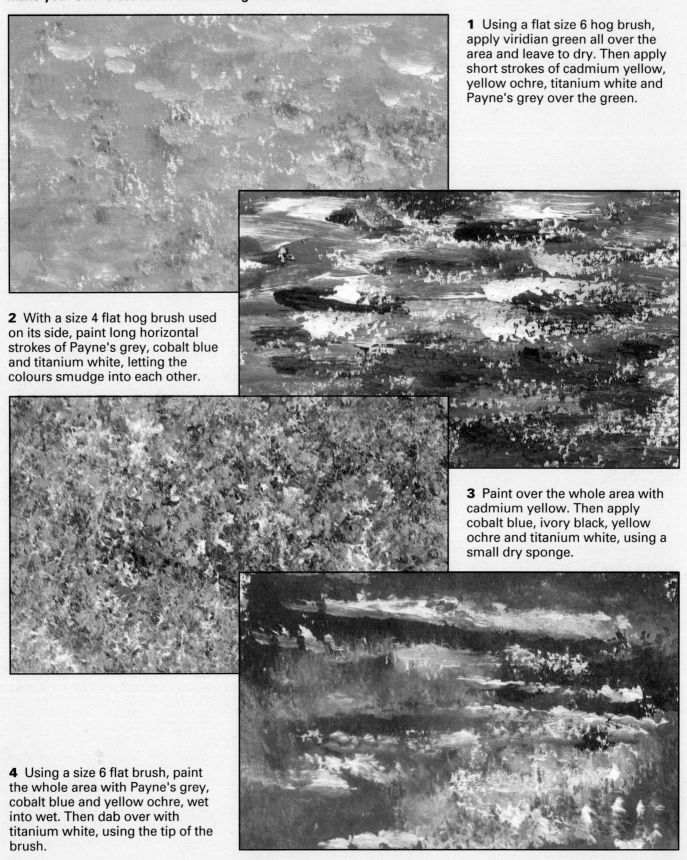

1 Using a flat size 6 hog brush, apply viridian green all over the area and leave to dry. Then apply short strokes of cadmium yellow, yellow ochre, titanium white and Payne's grey over the green.

2 With a size 4 flat hog brush used on its side, paint long horizontal strokes of Payne's grey, cobalt blue and titanium white, letting the colours smudge into each other.

3 Paint over the whole area with cadmium yellow. Then apply cobalt blue, ivory black, yellow ochre and titanium white, using a small dry sponge.

4 Using a size 6 flat brush, paint the whole area with Payne's grey, cobalt blue and yellow ochre, wet into wet. Then dab over with titanium white, using the tip of the brush.

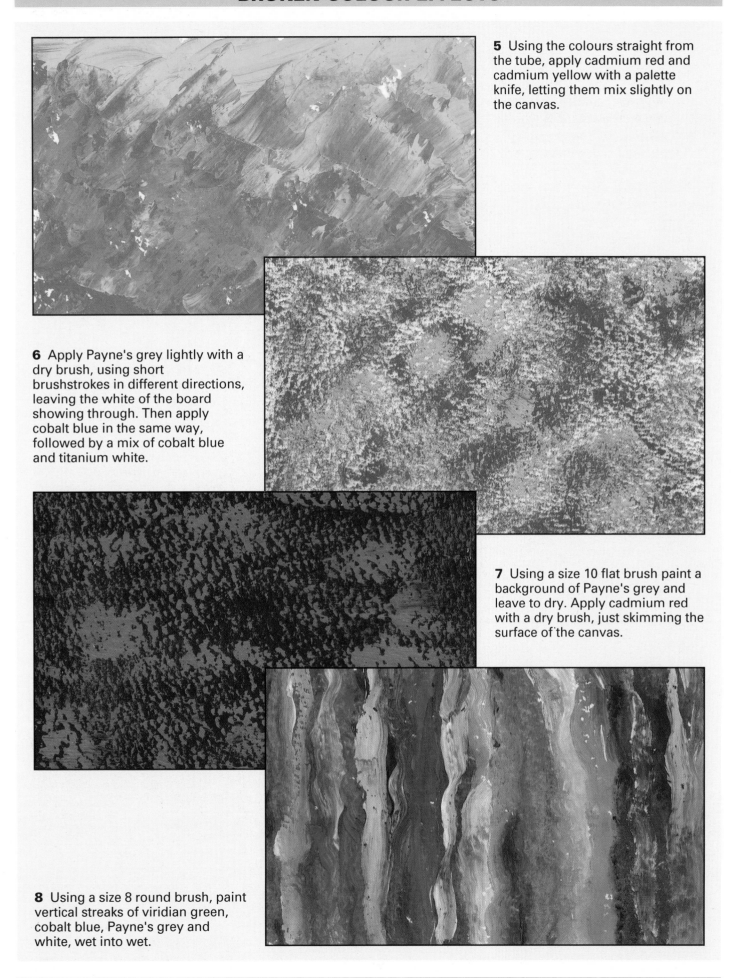

5 Using the colours straight from the tube, apply cadmium red and cadmium yellow with a palette knife, letting them mix slightly on the canvas.

6 Apply Payne's grey lightly with a dry brush, using short brushstrokes in different directions, leaving the white of the board showing through. Then apply cobalt blue in the same way, followed by a mix of cobalt blue and titanium white.

7 Using a size 10 flat brush paint a background of Payne's grey and leave to dry. Apply cadmium red with a dry brush, just skimming the surface of the canvas.

8 Using a size 8 round brush, paint vertical streaks of viridian green, cobalt blue, Payne's grey and white, wet into wet.

MARKET STALL

Our project painting for this lesson is a colourful market stall in the French resort of St Tropez, and is designed to give you more basic practice in painting in oils as well as serving as an introduction to broken colour techniques.

PREPARING THE CANVAS

Prepare your canvas by underpainting it the day before so that it has plenty of time to dry. Make a thin grey mix of 60% Payne's grey and 40% titanium white, thinned with turpentine substitute. Paint all over your white canvas with this and leave to dry overnight.

1 Draw up the outlines of the painting in pencil on your prepared canvas board. Prepare a thin, fairly dry, mix of ivory black and burnt sienna diluted with turpentine substitute and with the size 5 brush strengthen the pencil outlines and block in the dark areas as shown. Leave for about 20 minutes to dry (you can speed up the drying process by using a hairdryer).

MATERIALS

24 x 20in oil canvas board
palette for mixing
artist's flat bristle hog or nylon oil brushes: size 5 and $^{1}/_{4}$in, $^{1}/_{8}$in and $^{3}/_{8}$in
turpentine substitute or white spirit
mixing jars
tubes of oil paints: titanium white, ivory black, Payne's grey, yellow ochre, chrome orange, cadmium yellow, cadmium red, burnt sienna, raw umber, sap green, cobalt blue; viridian green
pencil
cloth or tissues for cleaning

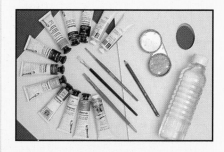

2 Paint the light flesh tones of the faces of the stallholders, using a $^{1}/_{4}$in flat brush and a mix of cadmium red, chrome orange and titanium white (plus enough turpentine substitute to make the colours mix well). Add more white for the lightest tones, and a touch of raw umber and cobalt blue for the darker flesh tones.

3 Clean the brush and then paint the yellow fruit using varying mixes of cadmium yellow and titanium white to give the various tones.

4 Clean your brush thoroughly and then paint the stallholder's jumper in various mixes of cobalt blue, Payne's grey and titanium white. Darken the blue mix by adding Payne's grey, and use this dark blue-grey colour to paint the dark awning at the top of the painting, the grapes, aubergines and other dark patches shown in step 5.

5 Paint the cloth in the foreground with viridian green, darkening the mix with Payne's grey for the shadows.

6 Using your clean ³/₈in brush, mix up cadmium red and apply this colour to the red awnings in the background, the red peppers in the foreground, and in other places as shown. Use the same colour to paint on some modelling of the lemons in the foreground.

7 Paint the tree trunks and branches with raw umber and dabs of titanium white. Clean the brush and then paint the fruit boxes with a mix of yellow ochre, raw umber and titanium white.

8 Complete the modelling of the fruit in the foreground by adding brushstrokes of darker tones (mixed by adding Payne's grey to your original colour) and highlights of titanium white. Now paint in the range of greens, using mixes of sap green (darkened with Payne's grey for the dark tones) for the white grapes, and mixes of viridian green and Payne's grey for the darker greens. Use titanium white for highlights.

9 The painting is now almost complete. Brighten the yellow fruit in the centre by overpainting with chrome orange. Overpaint the leaves of the tree with the $1/8$in brush, using dabs of sap green, raw umber and white, to create a dappled effect. Use titanium white with a touch of cobalt blue for the white overalls of the two stallholders, and for the pale background in the far distance. Now work over the painting adding final details and modelling — by now you should have a good idea of what mixes to use to match our artist's colours.

PAINTING FLOWERS

Flowers are a very popular subject for painters, and oils are excellent for capturing their glowing colours and intricate modelling. We show you how to set up and paint a floral arrangement, and give you tips on mixing colours for a range of favourite garden flowers.

For your first flower painting project, it's wise to select a single flower variety, and concentrate on the unique qualities of each individual flowerhead.

Once you have chosen your flowers, you will need a container to hold them. Choose something plain that will not dominate the flowers — a simple, undecorated vase is often the most effective. And make sure that it is deep enough for at least one half of the stems to be covered with water.

You may need to keep your arrangement fresh for several days while you paint it, so take special care when setting it up. To make flowers last as long as possible, florists 'condition' them by keeping them overnight plunged to the neck in cold water. Then they cut the bottom of the flower stems on a diagonal line, using a sharp knife, and remove all foliage that will be below the waterline. They also remove some of the upper foliage because the leaves take water away from the flowers.

To keep the flowers in place while you paint them, you can put a piece of plastic arranging foam (which can be bought from florists) in the bottom of your container; let the foam soak up water for ten minutes before pushing the flower stems into it.

Flowers with weak or broken stems can be wired. You can push florist's fine green wire through the stem and into the flowerhead, and the strengthened stem can then be bent to a graceful curve.

Don't arrange your flowers too formally, however. The most pleasing arrangements are often the most natural looking.

Keep your finished flower arrangement in a cool place, and don't forget to top up the vase regularly with clean water.

This painting *above* of old-fashioned roses by the master of flower painting, Henri Fantin-Latour (1836-1904), glows with life and colour, giving the impression that the flowers are just picked fresh from the garden. Note that the background is very plain, so as not to detract from the flower colours. Our project painting of gerberas, *below*, also concentrates on one type of flower seen against a simple background.

To help you paint flowers, we give you on these pages examples of colour mixes for various shades of a range of popular garden flowers. If you are planning to do much flower painting it's worth investing in some special pigments: permanent mauve, magenta and cadmium orange will be particularly useful.

LILY

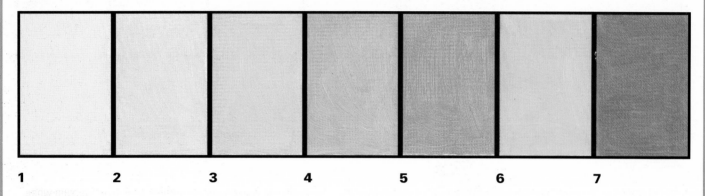

1 Titanium white, lemon yellow and yellow ochre. **2** Titanium white, lemon yellow and yellow ochre, plus a minute dash of alizarin crimson. **3** Lemon yellow, cadmium yellow and yellow ochre. **4** Cadmium yellow and yellow ochre. **5** Cadmium yellow, yellow ochre and scarlet lake. **6** Cadmium yellow, yellow ochre, scarlet lake and titanium white. **7** Cadmium yellow, alizarin crimson and burnt sienna.

ROSES

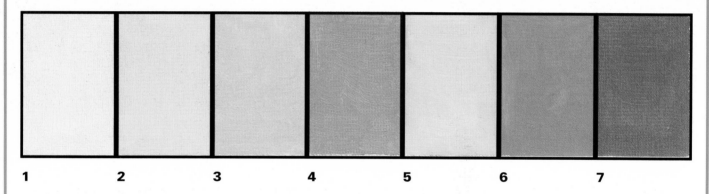

1 Titanium white, lemon yellow and yellow ochre. **2** Lemon yellow, yellow ochre and titanium white. **3** Titanium white and alizarin crimson. **4** Lemon yellow, alizarin crimson and cadmium orange. **5** Lemon yellow, alizarin crimson, cadmium orange and titanium white. **6** Rose madder and titanium white. **7** Scarlet lake and alizarin crimson.

SWEET PEA

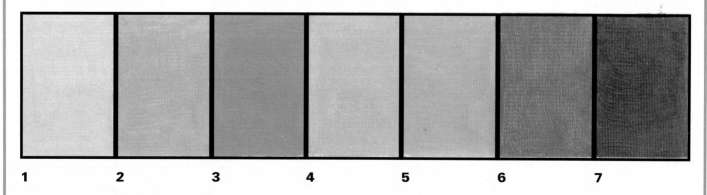

1 Titanium white, rose madder and permanent mauve. **2** Titanium white and permanent mauve. **3** Titanium white, magenta and rose madder. **4** Titanium white, magenta and lemon yellow. **5** Titanium white and magenta. **6** Permanent mauve and a touch of titanium white. **7** Alizarin crimson, raw umber and magenta.

IRIS

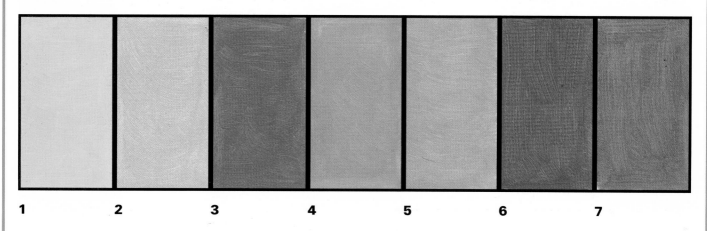

1   **2**   **3**   **4**   **5**   **6**   **7**

1 Lemon yellow and cadmium yellow. **2** Titanium white and cobalt blue. **3** Cobalt blue with a touch of titanium white. **4** Titanium white, burnt sienna and permanent mauve. **5** Cerulean blue and titanium white. **6** Permanent mauve and cobalt blue. **7** Burnt sienna and chrome orange.

CARNATION

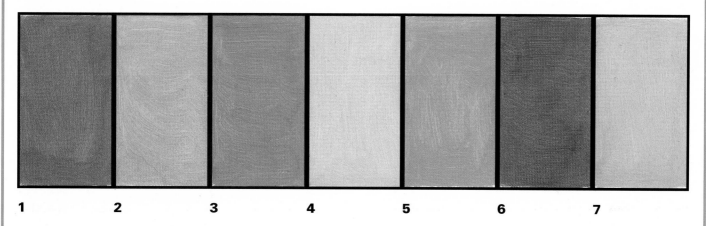

1   **2**   **3**   **4**   **5**   **6**   **7**

1 Cadmium red and burnt sienna. **2** Lemon yellow, cadmium yellow, burnt sienna and titanium white. **3** Rose madder, yellow ochre and titanium white. **4** Titanium white, magenta and permanent mauve. **5** Titanium white, magenta and yellow ochre. **6** Alizarin crimson. **7** Alizarin crimson and titanium white.

ANEMONE

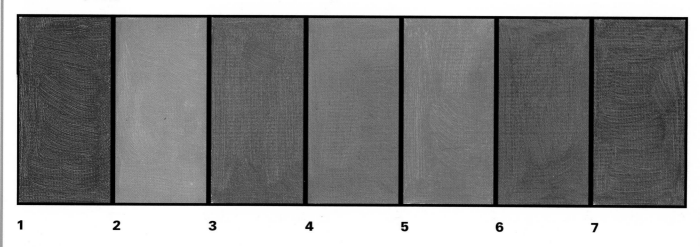

1   **2**   **3**   **4**   **5**   **6**   **7**

1 Permanent mauve. **2** Cobalt blue and titanium white. **3** Cadmium red and alizarin red. **4** Magenta and titanium white. **5** Permanent mauve and titanium white. **6** Magenta. **7** Alizarin crimson.

GERBERAS

Gerberas — also known as **Transvaal or Barberton Daisies** — make a wonderful subject for our painting project. If you are painting from life, keep your background fairly plain as a foil for the vibrant, glowing colours of the petals.

1 Sketch the outline of the gerberas, vase and tabletop. Squeeze on to the palette dabs of titanium white, cadmium yellow and yellow ochre plus a tiny amount of burnt umber for the pale wood tabletop. Dip the size 4 brush into each colour and paint quickly, letting the colours mix on the paper rather than the palette for a rough effect. Wipe your brush clean on a rag. Paint the shadow of the vase in cobalt blue mixed with burnt umber, painting wet-in-wet to get a soft edge. Wipe your brush clean and then dip into viridian, cerulean blue, hooker's green and white and, mixing the colours on the paper as before, paint in the background, following the rough outline of the flowers. Use less white to make the background colour darker towards the top of the picture.

MATERIALS

Daler fine grain oil painting paper size 16 x 12in (406 x 304mm)
oil colours: titanium white, cadmium yellow pale, yellow ochre, burnt sienna, cadmium orange, rose madder, cerulean blue, cobalt blue, hooker's green, viridian, burnt umber
3 brushes: flat hog's hair sizes 4 and 7; round nylon size 5
disposable palette
H pencil and eraser
cleaning rag
turpentine or white spirit

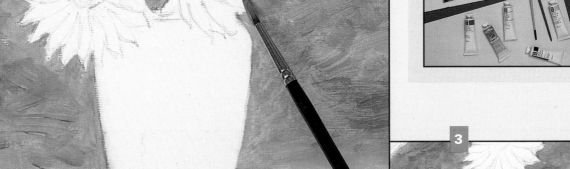

2 Using the size 5 round brush and the same background colour, carefully fill in the area around the stalks and flowerheads. Keep the paint thick enough to completely cover the white paper.

3 With the size 4 brush, mix cadmium yellow and yellow ochre. Keeping the paint fairly thick apply it in streaks over the background colour.

4 Add more streaks with the size 5 brush loaded with viridian. This serves to break up the strong background colour and add interest to the composition, which could otherwise appear rather flat.

5 Clean your brush and, working light to dark, mix cadmium yellow, yellow ochre, hooker's green and white and paint in the stalks and the bracts (the part of the stem that supports the flowerhead). To this ochre shade add burnt umber and paint the shadows on the stems and bracts.

6 With the cleaned size 4 brush mix cobalt blue and white, aiming for a smoother consistency than before. Paint in the left side of the vase, where the main light falls. Add more blue to the mix for the front of the vase. Add a touch of rose madder to the cobalt blue and white mix and paint in the deepest shadows on the right edge of the vase.

7 With the size 5 brush paint the unpainted part of the vase between the overspilling flowers. Paint in the vase highlights with white thinned with white spirit. To paint the light tones of the pink petals, mix titanium white with a little rose madder to get a pale pink. Paint the pink flowers with this, and add more rose madder for the deeper pink flowers. Leave the centres white for the moment. Paint the rest of the flowers using a mix of white and cadmium yellow for the pale yellow flowers; white, rose madder and burnt umber for the darker pinks; and white, cadmium yellow and cadmium orange for the others, varying the mixes to match the flower colours.

8 Now paint in the darker tones of the petals by using the same mixes as before, with less white, and laid on more thickly.

9 Paint the centre of the middle pink flower with cadmium yellow mixed with a little white; for the darker flower centres mix rose madder and burnt umber. Now taking the size 4 brush, dip it into the rose madder and cadmium yellow and stipple the paint around the flower centres.

10 With the cleaned size 5 brush, continue to build up the flower centres, darkening each colour you have used with burnt umber to add definition.

11 Darken the petals and the petal roots of the lightest blooms, mixing hooker's green and burnt umber. Use the brush as flat as possible, letting it lie along the petal length.

12 Enhance petal highlights and shadows, mixing white with the base colour used for each different shade of flower.

13 Work over the entire composition, adding the remaining highlights and shadows, taking note of where the light falls on the each bloom.

This flower study may take you several days to paint — but it is well worth spending time on the petal details. Your final painting should merit a prominent place on your wall.

INTRODUCING ALKYDS

Alkyd paints are a new kind of oil paint that have an overwhelming advantage over traditional oil colours — they dry much faster. And yet a painting done with alkyd colours will be indistinguishable from one done with oils. This makes alkyds a good choice for some specialist techniques.

Synthetically produced alkyd paints have been especially formulated to have all the qualities of oil colours. But with alkyds you can complete your painting in one sitting and it will be completely dry in 24 hours. This is in contrast to oils, which must be left to dry overnight between coats of paint, and in some cases you may have to wait a week before adding fine details. And yet alkyd colours remain workable on the canvas or palette for at least four hours, so there is no need to work in an unnecessary rush.

Special effects

This fast drying time lends itself to various specialist techniques. Scumbling (an impressionistic broken colour effect) translates well to alkyds and you will practise this technique in the painting project for this lesson.

Alkyds are also excellent for impasto, where paint is applied very thickly so that the brushstrokes are clearly visible. And they have the added advantage that as the drying times of the different colours are consistent (unlike oil paints) the possibility of cracking is reduced.

The paints are ideal for outdoor painting and portraiture. You can work from real life

and yet still finish the painting in one sitting — avoiding the need to work from sketches or photographs.

Alkyds are interchangeable with traditional oil colours. To save time, many painters use alkyds to underpaint their canvas and then complete the painting with oil paints. As with oil painting, you should observe the 'fat over lean' rule — each successive layer of paint should have slightly more oil in the mixture.

Apart from the actual colours themselves, you don't need to buy any extra equipment to paint with alkyds. The same brushes and canvases can all be used; oil colour liquin is a convenient medium and artist's white spirit or turpentine will thin or remove the paint.

The painting *above* **of 'Twilight in the forest' by Adrian Stokes (1854-1935) is a good example of the kind of painting that would be easier to execute with alkyd paints. The rich textural effect of the forest floor and the rocky outcrop have been created by scumbling — superimposing layers of paint — which is much easier to do with alkyds since they dry quickly. Our project painting for this lesson of a Highland scene,** *left,* **is a demonstration in the use of alkyd paints that exploits this property by laying colours one over another.**

ALKYD COLOUR CHART

The full range of alkyd colours (except for titanium white and flake white) is illustrated on this page. Although the range is smaller than that of traditional oil colours, this need not limit your colours on the canvas. As we demonstrate in the painting project for this lesson, a wide range of colours can be mixed from just a few tubes of paint. Because they dry quickly alkyd paints can be used instead of, or in conjunction with, oil paints to speed up painting time, and are particularly helpful for special techniques such as glazing and scumbling.

Cadmium lemon	Cadmium yellow light	Cadmium yellow medium	London yellow	Cadmium yellow deep
Cadmium orange	Cadmium red light	Cadmium red medium	Vermilion hue	London red
Cadmium red deep	Permanent rose	Alizarin crimson	Rose madder	Flesh tint
Cobalt violet hue	Dioxazine purple	French ultramarine	Phthalo blue	Cobalt blue
Prussian blue	Cerulean blue hue	Phthalo green	Viridian	Permanent green light
Sap green	Terre verte	Olive green	Naples yellow hue	Yellow ochre
Raw sienna	Burnt sienna	Raw umber	Burnt umber	Indian red
Light red oxide	Vandyke brown	Payne's grey	Ivory black	Lamp black

SCOTTISH LANDSCAPE

Our project painting of an atmospheric Scottish landscape exploits the quick-drying property of alkyd paints. You will also practise the technique of scumbling, which is an effective way of building up colour.

MATERIALS

canvas board 24 x 18in (610 x 457mm)
alkyd colours: sap green, olive green, raw umber, yellow ochre, cadmium lemon, French ultramarine, alizarin crimson, light red oxide, titanium white
brushes: round sable/synthetic sizes 2, 5, 6; hog's hair long flat sizes 4, 6; filbert size 10; short flat size 12
palette
white spirit
oil colour liquin
palette knife
rag

1 Dilute French ultramarine with white spirit to a very thin consistency. With the size 6 round brush, sketch in the outlines of the landscape.

2 With a palette knife mix French ultramarine, titanium white and a touch of alizarin crimson and using the size 10 brush paint in the sky. Wipe the brush on a rag. For the clouds use varying amounts of cadmium lemon, yellow ochre and titanium white. With a pale mix of French ultramarine and titanium white add shadows to the clouds.

3 Add a touch of light red oxide to your pale blue mix and, using the flat size 6 brush, paint in the peaks of the distant hills. Add a little more titanium white to the mix and use this to block in the entire remaining area of the background hills.

4 To paint the hillside by scumbling, first add cadmium lemon and yellow ochre to your mix and work over the area with this. Add a tiny amount of light red oxide to the mix to give more depth and texture to the hillside. For the pocket of trees behind the cottage use a mix of yellow ochre and light red oxide. Add raw umber to this mix and with the size 2 brush draw in the suggestion of tree trunks. Mix titanium white and French ultramarine with a touch of light red oxide and yellow ochre, and with the size 12 brush paint in the cottage roof. Use titanium white for the chimneys and add a hint of cadmium lemon for the left side of the cottage. For the cottage front add a touch of light red oxide and yellow ochre. Paint the windows with olive green thinned with liquin.

5 Paint the shadows on the cottage with the same shade. Block in the entire area of the middle ground with the filbert brush and a mix of French ultramarine, yellow ochre, cadmium lemon and a touch of light red oxide. Then add a touch more cadmium lemon to your mix and scumble with this shade, using the flat size 6 brush. Add a little more light red oxide, then some olive green and lastly raw umber, scumbling over the righthand hills with each mix. For the track in front of the cottage use a mix of French ultramarine, light red oxide and titanium white.

SCUMBLING

Scumbling is the term given to a broken colour effect in which semi-transparent layers of paint are applied over a base colour, allowing patches of the base coat to shine through. The layers of superimposed colours mix in the eyes of the viewer to give an atmospheric, textured effect. Use short, firm strokes, applying the colour irregularly over the area being worked. Use the paints thinned down with white spirit and take care not to overblend the colours. In our project a number of different shades are scumbled over a paler base colour. In some places you will be working wet-in-wet. Using this method the colour and texture of the hills and grassland can be quickly built up.

6 Scumble colour on the bank below the cottage as in Step 5. For the adjoining field use a mix of yellow ochre, light red oxide and titanium white. Dilute raw umber with liquin and put in the fence posts with the filbert brush; for their shadows add some yellow ochre and titanium white to this mix. Block in the dry-stone wall with raw umber and titanium white. Then, using the flat size 6 brush dab on touches of raw umber. Touch in titanium white with the round size 6 brush. Mix yellow ochre, cadmium lemon, light red oxide and titanium white and block in the righthand foreground. Add yellow ochre and scumble over the base colour with the flat size 6 brush. Add light red oxide to your mix, then olive green and lastly raw umber, scumbling with each different shade. Now use this dark colour to emphasise the right bank of the river.

7 Block in the river using the filbert brush and titanium white. Paint in the reflections of the river bank using the size 12 brush and a combination of olive green and titanium white. Put in the steps of the small waterfall with the same shade. Now add a little more titanium white to this mix and use light horizontal strokes to give the water a sense of movement. Add the sky's reflection using a mix of French ultramarine and titanium white.

8 Make a mixture of French ultramarine, light red oxide, yellow ochre, cadmium lemon and titanium white and block in the left foreground with the flat size 6 brush. Scumble over this first with a mix of yellow ochre and titanium white, then with a mix of olive green, French ultramarine and light red oxide, and lastly with raw umber thinned with liquin. To this shade add a little light red for the foreground stony outcrop. Put in the waterside reeds using sap green and the size 4 brush. Add highlights with a combination of cadmium lemon and yellow ochre.

9 Paint the reflection of the trees in the river using olive and sap green thinned with liquin. With the flat size 6 brush, block in the island with a mix of cadmium lemon, yellow ochre and titanium white. Add more cadmium yellow and a touch of sap green for the lightest areas; for the darkest areas use a mix of raw umber and light red. With a mix of sap green and cadmium lemon work on the right-hand foreground, then darken your mix with French ultramarine, olive green and titanium white and complete this area.

10 With olive green and titanium white, paint the right and darker side of the tree trunks using the round size 6 brush. For the left and lighter side of the trees use olive green, titanium white and yellow ochre. With the size 2 brush draw in the highest branches and twigs. Add some more titanium white and add highlights to the trees using the size 5 brush. Touch in some light red oxide on the trunk of the dead tree on the left.

11 Lighten the tree trunks with some dabs of sap green, and then with a mix of cadmium lemon and yellow ochre. Put in the chimney pots on the cottage with light red oxide. For the leaves, work wet-in-wet. Make quick short dabs with the filbert brush using varying amounts of yellow ochre, cadmium lemon and titanium white. Add some sap green to your mix and apply more leaves. With a mix of cadmium lemon and titanium white, add specks of sunlight to the left side of the foliage.

12 Using a mix of cadmium lemon, yellow ochre and titanium white, add some more colour to the background hills. Work over the painting adding highlights with a mix of cadmium lemon and titanium white.

Now that you have completed your first painting with alkyds you will understand how they can help by cutting down on the drying time that oils need.

UNDERPAINTING

Underpainting is a traditional technique that greatly simplifies the process of painting a portrait in oils. It consists of making a preliminary painting in the tones of one colour only, so providing a firm foundation on which to build up realistic flesh tones.

For many centuries portrait painters have employed the tried and tested method of making a monotonal underpainting of their subject. The composition and tonal relationships are established at the outset, and the artist is then free to concentrate on a detailed application of colour.

This method separates the physical painting process into two distinct phases, requiring the canvas to be painted twice. Tones of just one colour are used for the first layer of paint — the underpainting. The aim of this exercise is to map out the composition, delineating areas of light, shade and emphasis.

Once the monotonal representation is complete, you can give your full attention to mixing up the colour tones, matching them to the equivalent monotones of the underpainting.

There are a few guidelines to observe

when making an underpainting. Bear in mind the 'fat-over-lean' rule and dilute the underpaint with plenty of white spirit or turpentine; use a slightly thicker consistency of paint for the overpainting. Keep the tonal gradation subtle, but don't blend the colours in with one another. Use a fairly large brush for the underpainting — a 1/4-inch brush is ideal — and work quickly with confident, fluid brushstrokes. Ensure that the undercoat is completely dry before overpainting; this may take up to two days.

Beware of adding too much detail to your underpainting — remember that virtually the entire canvas will be overlaid with colour. On the other hand, don't worry if small areas of the underpainting show through in the final work. They will have the correct tonal value and will add interest and texture to the finished portrait.

Grisaille is the term applied to underpainting in tones of grey, as in our project portrait of an old man, but you could use tones of any colour. Earthy browns, greens, blues and reds were all colours that the Old Masters favoured.

This late self-portrait by Rembrandt (1606-69), *above*, is one of a series of nearly a hundred self-portraits that he painted, all of which illustrate his mastery of light and colour. Here his tonal range extends from sparkling white through mid flesh tones and velvety brown to darkest black, and the use of underpainting helps to give vibrancy to the whole portrait. Until the late 19th century, virtually all oil paintings were built up in a series of layers, with the initial stage being an underpainting to provide the half-tones. Our project portrait of an old man, *left*, shows you how to use this time-honoured method of oil painting.

We have already looked briefly at tonal scales on page 10. Every colour tone has an equivalent tone of grey; this is the principle that is used when underpainting. Before starting on the project painting of a portrait of an old man, it will be helpful if you practise the exercises on these pages. They will familiarise you with the subject of tonal value — an understanding of which is crucial to the painter.

1 First, make a monochrome tonal scale like this — start just with Payne's grey and gradually add more titanium white. Each tone should be halfway between its neighbours. To help evaluate different tones, half close your eyes. Our tonal scale has 14 gradations, but you could also practise making a scale with more or less gradations.

If you are having difficulty creating your tonal scale, try squeezing out measured lengths of the two colours from the tubes and mix them very carefully.

2 Now, by mixing cadmium red and titanium white, make another tonal scale, taking care to match each pink tone to the equivalent grey tone in your first scale.

3 When you are confident about mixing tones with just two colours, you are ready to add a third colour. By mixing various amounts of yellow ochre, cadmium red and titanium white, you will achieve basic flesh tones. You can add tiny amounts of other colours for more subtle skin effects, but this basic mix will give you essential practice. As before, make up a tonal scale of skin colour with 14 gradations.

EQUIVALENTS

To help you to assess tone, practise mixing up the equivalent grey tone to:
1 Cadmium yellow. **2** Viridian. **3** Cobalt blue. **4** Mauve. **5** Cadmium orange. You might like to continue this exercise by mixing up the equivalent grey tone to every oil colour in your palette. Study the results carefully; you may be surprised by which colours have equivalent tonal values. This exercise will help you to familiarise yourself with the colours you use most frequently.

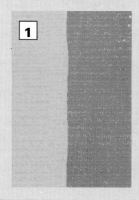

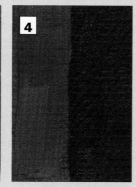

Now try painting the details *below* of an eye and an ear. This will give you useful experience of painting features, as well as more practice in mixing up and painting with flesh tones.

THE EYE

1 Make a dark mix of cobalt blue, cadmium red and ivory black. With a ¹/₈in flat brush paint in the pupils, shadows and main wrinkles.

2 Add titanium white and a little yellow ochre to the mix. Paint in the mid tone shadow around the

eye. Add some ivory black and darken the eye.

3 The lightest flesh tone is made by mixing cadmium red, yellow ochre and titanium white. Add a little more cadmium red and yellow ochre to the mix for the highlights.

1

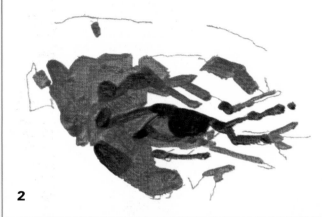

2

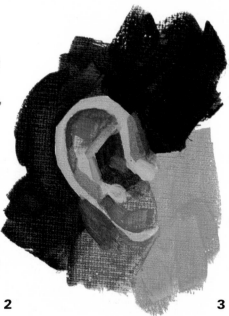

3

THE EAR

1 Using yellow ochre, cadmium red and titanium white mix a basic skin tone and paint the lightest part of the ear lobe, as shown. Add some cobalt blue to the mix and paint the mid tone.

1

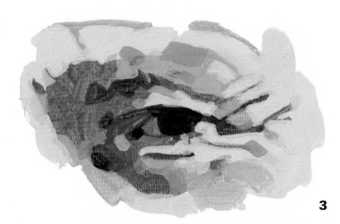

2

3

2 Darken the area below the ear by adding burnt umber to your mix. Add a little more cadmium red to the basic skin mix and paint in the ear lobes. Paint in the hair using a mix of ivory black and burnt umber.

3 Add ivory black and cadmium red to the basic skin mix for the darkest part of the ear. Add more yellow ochre and cadmium red to the basic skin mix for the parts of the ear in shadow and more titanium white for highlights.

OLD MAN

An old Spanish man is the subject of our first portrait in oils. Although the monochrome underpainting is no longer visible in the finished work, it is by using this technique that the subtlety of human skin is captured, bringing the old man vividly to life.

MATERIALS

stretched canvas or canvas board
oil colours: titanium white, ivory black, cadmium yellow, yellow ochre, chrome orange, cadmium red, raw umber, burnt sienna, cobalt blue, Payne's grey
brushes: synthetic long flat sizes 1/4in, 1/8in; flat hog's hair size 4
disposable palette
compressed charcoal stick
cleaning rag
white spirit
container for white spirit

1 Sketch the main outlines of the old man in charcoal. Lightly brush over the canvas to remove any charcoal dust.

2 Using the 1/4in brush and Payne's grey thinned with a little white spirit, paint in the darkest shadows, as shown. Note that the light is coming from the left. With the size 4 brush and the same mix block in the man's jacket. Don't forget to dip your brush frequently into white spirit to thin the paint.

3 Add a little more titanium white to the mix and using the 1/4in brush paint in the next lightest tone. Block in the background using the same colour mix and the size 4 brush.

4 Add more titanium white to the mix and with the 1/4in brush add highlights to the right side of the face, then build up the lighter tones on the left side.

5 Continue to build up the lighter tones as shown by adding small amounts of titanium white to your mix. For the man's hair and the highlights use titanium white with just a hint of Payne's grey. Noting where the shadows fall, touch up the highlights and shadows. You have now completed the underpainting and the canvas must be left for 24 hours or until it is quite dry.

6 Mix burnt sienna with ivory black and paint in the eyes using the 1/8in brush. Add a little cadmium red and titanium white to this mix for the detail around the lefthand eye. Make a basic skin tone by mixing yellow ochre, cadmium red and titanium white and begin working over the original monochrome underpainting. Add a little more cadmium red and titanium white to the basic mix for the next darkest tone, and then add a little burnt sienna to this mix. Use overlapping planes of paint and don't blend the colours.

7 By adding tiny amounts of chrome orange, cadmium yellow, titanium white, cadmium red, cobalt blue and burnt sienna to the original skin mix in varying quantities, build up the flesh tones on the left, and lighter, side of the face. Use the 1/4in brush for the larger areas of colour and the 1/8in brush for adding detail.

8 For the righthand side of the face work with the same colour mixes as before, but add a little raw umber and cobalt blue to darken the tones. For the darkest shadows add ivory black, more cobalt blue and a touch of cadmium red. Now touch up the flesh tones.

9 Use pure titanium white for the lightest sections of the man's hair; mix titanium white, cadmium yellow, ivory black and cobalt blue for the darker sections. For the lefthand shirt collar use a mix of cobalt blue and titanium white; add Payne's grey to this mix for the darker areas of the shirt.

10 Add ivory black to the mix and using the size 4 brush block in the man's jacket, neatening the outline with the 1/8in brush. With a mix of cadmium yellow, ivory black, cadmium blue, titanium white and Payne's grey block in the background with the size 4 flat brush, using the 1/8in brush to carefully trace around the outline of the old man.

11 Finish off the portrait by touching up the shadows, freckles, wrinkles and highlights.

Now that you have successfully completed your first portrait in oils, you should have the confidence to undertake your own project. Try painting one of your family or friends from a close-up photograph, or you might even like to attempt a self-portrait!

PAINTING WITH A KNIFE

This painting by Les Nind, *left*, shows how exciting and vibrant a knife painting can be. The thick layers of paint give a depth and three-dimensional quality to the scene, while fine detail is achieved by using the tip of the painting knife.

Painting with a knife is an exciting way to extend your techniques in applying paint to canvas, and it gives freedom and spontaneity to your strokes. In this lesson we introduce you to painting with this surprisingly versatile tool.

Now that you have gained experience in using brushes in a variety of ways it is time to try how a knife feels as a painting tool. Used with oil or acrylic paint straight from the tube, the broad, free strokes of the painting knife add interest and texture to a painting, and give the artist a sense of exhilaration. When experimenting with knife painting, many people discover a new confidence in using colour and with laying on the thick coats of paint that are known as impasto.

Large areas of canvas can be covered using sweeping movements of the trowel-shaped knife blade. Textural effects and forms can be created in the thick paint and interesting surface patterns moulded with the tip. Big slablike strokes are particularly useful when painting a landscape for rocks or brilliant patches of light on water.

Speed and decision

Knife painting is not about intricate detail. The bold, impressionistic effect that is achieved is part of its pleasure. The speed and decisiveness with which you need to work, covering the canvas and building up layers of paint that retain their sharp edges, are also special qualities. Painting with a

knife presents its own special challenge. It is an opportunity to think big about your subject matter, simplifying it down to the essentials in terms of line, light and shade or to venture into the abstract, responding to pattern and shape.

Our painting project for this lesson, *below*, is a still life of 'Winter pansies' executed entirely with a knife and designed to demonstrate the adaptability and versatility of this painting tool.

PAINTING KNIVES

The palette knife with a narrow blade used for mixing paints is not suitable for painting. A painting knife has a broad blade and rounded tip, and most have a cranked handle to raise the hand away from the wet canvas. The knife is made of steel which is finely ground down to the tip, giving it spring and flexibility and allowing sensitive control. Many knife shapes and sizes are available and you should try out several to find one that you feel comfortable with. The same knife is used for the entire painting.

Pictured here is the full Winsor and Newton series of six knives numbered (from left to right) 13 to 18. Other manufacturers will supply similar series.

KNIFE STROKES

A painting knife is a versatile instrument, and by using different parts of the blade you can achieve quite different strokes and effects. You can also achieve interesting results by holding the knife at different angles and by varying the pressure you apply. Try these three examples to help you get the feel of painting with a knife, then experiment with other methods of using your knife.

1 Hold the knife at a slight angle to the canvas, applying the paint with firm pressure so that the texture of the canvas shows through the paint.

2 Use just the very tip of the knife to scratch through a layer of paint. A surprising amount of detail can be achieved using this method.

3 Paint with the entire base of the knife, spreading the paint very thickly. This produces a very smooth surface that reflects the maximum amount of light.

SPECIAL TECHNIQUES

Many of the techniques that are used when painting with a brush can be adapted to knife painting. Two methods that we will use in our project painting are impasto and glazing, so it is a good idea to practise these techniques using a knife.

1 Impasto (thick paint that sits in relief on the surface of the canvas) can be taken to its extreme when working with a knife. In this example burnt umber, yellow ochre and titanium white have been mixed directly onto the canvas with a wavy motion of the knife, producing an expressive textural effect.

2 Glazing (applying thin layers of colour over one another) is very effective when painted with a knife. In this example, partly transparent strokes of titanium white have been carefully scraped over a layer of sap green, painting wet-in-wet. The impasto ridges add interest to the paint surface.

2

PAINTING AN APPLE

Practise this step-by-step exercise of painting an apple; it will help your knife control and prepare you for our project painting of a still life.

1 Sketch in the shape of the apple and then paint the yellow half of the fruit with Winsor yellow and titanium white.

1

2 With alizarin crimson, apply a thin glaze of colour over the yellow, painting wet-in-wet. Hold the heel of the knife still, moving the knife-tip in an arc.

2

3 Refine the modelling on the apple, adding highlights with a mix of alizarin crimson and titanium white. Paint the stalk with a mix of sap green and raw umber, then use a mix of sap green, Winsor yellow and titanium white to form the indentation around the stalk.

3

WINTER PANSIES

Our painting project for this lesson is a colourful still life featuring flowers and fruit. The fine subtleties of tint are achieved by only partially mixing the colour on the palette before applying it to the canvas, and this technique gives an impression of fine detail.

MATERIALS

oil canvas or canvas board
oil colours: burnt sienna, raw sienna, cadmium yellow, Winsor yellow, cadmium orange, French ultramarine, alizarin crimson, raw umber, sap green, titanium white
painting knife size 16
brushes: hog's hair long flat size 4; sable/synthetic short flat size 6
palette
white spirit and dipper
tissues

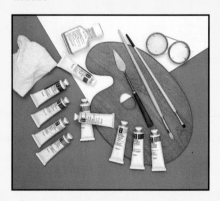

1 Sketch in the main objects in the still life with the size 4 brush and French ultramarine mixed to a thin consistency with white spirit; then with the size 6 brush indicate the position of the main flowerheads.

2 With the knife, mix varying amounts of titanium white, raw sienna and burnt sienna and begin work on the earthenware vase, applying the paint thickly. Wipe your knife on tissue in between each colour mix. Add cadmium yellow to your mix for the highlights. For the two clay pots, use varying amounts of raw umber, burnt sienna and titanium white, again adding cadmium yellow for highlights.

3 Mix French ultramarine, titanium white, burnt sienna and cadmium yellow and paint the newspaper 'basket' containing the pansies. Add more titanium white to this mix for the lighter areas.

4 For the inside of the vase, mix titanium white, raw umber and a hint of raw sienna; for its rim mix raw sienna with titanium white. Now, using the same colour mix as in step 2, complete the earthenware vase.

5

6

5 The background is painted with pale mixes of all the colours used in the painting. Use complementary colours around the objects in the still life; otherwise, apply colour randomly but try to balance areas of colour across the canvas. (For how to find a complementary colour, see page 130). Don't forget to clean your knife regularly.

7

6 Mix French ultramarine, burnt sienna and cadmium yellow for the soil in the newspaper basket. Mix sap green and titanium white and paint the green apple, adding Winsor yellow to your mix for highlights and a touch of alizarin crimson for the reflection of the red apple.

7 Using a mix of Winsor yellow, titanium white and a touch of sap green, indicate the shapes of the two red apples. For the shadow of the newspaper basket, mix French ultramarine, titanium white and a touch of raw umber; add more raw umber to this mix for the shadows cast by the fruit. Now apply a glaze of alizarin crimson over the two red apples. Paint the apple stalk and blossom with raw umber, then use sap green to refine the modelling around the indentations.

8

9

8 Mix raw umber and titanium white for the darkest green of the foliage; sap green, raw umber, raw sienna and titanium white for the mid green; sap green, Winsor yellow and titanium white for the lightest area of foliage. Add a little more Winsor yellow to your mix and use the tip of the knife to draw in the flower stalks.

9 With the same colour mix, use the entire base of your knife to paint the leaves. For the yellow pansies, mix Winsor yellow and titanium white, applying the paint very thickly. Add touches of cadmium orange to the petals.

10

11 Using the same colour mixes as in steps 9 and 10, paint the yellow pansy on the tablecloth, and add two blue flowerheads in among the yellow pansies to balance the colour. Now paint the tablecloth, using titanium white mixed with tiny amounts of French ultramarine and raw umber. Add more raw umber to this mix for the shadows of the clay pots.

11

12 Complete the background, using the method outlined in step 5. Paint the reflections of the apples on the vase and basket using sap green and titanium white for the green apple and alizarin crimson and titanium white for the red apples. Using a mix of sap green and Winsor yellow paint the moss on the pots. Refine the modelling on the pots using a mix of alizarin crimson and burnt sienna and a few touches of titanium white.

10 Mix French ultramarine, titanium white and a touch of alizarin crimson for the blue flowers. For the faces of the yellow pansies and the dead blossom use raw umber. The centres of the blue flowers are Winsor yellow.

12

Because the paint is used thickly, your painting will take a long time to dry. If you leave it in a warm, dry place it will be touch-dry within a month, but you shouldn't apply varnish for at least six months.

WARM AND COOL COLOURS

On pages 129–34 we introduced you to colour theory, with the emphasis on effects produced by using complementary colours. Now we look at how the use of warm and cool colours enables you to create a sense of space, depth and mood in your paintings.

Colour temperature is based upon the principle that different colours evoke sensations of cold and heat. In order to prove this subjective response to colour, experiments have been carried out on humans, animals and even insects.

Hot and warm colours — browns, reds, pinks, oranges and yellows — have red in their composition and are sometimes referred to as the fire colours. Cold and cool colours are blues, greens and violets, and are often associated with water. Warm and cool colours evoke quite different moods; cool colours are calming, and a painting in this colour key will be atmospheric — perhaps mysterious or sombre. Warm colours, by contrast, are associated with sunshine and are more lively. Circumspect use of warm and cool colours can be used to suggest or emphasise the emotional message of a painting.

Another property of these two colour groups is that warm colours advance, jumping off the page towards you, whereas cool colours recede. By using warm hues in the foreground and cooler ones in the background, a sense of distance and space can be achieved with colour alone. In the 17th century many landscape painters applied this principle to their paintings, using browns for the foreground, greens and yellows for the middleground and blues for the background.

However, both red and blue pigments vary from warm to cool. For example, French ultramarine, a violet-blue, is warmer than the green-blue of Prussian blue — and cadmium red is warmer than alizarin crimson, which contains some blue. Furthermore, colour temperature is relative, and one colour will be affected by other colours adjacent to it.

Above left: This atmospheric picture by Jane Corsellis, entitled 'Interior in Malacca', is painted in predominantly cool blues and greens, with just a few hints of warm yellow where the sunshine filters through the heavy shutters. Note how the merest touch of vivid red in the distance reduces the depth of the picture, while also serving to draw the eye to the outside world. If you cover the patch of red with a fingertip, the interior loses a surprising amount of impact. Our painting project, shown *above*, uses a more even balance of colour temperature to give you practice in using warm and cool tones.

In our project painting, dots and dashes are used to convey foliage. First practise these brush techniques using cool colours, then try the same brush techniques using warmer colours. Study the effects carefully; the example painted with warm colours, *top,* is autumnal, decorative and lively, while the example in cool colours, *above,* is calmer and less demanding on the eye.

Warm colours are those with red pigment in their make-up — browns, reds, pinks, oranges, yellows. Study the top band of colours, *above,* showing a warm spectrum, and note the images that come to mind — earth, fire, sunshine. Cool colours are blues, greens and violets. Now look at the lower band of cool colours — this has a relaxing and calming effect, summoning up images of sea and sky.

Now look at both colour spectrums together, and note how the warm colour band appears to jump forward, while the cool colour band recedes into the canvas.

GLAZING

Glazing is a technique in which a transparent layer of paint is applied over a dry colour or ground, creating a special luminosity. Blues, especially French ultramarine and Prussian blue, give very successful results, and these are the colours used for glazing in our project painting. The technique is looked at in detail on pages 171–6.

AIDS FOR PAINTING STRAIGHT LINES

Masking tape

Masking tape can be used to simplify and speed up the process of painting straight lines. Masking tape can be bought in different widths from art shops and builders' merchants. Practise sticking down long strips of masking tape in a straight line; hold the tape taut and stick one end in position first, then lay down the entire remaining length in one movement. When painting over the masking tape, use a fairly dry brush so that the paint does not seep under the tape and ruin the hard edge you are trying to achieve. Let the paint dry for a few minutes before removing the masking tape.

Mahl stick
A mahl stick *(below)* can be used as a rest for the painting hand when working on a large canvas. It keeps the hand off the work and can also be used as an aid for painting straight lines. Traditionally made of bamboo with a chamois leather pad, modern versions have extending aluminium handles and a leather or rubber pad. Rest the pad on the canvas and, if you are righthanded, hold the stick in your left hand, then use the mahl stick to steady your painting arm. You can make your own mahl stick by tying a bundle of rags to the end of a garden cane.

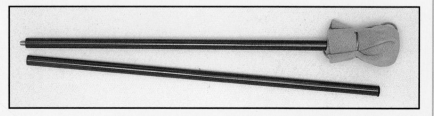

THROUGH AN OPEN DOOR

A charming garden scene viewed from within an artist's shadowy studio is this lesson's inspirational project painting. The impression of fine detail is an illusion created by the juxtaposition and interplay of warm and cool colours.

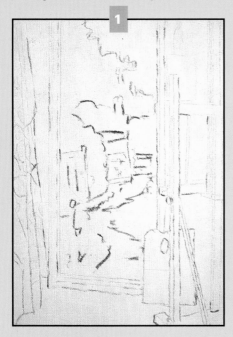

1 Sketch the main outlines of the composition with the compressed charcoal stick. Lightly brush over the canvas to remove any dust.

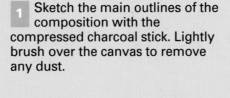

2 Varying amounts of ivory black and titanium white are used for the foreground underpainting. The long flat size 5 brush is used for detail, and the size 4 brush for larger areas. Work from the left of the canvas to the right, sticking down strips of masking tape to help you paint the straight lines of the door frame and easel.

MATERIALS

canvas board 51 x 71cm
oil colours: ivory black, titanium white, French ultramarine, Prussian blue, cerulean blue, cadmium red, cadmium red deep, cadmium yellow, lemon yellow hue, Vandyke brown
brushes: hog's hair short flat size 4; sable short flat size 5; sable long flat size 5; synthetic short flat size 1; synthetic long flat size 8
compressed charcoal stick
palette
dipper
linseed oil
turpentine
masking tape
mahl stick
tissues

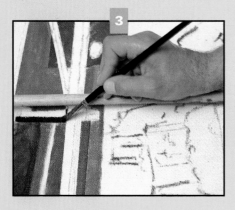

3 After painting the main vertical lines, paint the horizontals; stick down masking tape where the canvas is unpainted, but where this is not possible use the mahl stick, holding it just above the canvas (laid flat) and resting your painting hand on the stick.

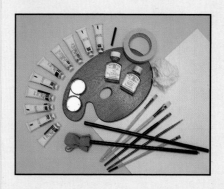

4 Complete the grey tones of the underpainting.

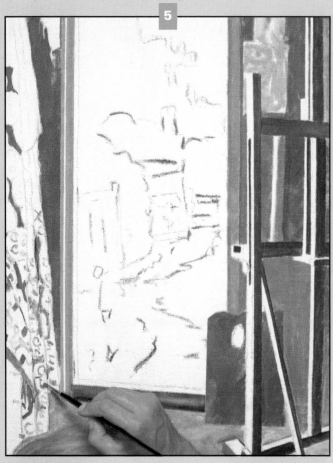

5 Roughly indicate the pattern of the foreground curtain using French ultramarine and a mix of cadmium red deep and cadmium yellow. Use the size 1 brush, and paint very loosely, wiping your brush on the tissues between each separate colour application. Leave the painting to dry — this will take at least 48 hours.

6 Stick strips of masking tape around the inside of the door frame to protect the unpainted canvas. Make a quantity of glazing medium, mixing linseed oil and turpentine in the proportions 60:40. With the size 8 brush, apply a glaze of French ultramarine mixed with glazing medium over the foreground grey tones, glazing only the parts of the lefthand curtain that are in shadow. Remove the masking tape.

7 Mix cadmium yellow with a touch of cadmium red and titanium white then, with the size 1 brush, complete the pattern on the curtain, painting only the areas that catch the sunlight. With a mix of Prussian blue and glazing medium, and using the size 8 brush, emphasise the folds of the curtain. Using the same mix, paint over the areas of the foreground that are to recede — the areas behind the easel and the palette.

8 Lay thin strips of masking tape around the inside of the door frame. With titanium white, paint over the entire sky area and the distant trees, using plenty of paint. Mix French ultramarine and titanium white with a touch of cerulean blue and, with rough strokes, paint into the sky area wet-in-wet, painting down to the treeline.

9 Use varying amounts of French ultramarine, cadmium yellow and titanium white to paint the distant trees and foliage, painting wet-in-wet into the

titanium white applied at step 8. Add a few touches of ivory black to give the impression of branches, and use titanium white for the highlights.

10 Mix cadmium red deep and French ultramarine and paint the pergola and table legs using the size 1 brush. Add cadmium yellow and cadmium red to the mix and paint the highlights on the pergola. Paint the fence with a mix of cadmium yellow, cadmium red and a little French ultramarine. Add the slats on the fence in titanium white, painting wet-in-wet.

11 Paint the shadows on the fence with a mix of French ultramarine, ivory black and titanium white. Add a few touches of cadmium red mixed with titanium white. For the bush behind the fence, mix French ultramarine with lemon yellow hue, and apply it in quick, dry dabs. Add a little more French ultramarine to your mix and build up the bush. Mix cadmium red with titanium white for the flowers, again using dabs of colour. Add some cadmium red deep to the mix for more flowers. Mix French ultramarine, cadmium yellow and ivory black for the darkest areas of foliage.

12 Mix cadmium red deep and titanium white for the patio under the pergola. Use varying amounts of French ultramarine, titanium white and cadmium yellow for the foreground flower bed; for the path, use varying amounts of cadmium red, cadmium red deep, titanium white and cadmium yellow. Apply the tones randomly, using the long flat size 5 brush and long, firm strokes of colour. Paint the foreground tulips with a mix of cadmium red deep and titanium white.

13 Paint the lightest leaves in the flower bed using the short flat size 5 brush and a mix of cadmium yellow and titanium white, painting wet-in-wet. Add French ultramarine to the mix and paint the darker leaves. Add Vandyke brown to the mix and complete the flower bed. Paint the shadows on the path with Vandyke brown.

14 Add a few touches of cadmium yellow mixed with titanium white to the path, and then with a pale mix of cadmium red deep and titanium white work over the path, blending the colours together. Paint the fallen petals with cadmium red deep. Paint the table-top beneath the pergola with a mix of cadmium red and titanium white. For the foliage in the sky, mix French ultramarine, cadmium yellow and ivory black, painting with quick, light dabs of colour. Gradually add more cadmium yellow to the mix and build up the green tones.

Finally, remove the masking tape around the door frame and paint the canvas beneath with a mix of cadmium yellow, titanium white and a touch of cadmium red.

For more practice in colour temperature you might like to try painting a scene entirely in warm or cool colours — such as a desert or arctic scene. You will find that you need to add touches of the opposite temperature key to give balance and depth to your painting.

GLAZING

A glaze can completely transform a painting, imparting a rich translucence to the surface and intensifying shape and form. An understanding of glazing — one of the oldest techniques in oil painting — is crucial to the painter, and in this lesson we show you basic glazing techniques and how to paint glowing copper pans.

A transparent layer of colour painted over dry, opaque colour is called a glaze. The two colours combine optically, assuming a vibrancy and depth quite different to the effects achieved when two colours are mixed together. The reason for this is that light passes through the transparent glaze and reflects back from the colour underneath, giving the paint a three-dimensional quality.

Glazes can be used in a number of different ways. They can be applied over an underpainting or laid over areas of opaque, even dark colour. Painted over impastos — areas of very thick paint — a glaze will enhance the textural effects. A glaze can be used to modify tone and to soften contrast, to give shadows a luminosity or to enliven areas of flat colour. Glazing was widely used until the 19th century; and Rembrandt, Rubens and Turner were all exponents of the technique. Since the 19th century, however, many artists have preferred a more inspirational and less elaborate approach, painting directly on to the canvas in a method called alla prima.

Glazing is a wet-on-dry technique, and it is absolutely essential that an area to be glazed is bone-dry. Because of this,

paintings to be glazed must be worked in stages, and you may have to wait for a week before the canvas is quite dry. Impatience will ruin the translucent effect of a glaze: if even slightly wet the underlying colour will be disturbed and the colours will mix.

Always use plenty of colour mixed together with your glazing medium. If you are unhappy with the colour of a glaze when it is dry, simply apply another glaze over the top. In this way a number of glazes can be painted one over another — Titian sometimes used as many as thirty!

An understanding of how different colours react with one another is essential for successful glazing. Make your own experiments by glazing one colour over another, and keep careful notes of what you do.

Joe Anna Arnett has used a traditional glazing medium mixed with reds and golds to achieve the burnished surface of the copper pot in her painting 'Parrot tulips', *above left.* **Our project painting** *below,* **in a more modern style, uses a proprietary glazing medium to achieve the gloss of the metal objects.**

Make sure that you add plenty of colour to the glazing medium — the proportions should be approximately half and half. Mix them together very thoroughly; if this is not done, some separation may occur which will ruin the glazing effect. You should practise mixing colour with glazing medium until you achieve a thin but oily consistency. Remember that the underpainting must be completely dry before any glazing is done. Position your canvas or board flat or at a slight angle to avoid any drips or runs, and use a large, soft, flat brush for glazing.

Mix Payne's grey and titanium white and paint four blocks of graduated grey tones (light grey at the top, graduating to darker grey at the bottom). Leave to dry. Now mix the following colours with glazing medium and apply a different coloured glaze over each of the monochrome underpaintings:

GLAZING MEDIUMS

To make the paint easier to handle and give it the lustre characteristic of a glaze, a medium is always used when glazing. To start with, you will probably obtain more satisfactory results by using a proprietary glazing medium. Based on synthetic alkyd resins, these have a quick drying time and special film-forming ingredients that impart a gloss to the paint surface. Traditional glazing mediums might have contained stand oil, beeswax, damar varnish, mastic varnish, etc. An equal mix of linseed oil and turpentine can also be used as a glazing medium, but the proportions must be right: too much linseed oil and the glaze will move about on the canvas; too much turpentine and the glossy effect will be impaired.

1 Cadmium yellow   **2 Viridian**   **3 Cobalt blue**   **4 Alizarin crimson**

Surprising results can be achieved by applying different coloured glazes over the same opaque colour. Try these two comparisons, and then experiment with some of your own colour effects.

Roughly mix alizarin crimson and titanium white on your palette and paint two blocks of colour with a textured surface. Leave to dry. Now glaze over each colour block with a different mix: **5a** Cobalt blue and glazing medium. **5b** Cadmium yellow, a touch of alizarin crimson and glazing medium.

With French ultramarine and titanium white, paint two blocks of colour, mixing the colours directly on the canvas and using the paint quite thickly to produce a textured surface. Leave to dry before glazing with a different mix: **6a** Cobalt blue, alizarin crimson and glazing medium. **6b** Cadmium yellow and glazing medium.

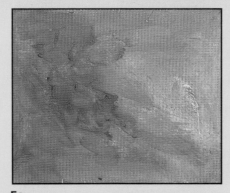 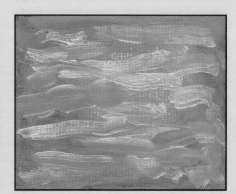

5a   **5b**

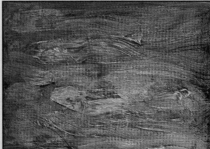 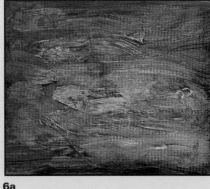

6a   **6b**

PAINTING SKIES

An impressionist effect of a sky seeming to sparkle with warm sunlight can be achieved by applying a blue glaze over a yellow underpainting.

1 With cadmium yellow and titanium white paint a broken surface effect. Don't mix or blend the colours on the palette. Leave to dry.

2 Mix cobalt blue and titanium white and then mix this with glazing medium and glaze over step **1**.

PAINTING FLESH TONES

A traditional method for painting flesh tones that can be seen in many 14th-century paintings involved underpainting in green, and then applying a pink glaze over this. Where the green shines through it complements the pink flesh tones.

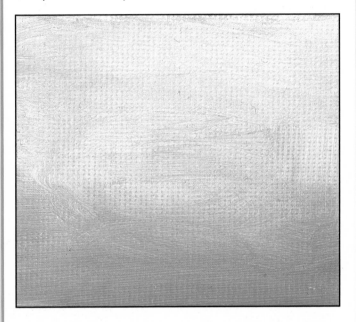

1 Mix viridian and titanium white in varying quantities and paint graduated tones of green. Leave to dry.

2 Mix alizarin crimson, titanium white and a touch of cadmium yellow. Now mix in some glazing medium and lay a glaze of colour over the green tones.

COPPER KETTLE

This project painting features a traditional copper kettle and two decorative moulds. The high gloss and shimmering reflection of the metal objects have been achieved by applying different coloured glazes over a monochrome underpainting.

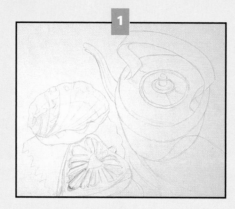

1 Use the 4H pencil to sketch in the outline of the kettle and two moulds.

2 With the size 4 brush and titanium white paint round the objects where there are no shadows. Add Payne's grey to make a pale mix and paint the background shadows. Use pure Payne's grey for the darkest shadows cast by the objects, gradually adding more titanium white to your mix as you move away from them. Where the shadows blur into the background use your finger to blend the edges.

M A T E R I A L S

oil sketching pad or canvas
oil colours: titanium white, Payne's grey, raw sienna, burnt sienna, raw umber, cobalt blue
brushes: round synthetic size 6; short flat hog's hair size 4; ¼in short flat synthetic
4H pencil and eraser
Wingel or other quick-drying proprietary glazing medium
disposable palette
white spirit and jar for cleaning brushes
tissues

HELPFUL HINT

Strong definition of the shadows is essential because they determine the degree of highlight that can be created later with the glazing.

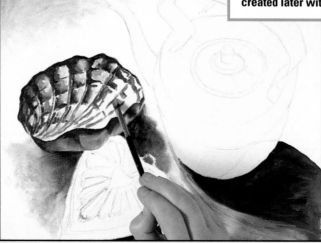

3 Outline the shell mould using the ¼-inch brush and Payne's grey. Add titanium white and shade in the moulded segments and, with the same mix, indicate the ribbing on the shell mould. Define the dark shadow between the two moulds with Payne's grey.

4 Paint the heart mould with varying mixes of Payne's grey and titanium white.

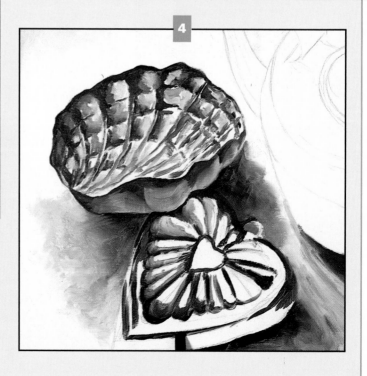

5 With a dark mix of Payne's grey and titanium white, paint the shadows on the kettle. Add a little titanium white to the mix and outline the kettle handle and spout. Add more titanium white and finish painting the kettle.

6 The underpainting is now complete and the painting must be left for a week, or until it is completely dry, before you can move on to step 7 and apply the glazes.

7 Mix raw sienna with glazing medium and with the size 4 brush paint over the entire inside of the shell mould. Use a mix of burnt sienna and glazing medium for the heart-shaped mould.

8 For the underside of the shell mould, use the ¼-inch brush and a mix of raw umber and glazing medium. Now check that the glaze on the heart mould is tacky to the touch, and then with a tissue lift off the glaze where the mould catches the light. Use a clean piece of tissue for each 'stroke'.

9 The kettle is glazed with burnt sienna mixed with glazing medium. Use the 1/4-inch brush for larger areas and the size 6 brush for fine detail.

10 Add some colour to the shadows cast by the objects with raw sienna mixed with glazing medium and the 1/4-inch brush. Mix cobalt blue, raw umber and glazing medium and dab a few light brushstrokes over the white tablecloth to remove its starkness. With the size 6 brush and raw umber, paint the hooks on the two moulds. Leave to dry.

11 Emphasise the detail on the lid of the kettle using the 1/4-inch brush and raw umber mixed with glazing medium. Add the highlights on the kettle and the heart-shaped mould with titanium white.

Now that you have learnt the technique of glazing, you will wonder how you ever managed without it! Why not take another look at any of your paintings you feel dissatisfied with, and ask yourself whether they could be transformed with glazes?

SECTION 2

Drawing

SEEING THE LIGHT

This kitchen composition, drawn in 4B pencil on a paper with a fairly rough surface, shows how effective a simple pencil drawing can be.

In the corner of any kitchen can be found subject material for a compelling still life. The everyday components of a casual scene can be depicted vividly using just pencil and paper to create an image of daily life that becomes a picture. For anyone who has ever wanted to try their hand at pencil drawing the adventure starts here!

Everyone can draw, but not everyone has had the chance to develop their skill to a point where the results are satisfying. When people first begin to draw, they tend to produce something that looks flat and two-dimensional. However, the real world is full of three-dimensional objects which change in appearance as the observer moves round them.

Drawing with pencil is the ideal way of starting the exciting process of improving your drawing skills. Drawing involves looking, observing patterns of light and shade, and translating what you see into lines and marks on a sheet of paper.

These lines and marks form a map; their directions and shapes are very important. Curiously, if you try to draw an object, say an arrangement of fruit, with too much concentration on the fact that it is fruit, success can elude you. What is important is to observe shapes and proportions, and

how the areas of dark and light fit together.

The pencil is a marvellous instrument. With it you can make broad lines and fine lines, dark lines and faint lines. By drawing lines close together you can build up areas of shading, or you can achieve a multitude of different effects with cross-hatching and other techniques. It is truly astonishing how many different linear and tonal qualities are possible using just a graphite pencil.

Process of addition

As your skill in pencil drawing increases you will find that you need to use the eraser less and less. As in watercolour painting, you can build up a tonal composition, ranging from the white of the paper, through varying degrees of grey, to very dark. By this process of addition, the depicted object or scene gradually seems to acquire a three-dimensional quality.

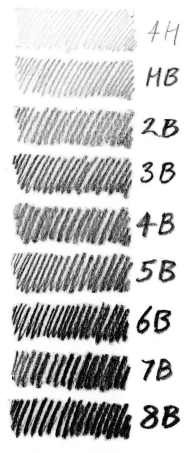

Sample grades of pencil showing the range of qualities between 4H and 8B. The 4H will keep its point longest, but even under pressure will only produce a pale grey mark which may dent the paper. The 8B will produce the darkest, richest black but will lose its point quickly.

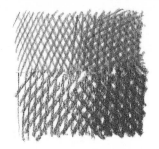

In these samples the upper part was made with a 2B pencil, the lower with a 6B. The line made is a 'scribble' backwards and forwards with the pencil touching the paper all the time.

This sample shows lines that stop cleanly. Control of the hand for even spacing needs practice, but over-shooting the end is not 'bad'; indeed it may prevent a drawing looking mechanical.

Working lines over one another and laying them in different directions is called 'cross-hatching'. It is an ideal way to build up dark areas by stages, thereby avoiding overworking.

Shading (i.e. creating a tonal area) can be built up gradually. To keep the transition soft and even, you will need to practise. If you do overwork an area, 'lift' using a putty rubber.

SHARPENING YOUR PENCIL

Sharpening your pencil with a knife produces a long tip, which in turn can be given a flat face or a chisel type end, making it a more versatile drawing instrument. Pencil sharpeners produce a short, round point which quickly blunts. Some brands of knives have replaceable, retractable blades, others have blades that can be broken off.

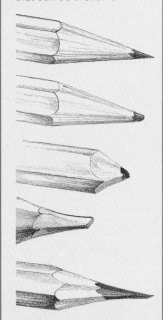

Top to bottom: **Pencil sharpened with a pencil sharpener; same pencil blunted; badly sharpened pencil; chisel end made with a knife; long point made with a knife.**

Pencil drawing at its simplest is monochrome (one colour). But within that one colour it is possible to express a range of tone.

'Tone' is the term used for the degree of lightness or darkness of a particular colour. In the case of a pencil drawing the tonal range will be from white, through varying shades of grey to black. But all colours have a similar tonal range, depending upon how much light is falling upon them. In order to be able to draw (or paint) you need to train your eye to see objects in terms of tonal areas rather than outlines filled in with solid colour.

To get an idea of tone, hold a piece of white paper up against a bright sky. The white paper will appear dark in comparison with the sky. Now look at any simple object, such as a mug or an apple, and try to see it simply in terms of tonal values. Closing one eye and looking at the object with one eye only will help you to see it in terms of tonal areas.

As a first exercise in rendering tone with pencil, try to reproduce the examples shown, *above*. This will give you the experience of producing different tonal values using different techniques. When drawing with pencil the range of tones is limited to what pencil and paper are capable of delivering.

HOLDING YOUR PENCIL

There is no right or wrong way to hold a pencil. Everyone has their own way which is natural to them, but it is useful to try out different ways to give yourself greater flexibility in your drawing.

Try to avoid holding the pencil too tightly and too close to the tip (**1**). When you hold the pencil this way you can only make small marks with a limited range of movement. The hand also covers the drawing close to where you are working, making it difficult to see the overall result. Instead, hold the pencil lightly halfway along its length. In this position

the pencil lies between the thumb and first finger (**2**). Another variation is to place the pencil in the palm of the hand and to rest the thumb on top of it (**3**). When you hold the pencil like this you can use it at a lower angle to the paper. And if you sharpen it to a long, flat tip you can make very broad marks and shade large areas more easily.

Smudging can be a problem when you are drawing with pencil. You can avoid this by putting a piece of paper between your hand and the drawing, but this obscures the drawing. Tracing paper or clear film is a better option, but it is still inhibiting and has to be held and moved by the other hand. The best solution is to hold the pencil without the hand touching the paper (**4**). This also means that the hand can move freely and this gives the drawing an expansive quality.

To get your hand moving freely, try writing the alphabet in large letters, holding the pencil at mid-length position (**5**). Make the movement from shoulder or elbow rather than from your wrist.

SIMPLE STILL LIFE

For your first drawing project, we show you how simple it is to produce a satisfying still life using one grade of pencil only. The different tones in the drawing are achieved by varying the pressure when making marks. Use a 4B pencil and a watercolour paper with a fairly rough surface.

MATERIALS

4B pencil
pad of watercolour paper
putty rubber
bulldog clip
retractable blade knife

1 First select a bunch of bananas and a few apples of uniform colour. Arrange them as shown above so that the bananas cover at least one of the apples. Place the group near a window, or use a table lamp or spotlight, so that the group is lit from one side only. Position yourself so that you are looking obliquely down on the arrangement. Although the fruit may be seen as a collection of individual items, it is best to think of them as a group in order to draw them. Look carefully at the individual shapes of the fruit, and how they create the overall shape of the group, and then lightly sketch the boundaries of the cluster of shapes.

2 Look at the way the light falls on your grouping, and note which are the light areas and which are the dark areas. At this stage don't think too much about the boundaries of the fruit, but try to see the whole composition in terms of light and shade. Close one eye if that helps. Now sharpen your pencil to a flat chisel tip and, letting your hand move freely, start to shade in the palest shaded areas using a light pressure. Start from the left (if you are right-handed), or from the right if you are left-handed, and work across the drawing, thinking about where the light is coming from and where each fruit turns away from the light. Run the shading on to the table surface where there are cast shadows. You can vary the direction of the pencil marks, but don't feel that all the marks have to follow the contours of the fruit.

HELPFUL HINT

A simple composition of fruit (taken from our opening drawing) is the subject of our project. Sit so that you are looking down on it from an angle.

3 The next step is to shade in a darker tone where the objects cast shadows on each other, and on the table surface. In the darkest areas the fruit and shadow will fuse together, and if you half close your eyes you will be able to see this simplification of the tones — object and shadow becoming one. Using your chisel tip and a backwards and forward 'scribble' technique, shade over the darker areas using a medium pressure. This will result in a darker tone than the first shading.

4 Now look critically at your drawing and decide where the very darkest areas are. It helps to prop it up and look at it from a distance, comparing it with the subject. Note that the highlights are depicted by the white of the paper. What you are doing is gradually shading in darker tones. Make a careful note of where the very darkest tone occurs, and gradually work over your drawing, shading in the darkest areas, using a heavier pressure.

5 Continue shading in the darkest areas, taking care not to work over the highlights, which appear as 'shine'. As you shade in the darker tones, the light areas will appear brighter by contrast. If you overwork an area, lift off some of the graphite with a putty rubber, using a dabbing action rather than rubbing backwards and forwards. As the drawing develops, so will the danger of smudging, so take care to keep your hand clear of the paper. As soon as you feel your objects have a solid, three-dimensional look to them, stop!

You will have learnt a great deal from your first project: how to set up a composition, how to observe the way light falls on it, how to distinguish tones. Increasing skill will come from constant practice. Carry a small sketch book with you and get into the habit of making lightning sketches of everyday scenes. Drawing is based on observation, and the more you understand what you are observing, the better you will draw.

TEXTURED SURFACES

This atmospheric woodland scene, *left*, with its multiplicity of leaf, grass and bark textures, was drawn with 4B and 8B pencils — showing just how versatile pencil technique can be.

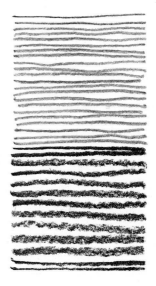

Textural effects made with pencil vary with the technique used, the grade of pencil, and the texture of the paper. *Above*, lines drawn with an HB pencil (*top*) and 8B pencil on rough watercolour paper.

The texture of grass, leaves and tree bark are immediately apparent when you are standing in a woodland glade, but how do you describe them on paper? In this lesson we look at pencil techniques for suggesting texture, and show you how to use some of them in our step-by-step project.

The world we see around us, and that as artists we try to reproduce on paper, is composed not only of shapes, hues and tones, but also of textures. Woolly, silky, soft, shiny, hard, knobbly, smooth, gritty — every surface has its own particular quality. To give expression to these various textures on paper is one of the most challenging aspects of drawing with pencil.

On the next two pages you will find examples of textural techniques. As we saw on page 180, when we looked at various means of expressing tone, there are many ways of combining pencil marks to create different effects. While it is useful to practise these techniques so as to have them at your disposal when needed, it is important not to get carried away by them. In any one drawing you will probably not need to use more than three or four at the most — otherwise the whole effect may end up looking like a patchwork quilt!

Remember too that there are no set rules for using textural techniques. For instance, the first example shown on the next page is a series of wobbly parallel lines. The subtle variations in the lines might suggest to one person a moving texture, and so be used to depict the surface of the sea, or an uncut hayfield ruffled by a breeze. But another person might see it differently, and use it for the sky, or a beach, or stone wall.

Seeing and perceiving

Once again we are brought back to the crucial element in drawing — seeing and perceiving. How you perceive the textures of a given scene, and how you perceive the qualities of the textural exercises on the next page, will be unique to you. The way you perceive textural quality, and the techniques chosen to depict those qualities, will help you to develop your own style of drawing.

The two-tone textures *above* were drawn with 2B pencil (*top*) and 6B pencil on good quality writing paper (*top left*), Ingres paper (*top right*), watercolour paper (*bottom left*) and thin card (*bottom right*).

SIMPLE TEXTURES (using 4B pencil)

1

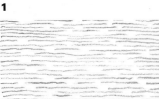

2

3

4

1 Drawing flowing, parallel lines needs careful control. Too close together they make a dark texture. Too far apart they lose their relationship with one another and cease to be a texture as such.

2 Lines drawn in the same way as continuous lines, but with breaks, create 'lights'. This is a classic technique used for the sparkle on water.

3 Short, crisp parallel lines drawn in the patterns shown can create the effect of movement and a feeling of overlapping areas.

4 Short runs of zigzag lines create a similar feeling to 3, but note how the triangular white patches between the actual pencil areas create a strong feeling of movement and a sense of activity.

5 Dots are an effective minimal treatment, but notice how, when applied quickly, they take on the direction of the hand movement. In the lower part of the sample the movement has evolved suggesting a much thicker texture.

6 Small circles relate strongly to round objects and can be used in conjunction with other textures in a drawing. Round blobs make a tonal contrast .

5

6

7 A pattern of continuous wriggly lines across the page lends itself to considerable variation. The spaces become as important as the lines themselves, creating their own individual effects.

8 A continuous scribbled line drawn in all directions without ever lifting the pencil from the page will form dark areas suggesting a rough, abrasive texture.

7

8

COMPLEX TEXTURES

1

2

3

4

1 A texture built up from 4B lines in different directions. The long smooth lines are drawn with a swinging curve, the other lines are short, jabbing marks.

2 Wavy 4B lines drawn with changes of pencil pressure. All texture techniques can be varied by the pressure used.

3 A texture composed of curved 4B lines moving in different directions. The white spaces left between the lines can suggest quite a strident texture that is not always sympathetic when used on a large scale.

4 More or less parallel, curving 4B lines that follow form give a strata-like effect.

5 Thick marks made with a soft, 8B pencil create a bold, chunky texture. The size of the marks also suggests a spatial quality — the smaller marks at the top seem to suggest the surface is receding into the distance.

6 These rectangular marks, made with an 8B pencil, make the white spaces between them seem more dominant than the marks themselves.

5

6

7 Powerful, thick, 8B pencil marks are so insistent that they become a feature in themselves. When strong feelings invade your drawings, you may find a use for them.

8 This last textural technique involves a 4B swinging line overlaid with heavy jabs from an 8B pencil. This is another technique that can add a sense of vitality to a drawing.

7

8

A WOODLAND SCENE

MATERIALS

4B and 8B pencils
pad of watercolour paper
eraser
scalpel

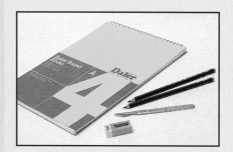

A wood is full of fascinating textures, overlapping each other in great profusion. Part of the skill involved in drawing such a scene lies in the way you depict textures in the foreground and background. Leaves, grass and tree bark in the foreground can be defined clearly, but deeper into the wood we need a vaguer impression of foliage and dappled light merging into the distance. The twisted tree trunk is the heart of the composition and should be sketched in first. When drawing any outdoor landscape, it is important to establish the main shapes and their position on the page right from the start.

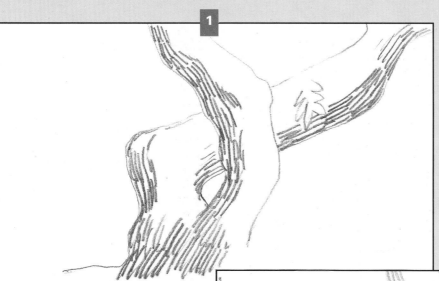

1 With the 4B pencil, lightly draw in the outline of the twisted tree trunk. Then start to indicate the texture of the bark on the surfaces in shade.

2 Draw a boundary round the area of your drawing and shade in some of the darker tones. Indicate some of the surfaces on which the light is strongest. Remember that these areas will be left white.

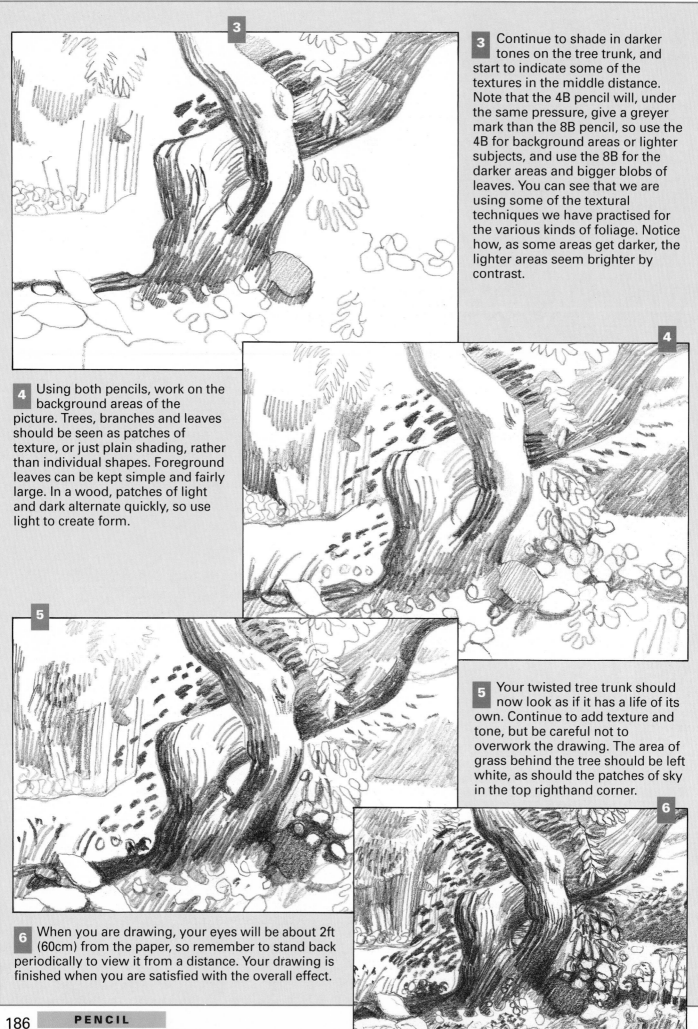

3 Continue to shade in darker tones on the tree trunk, and start to indicate some of the textures in the middle distance. Note that the 4B pencil will, under the same pressure, give a greyer mark than the 8B pencil, so use the 4B for background areas or lighter subjects, and use the 8B for the darker areas and bigger blobs of leaves. You can see that we are using some of the textural techniques we have practised for the various kinds of foliage. Notice how, as some areas get darker, the lighter areas seem brighter by contrast.

4 Using both pencils, work on the background areas of the picture. Trees, branches and leaves should be seen as patches of texture, or just plain shading, rather than individual shapes. Foreground leaves can be kept simple and fairly large. In a wood, patches of light and dark alternate quickly, so use light to create form.

5 Your twisted tree trunk should now look as if it has a life of its own. Continue to add texture and tone, but be careful not to overwork the drawing. The area of grass behind the tree should be left white, as should the patches of sky in the top righthand corner.

6 When you are drawing, your eyes will be about 2ft (60cm) from the paper, so remember to stand back periodically to view it from a distance. Your drawing is finished when you are satisfied with the overall effect.

SHADE AND SHADING

In our first drawing lesson we showed you how to produce a drawing in four tones using one grade of pencil and varying the pressure. In this lesson we look in more detail at how to render tones with pencil shading, and in the project we use different grades of pencil to depict four different tones.

The drawing of a bridge in an Italian landscape, *above,* by Sir Augustus Wall Callcott (1779-1844) shows how the skilful rendering of tones in what is an essentially simple drawing results in a very lifelike portrayal of a scene.

This lesson is about shade and shading. When light falls on solid objects you see a pattern of highlights, reflected light and cast shadows, all of which have different tonal values. It is the ability to see a scene in terms of tonal values, and to render those tones in pencil, that gives a realistic quality to your drawings.

In a pencil drawing we are only able to use the tonal range of grey. However, by choosing different grades of pencil — and varying the pressure used — you can achieve a wide variety of tonal effects, as we demonstrate overleaf.

The world around us is multi-coloured, but in pencil drawing we are, as we have said, restricted to the grey tonal range. It is therefore vital that you learn to see the tones (as opposed to hues) that are present in colours, and apply these to the grey tonal range. One of the exercises

overleaf shows you a coloured photograph translated into black and white. We suggest that you try and 'map' the tones of the black and white picture, using perhaps a maximum of five tones. Mapping is simply a term used in drawing to describe the technique of making a simple outline drawing of your chosen subject, and then shading in the areas that are dark and the areas that are light. These areas of light and dark are what give a flat drawing a three-dimensional quality. You could then try the same exercise with a black and white photograph of your own. Don't worry about detail — just shade in the areas of different tones.

When you have experimented with the different pencil tones, and have tried the mapping exercise, you are ready to move on to our project — a drawing of a bridge over a stream — which puts all this theory into practice.

Our drawing project, *top left,* is also of a bridge and is intended to give you more practice in depicting tones by means of shading with pencils of different grades. The chart overleaf, illustrating tones created by 10 grades of pencil using five different pressures, shows the enormous variety of pencil tones that can be achieved. Our project, however, uses just four tones, created by using four different grades of pencil.

TONES

Below: An example of the tonal range it is possible to achieve using just one pencil, in this case a 6B.

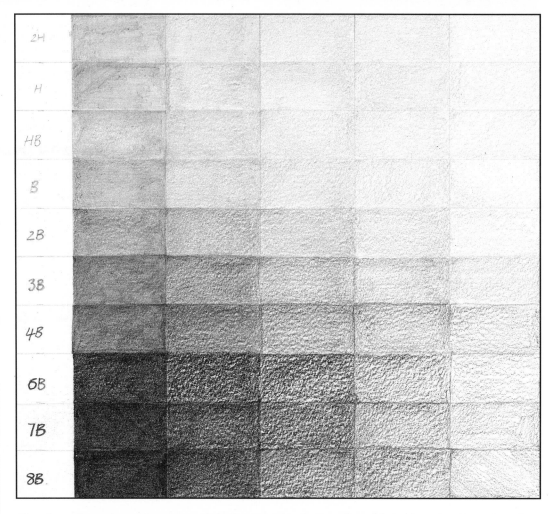

2H

H

HB

B

2B

3B

4B

6B

7B

8B

The chart *above* shows the great variety of grey tones that can be achieved by using 10 grades of pencil and five different pressures. Try reproducing this as an exercise in tonal shading.

COLOUR AND TONE

'Tone' means how dark or light a colour is, but as this still life (*right*) shows, it is often difficult to distinguish the tones in a complexity of colour, highlights and shadows. Until your eye becomes practised, you may have problems seeing the tones in colours.

In the same picture in black and white (*right*), the range of tones from light to dark is much easier to see. When you draw any subject in pencil it is a good idea to look at it through half closed eyes before you start. With practice this will help you to see the subject in terms of light, medium and dark tones.

BRIDGE OVER A STREAM

A bridge over a stream provides a wonderful natural subject on which to practise your powers of tonal observation. Here we use four grades of pencil to produce a simple, realistic scene in which the bridge stands out from its background to great effect — a result achieved simply by tonal pencil shading rather than by textural shaping.

1 Using the HB pencil, map out your scene by making a simple outline drawing of all the main shapes. Then draw a frame around it so that it is contained and you don't feel that you have to draw right to the edge of the paper.

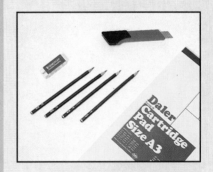

2 Half close your eyes and observe the tonal range of the scene. Try to reduce it to areas of light, medium and dark tone. Leave the lightest areas as white paper and, still using the HB pencil, start shading in the darker areas. Don't use too much pressure or overwork any areas — the form of the scene will emerge as you build up layers of different pencil tone.

3 Using the B pencil, begin to shade in the medium tones. Pay particular attention to the shading of the brickwork and the shadows cast on the banks of the stream. Roughly sketch in the trees on the horizon.

4 Now go over the medium tones with a 2B pencil. Because it is a softer pencil the shading will appear darker, so don't increase the pressure. Use it to highlight and soften the hard edges and build up the shadows on the building. You will find that your picture is beginning to have depth and come to life.

Don't be tempted to try and complete the bridge before moving on to other areas. The secret is to shade in each tone over the whole drawing before moving on to the next stage. This will produce an attractive finished drawing in which all the tonal values are in harmony.

5 Using a well-sharpened 3B pencil, finish off the drawing by shading in the fine detailing of the grasses on the bank, the ripples in the water, the trees and the country track and hedges. Shade under the eaves and down the side of the house, and finally go over the brickwork of the bridge to add definition to the stone and brickwork. You should press a little harder to achieve the darker shadows on the support arch.

PERSPECTIVE

To draw a landscape, street scene or any vista convincingly it is essential to master the rules of perspective. We explain the basic principles and, in our project, provide you with the underlying structure of guidelines to show you how to tackle any composition involving distance successfully.

When you look at any landscape, street scene or vista you can see a curious phenomenon. Things further away look smaller. This is one of the basic laws of perspective - and it is the laws of perspective that determine how we represent distance in a flat drawing. Drawing is basically about making lines on paper, and lines have directions. Lines drawn on paper to represent lines receding into the distance follow a clear set of rules — those of perspective.

A flat desert
Imagine a vast flat desert stretching away to the horizon — that is the imaginary background for all perspective principles. The desert's horizon is a horizontal line straight ahead of you — and everything in a perspective drawing is related to that

horizon. If a railway crossed the desert, the railway lines would be laid parallel to each other. If they were not, the trains would fall off! But in a drawing, the railway lines appear to converge as they travel further away, finally meeting at infinity on the horizon. So what we see, and draw, is not the same as what we know to be true about the railway lines in the real, three-dimensional world.

Diminishing posts
If a fence of posts and chain link were to be constructed alongside our imaginary railway line, we should see that although in the three-dimensional world the posts were evenly spaced, they appear to get closer together as they get further away. They also diminish in height until they too vanish on the horizon.

The drawing of a corner of a Norfolk village, *above*, relies on the principles of perspective to give a convincing impression of distance receding through the gates of the estate on the right. Although the underlying structure of lines leading to a vanishing point has been skilfully lost in the drawing, we should be immediately aware if they were not there. You have only to look at a drawing by a very young child who knows nothing of perspective to see that though it may be charming in its naivety, somehow the houses do not seem to stand up properly, and there may be a bizarre tendency for distant objects to be drawn the same size or larger than near objects, giving a surreal effect. When the rules underlying perspective are observed, drawings look more realistic.

HORIZON

As we have said, to understand perspective we must imagine a vast desert with a horizontal line as the horizon. This horizon is also considered to be your eye level when you are drawing (see **1**).

If we consider a railway line travelling straight towards the horizon the lines will appear to converge as they get further away, and finally meet at infinity on the horizon (see **2**).

If we imagine a fence of posts running alongside the railway line, these will appear to get closer together as they recede, and also diminish in height until they vanish at the same point on the horizon (see **3**).

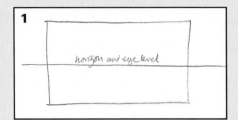

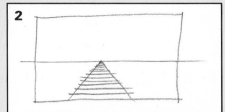

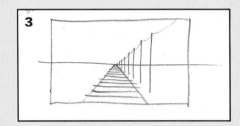

So, here are some basic rules to remember. Your eye level and the so-called horizon in your drawing are the same line. Lines that are understood to be parallel, but which are travelling away from you, will converge on your horizon. Those that are above your eye level will descend to the horizon, while those that are below your eye level will rise to the horizon.

BUILDINGS

When you are drawing a building, you will most probably see two walls, and they are likely to be at right angles to each other. The vertical ends of the walls will be drawn vertically, but the top edge of each wall, where the guttering might be, and the ground line will converge as the wall gets further away. Each wall will have a different vanishing point on the horizon (see **4**).

In order to see the direction of the receding lines more clearly, it helps if you hold up your pencil in front of you and tilt it so that it coincides with the line of the wall. This will make you more aware of the angle the line makes with the horizon. Remember that the vanishing point may be way off your drawing paper. A wall that is seen very obliquely will have a vanishing point fairly close to, but a wall seen nearly flat on will have a vanishing point way off the page (see **5**).

The line of the ridge of the roof is also parallel to the gutter line and the ground line, and will recede to the same vanishing point (see **6**).

Smaller parts of the building, such as doors, windows and chimneys, will follow the same rules. While all the vertical lines

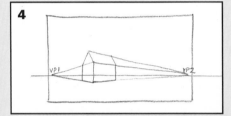

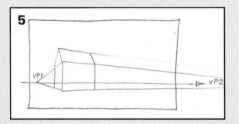

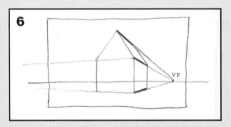

will be drawn vertical, the top and bottom lines will converge to the same vanishing point as the main lines of the wall in which they are placed (see **7**).

Different vanishing points

The first thing to do when starting a perspective drawing involving buildings is to block in the outline of the buildings and then project the lines to their vanishing points on the horizon. This may involve using a very large sheet of drawing paper! Remember that if you are drawing a group of buildings, each building will probably have a different set of vanishing points. So your underlying structure of guidelines

may become quite complex.

Pencil is the ideal medium for constructing perspective directions. You can use very fine, light pencil lines for constructing guidelines, and as the drawing progresses, these can be whisked away with an eraser.

In the drawing project opposite, guidelines have been drawn up for the main house in the foreground. Its vanishing point is VP1. The top lines relate to the chimneys and the one vertical line is the near corner of the two main walls. If you want to see exactly how the guidelines work you can trace off the diagram, and then see how it fits over the finished drawing.

A VILLAGE SCENE

Our step-by-step drawing project of a village scene is primarily aimed at showing you how the principles of perspective work in a finished drawing. Constructing the guidelines for the drawing is an essential part of learning about perspective.

MATERIALS

HB and 4B pencils
pad of cartridge paper
ruler
eraser and scalpel

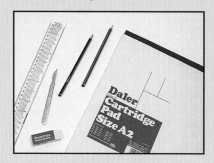

1

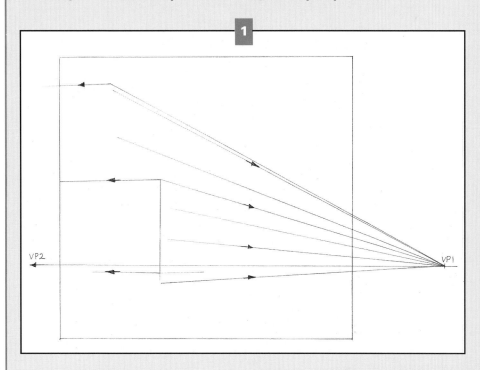

1 The first step is to construct a framework of guidelines running to their vanishing point. The guidelines above relating to the main building show the line of the chimneys, the ridge of the roof, the guttering, the bottom of the upper storey windows, the top of the lower windows and the ground line all converging at VP1 to the right. The lines of the flank wall and the other lines going off to the left will all converge at a vanishing point way off the page. It will help you enormously if you use a very large sheet of paper so that you can get at least one vanishing point in. Your actual drawing area will be quite small.

2 This shows the guidelines for the rail and posts in the foreground, which vanish at VP3. The horizontal line across the page is the horizon line, and your eye level. Remember that if the object concerned is above your eye level, then as it recedes from you it will be descending towards the horizon. If it is below your eye level, then as it recedes its lines will rise to the horizon. Draw

guidelines very faintly, so that if possible they merge into the finished drawing.

3 The third part of the basic scaffolding relates to the lodge building to the left of the gateway. The end wall, in shadow, is seen obliquely. At first sight it might seem that the roof line and the gutter line of the main view of the lodge are parallel to the horizon, but the fact that the end wall can be seen means that the lines of the main view must converge somewhere to the left. In fact the lines of the ridge and gutter descend very gradually to the horizon and vanishing point VP2 way off the page. It seems likely that VP2 serves both the main house and the lodge, suggesting that they were built parallel to each other. The ground line lies just slightly below the horizon line, and so will rise very gradually towards its vanishing point on the left, VP2. When a line is masked (as here by fences and plants) it is important to visualise what is happening underneath.

4 You are now ready to start drawing! Draw in the main elements of the scene, using your guidelines to help you position accurately the walls, windows and posts. In this kind of perspective exercise the guidelines may seem over-dominant at first. But as you add tone and detail the straight lines will become blurred. Try to put out of your mind your knowledge that doors and windows are rectangular. In this drawing they will assume the shapes dictated by the perspective guidelines. Note the bend in the fence rail in the foreground, which is a detail from real life that does of course deviate from the perspective line.

5 You can now start to add tone. Begin by shading in the tree behind the main house and the trees beyond the gate in the distance. Then add tone to the window wall of the main house, the garden wall up to the lodge, the side of the chimneys in shadow and the shaded parts of the rails and posts. Aim for three distinct tones. If you have difficulty identifying the tones when drawing from life, try looking at the subject through sunglasses. Areas that are painted white, but which lie in shadow, are likely to be much darker than first thought.

6 Continue to work over the drawing, adding light tone, mid-tone and dark tone. Resist the temptation to finish one area completely ahead of the rest of the drawing, otherwise the overall balance of tones may well be lost. In the final stages you can use some of the textural techniques learned in lesson 2 to suggest brick courses, shrubs, grass and road surface. As the drawing develops, do not forget to observe the underlying movement of the perspective lines.

Your finished drawing should have a feeling of depth and mystery in the distant grounds glimpsed through the arch. This illusion of depth on a flat page is the result of mastering perspective.

LIFE DRAWING: The head

In this lesson we make a start on life drawing with a study of the human head. Drawing a portrait is particularly challenging since it involves rendering both the physical form of the head plus the individual characteristics of the face to produce a likeness. And a self portrait can reveal how we see ourselves.

A self portrait is a good introduction to the pains and pleasures of drawing the human head. One advantage is that the model is immediately available and does not have to be cajoled into sitting for you, and can be guaranteed not to get up and walk away when you are only halfway through the drawing. As the drawing may take several hours, this is quite an important consideration.

Sitting comfortably

It is a good idea to set yourself up comfortably before you begin. You will probably find a hard, straight-backed chair is best, and you will also need a mirror propped up

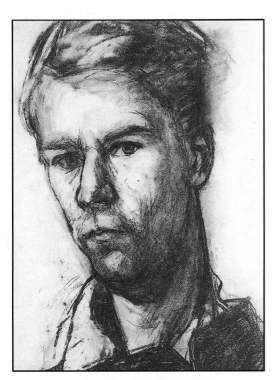

at a convenient angle and a good light source. You need to be able to see your reflection in the mirror and your drawing without moving your head.

Daylight is one of the best light sources, so if possible work during the day and arrange things so that your reflection is well lit. If you have to use artificial light, make sure that it is not too harsh. Fluorescent light is far too unflattering and should be avoided. Lighting from the side will throw facial shadows that emphasise form, while soft lighting from below will create a dramatic effect. But to start with it is probably best to use conventional lighting.

Right: The self portrait of Henri Gaudier-Brzeska (1891-1915) shows a drawing style influenced by his work as a sculptor.

Above: John Minton's self portrait has the wide-eyed look typical of many self portraits.
Left: David Michie's self portrait captures the concentration needed to produce a likeness.

Before beginning to draw the human head it is a good idea to study its basic shape and structure. Examine the silhouettes of the heads of people around you. If you look at them carefully you will begin to see the shape of the cranium beneath the hair.

If you look at the outline drawing of the head of a young adult (**1**) you will see that the facial features occupy quite a small area in relation to the cranium (the part of the skull that encloses the brain). However, this proportion changes with age.

In a baby (**2**) the cranium is very large compared to the facial area. And because an infant has no teeth, the distance between nose and chin is quite short.

In a young adult (**3**) the facial area has become larger in relation to the cranium. The presence of teeth forces the nose and chin further apart.

In extreme old age (**4**) the cranium appears to have shrunk, and the absence of teeth brings the nose and chin closer together again.

It is useful to keep this picture of the structure of the head in mind when drawing any portrait.

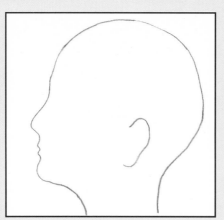

1

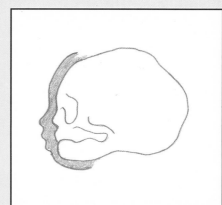

2

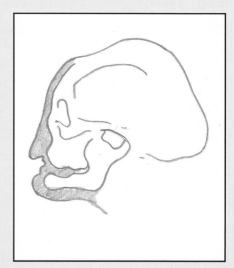

3

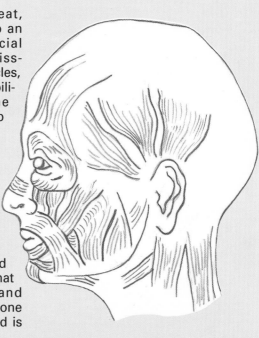

4

CLASSICAL PROPORTIONS OF THE FACE

In Classical Greece it was thought that the male head could be divided into eight units, *above*. The hairline was two units down, the brow line was the mid line and the nose filled two units.

THE MUSCLES OF THE FACE

In order that we can talk, eat, laugh, frown and give rein to an extraordinary range of facial expressions, the face is criss-crossed with a network of muscles, *right*, that give it form and mobility. The muscles around the mouth permit very delicate lip movements, enabling us to speak, while muscles around the eyes control eye movements such as blinking and altering the focus.

Muscles covering the forehead allow us to wrinkle the brow, while muscles controlling the movement of the cheeks enable us to smile and pull faces. The large muscle that runs from behind the ear and across the neck to the breastbone allows us to turn our head, and is very prominent when we do so.

SELF PORTRAIT

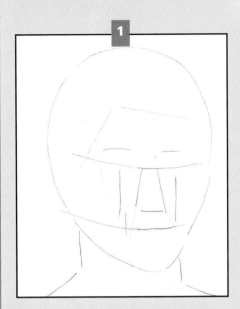

2 Now sketch in the hairline, brows, eyes, nose and mouth. Note that the position of all these does correspond quite surprisingly well with the Classical proportions.

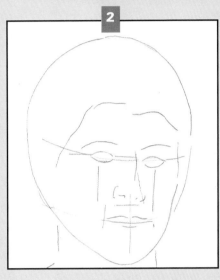

1 With an HB pencil, draw the outline of your head as an oval. Sketch in the line of the eyes and the line of the mouth as shown, remembering that as the face is rounded these lines will be curved.

Drawing your own face can be an interesting and revealing experience. Keep things simple by having only one light source, and try to arrange things so that you are not sitting square on to the mirror. Before you start, examine your face as objectively as possible from various angles and decide what your best features are and how your character is reflected in your face. Try to adopt an expression that conveys your personality. All this will be good experience for when you come to draw other people.

M A T E R I A L S

HB pencil
4B pencil
eraser
drawing pad (or paper and drawing board)

3 Using the 4B pencil, start to fill in the details of your features. This is the stage that will determine whether you achieve a likeness, so don't rush it.

MOUTH AND EYES

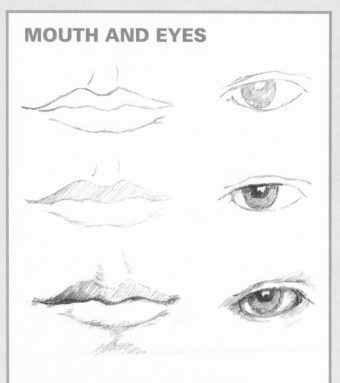

We show *above* in detail how to achieve the fine modelling of the mouth and eyes. Note that in normal lighting (from above) the upper lip is in shadow and the lower lip light. Spend plenty of time on drawing the eyes, as they give character to the whole face.

4 Still using the 4B pencil, start shading in tones to establish the contours and moulding of the face. Eyes and mouth can present particular difficulties, so we have given you some tips in the box *top left*.

5 Continue adding tone with the 4B pencil until you are satisfied with the overall effect. Take your time, and remember that mistakes are easily corrected with the eraser. Do not overwork your drawing — stop while it still looks fresh.

It would be an interesting project to draw yourself at regular intervals — say once a year. This would show both how your face changes over a period of time, and how much your drawing improves!

LIFE DRAWING:
The figure

Life drawing can often appear to be a rather daunting prospect, conjuring up images of lofty north lit art studios and bored models. However, if you approach it in the comfort of your own home with a relaxed and natural subject you will find it a rewarding and enjoyable activity and be pleasantly surprised by the results.

Before you begin to draw, make sure that your model is comfortable. Appearing relaxed while sitting in the same pose for an hour or so at a time is not easy, so it's a good idea to draw someone while they are reading, watching television or listening to music. To achieve a reasonable drawing you need about two and a half hours' drawing time. Most people will be prepared to sit for half an hour at a time, so you may have to plan your sessions over a few days, drawing for an hour a day with a break after half an hour. Art school tutors will often ask their students to do five-minute sketches, and this can be a useful exercise before you begin a detailed study.

Plenty of time
To start with, give yourself time. Time to think, time to look and time to draw. Life drawing isn't just about making a portrait of somebody. It is mainly about understanding how the human body works, and how the various parts relate to each other proportionally. Study the introduction to anatomy overleaf, and make a point of watching people to see what happens when they move about and assume different body positions.

Don't struggle too much for a likeness. The face is a powerful element in communication and we all think we know what it looks like. People have two eyes, a nose, mouth, ears and hair, and the inexperienced artist will try to show two eyes and put the nose in the middle of the face. But

in a drawing only one eye may be seen, and the nose may not appear to be in the middle of the face. If you give yourself time to consider shapes and proportions a likeness will miraculously evolve. As you follow our step-by-step drawing you will see that it is not about whether a nose is long or short, but about directions, sizes and sensitivity to the shapes that make up the human figure.

Above: This drawing of a seated figure by David Hockney, entitled 'Lila di Nobilis Paris 1973' is a powerful evocation of the sitter, achieved with great economy of line.

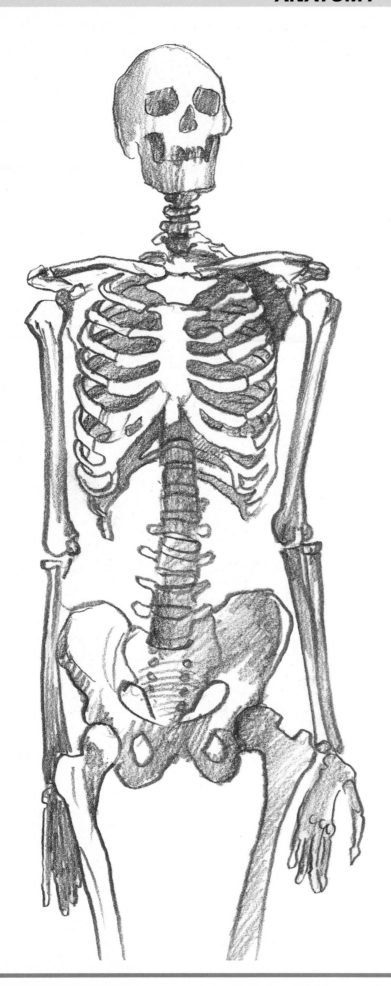

The human figure is a very complicated construction. If we can understand just a little about that construction it will help our figure drawing immensely.

The basis of the human figure is the skeleton of bones, *left*. These are connected by a complex of muscles, and as the body moves, so the arrangement of bones and muscles shifts to present different external forms. This may sound obvious, but it is the reason why life drawing from a nude model is the basic discipline for figure drawing.

It is not necessary to have a complete knowledge of human anatomy, but it helps if you understand some basic principles. The torso and head are supported by the spine, to which is connected the ribcage which protects vital organs such as heart and lungs. The pelvis, at the base of the spine, is a sort of bone bowl which holds the stomach.

Either side of the pelvis is the femur, a big bone which runs down to the knee, from which two bones continue to the foot. The feet, small as they are, are strong enough to support the standing figure. Each arm is attached to a shoulder blade or scapula, which can move about at the back of the ribcage. Covering these rigid bone elements are muscles and fat. So the artist has to be aware of what is rigid in itself, where a rigid part is hinged to another, and what is soft and yet vital in the control of movements.

MANNIKIN

You can buy a jointed wooden doll, called a mannikin, to help you with figure drawing. It has the correct proportions of the body and can be arranged in various poses, *below*.

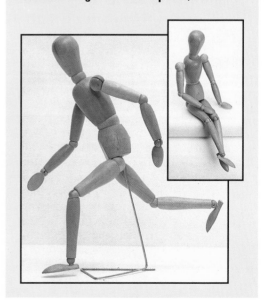

SIGHT MEASUREMENT

Sight measurement is a way of measuring the proportions of a figure by using your pencil as a sighting aid (see 'Using your pencil' *below right*).
To compare, say, the distance from the top of the head of your model to a point on the chest, and from the chest to the tip of the foot, hold up your pencil vertically with your arm fully outstretched. Line up the top of the pencil with the top of the head, *left*. Move the hand-hold down until the thumb is level with the chest. Then move the pencil down without changing the hand-hold until the top is lined up with the chest. The position of the thumb can then be compared with the tip of the foot. Ensure that the arm remains at a constant outstretched position, or the sizes will be changed. In fact in the pose *left* the dimensions are equal. In a similar way the head alone can be measured and its dimension moved downwards counting the number of 'heads' the body occupies, *below left*. In this case it is two and two-thirds.

SETTING THE SCENE

The best way to draw your model is from a three-quarter view — not a profile and not right in front but somewhere in-between. If your model is going to read, ask them not to move their head when turning pages — the eyes can move but the head must stay in the same position. And choose a pose that is easy to re-position after a break, because any change in the pose will change what you see. You can use markers such as pins or adhesive labels to help you with this. If you plan to work on more than one day you will need to make sure that your model wears the same clothes — and look out for visits to the hairdressers. You may find that you have to become quite tough on your model in order to get everything right, so find out if they're going to be amenable before you begin!

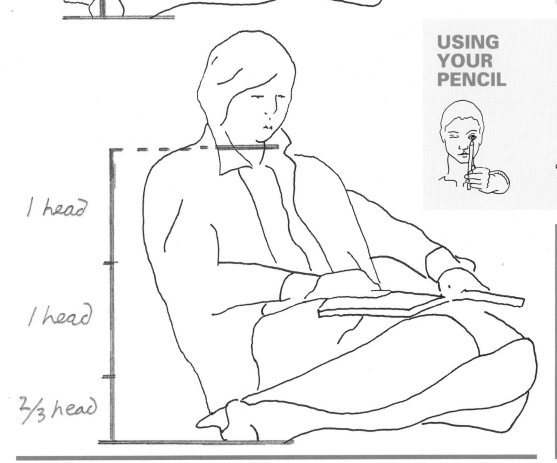

I head

I head

2/3 head

USING YOUR PENCIL

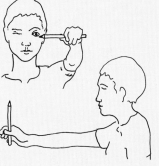

HELPFUL HINT

When using sight measurement as an aid, the edge of your sketch book should be parallel to the horizontal of your subject.

A SEATED FIGURE

MATERIALS

4B and 8B pencils
pad of cartridge or watercolour paper
eraser
scalpel

For our first figure drawing project we have chosen a seated figure, which is probably the most acceptable pose for your model. Place your model so that you see them in a three-quarter view if possible — not straight on or pure profile. And make sure your model is happy about holding the pose for half an hour at a time.

1 Use a reasonably large drawing pad (the original drawings here were done on paper 25 x 35cm) and block in the main lines of the pose with broad pencil lines. Take your time — most of it should be spent looking rather than drawing. This is by way of a preliminary exercise to get you looking at the pose carefully. You can discard this drawing once it is made.

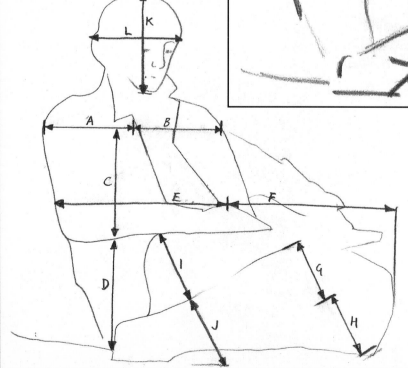

2 Now on a new piece of paper draw the main outlines of the pose and, using the technique of sight measurement described on page 201, establish some dimensions that are equal. You will see on our drawing that the equal dimensions are paired AB, CD, EF, GH, IJ, KL. Again, don't hurry this stage. The aim is to help you to get the proportions of your drawing right, and to draw what you see is there, not what you think is there. This again is a preliminary drawing. Keep it beside you as vital reference when you start your drawing proper.

3 The final preliminary exercise is to look at the overall shape of the pose in front of you and draw it as a map of main areas. The hair might form one shape, the face another, the dark jacket area nearest to you (including the sleeve) another main shape. Dividing the pose into basic shapes in this way will help you to see it just as it is.

4 You can now start your actual drawing, and by now you should have a fair idea of the main shapes in the pose before you and their relation to each other. Block in the main outlines lightly, and refer to your sight measurement drawing to get the proportions right. When you are satisfied your initial 'map' is correct, you can start shading in some of the tones.

5 Continue adding tones to your drawing, working over the whole drawing evenly rather than completing one part of it before the rest. This will give a better chance of achieving overall unity. Draw in some of the background details and remember to leave the lightest areas white.

6 Continue to add darker tone to your drawing until you are satisfied with the overall effect. Take care however not to overwork the face. In a figure drawing the head is only part of the whole, so you should not attempt to draw a portrait. Too much detail in the face will distract attention from the rest of the figure, so leave the face fairly understated.

When you are drawing, try to think of lines as simply places where volume and shape turn out of sight. In fact at the very point where we consider a line to be, there is nothing! What we see is in fact one shape stopping and another beginning, or one tonal area contrasting with another. When you begin to understand that lines do not really exist, you are well on the way to learning to draw.

INTERIOR PERSPECTIVE

On pages 191–4 we explained the principles of linear perspective and showed you how to draw up guide lines for a village scene. In this lesson we use these same principles in our project drawing of an interior, and give you some practical advice on how to depict the foreshortening effect of perspective on objects.

An important part of perspective is the foreshortening effect it can have on objects, and when drawing objects for the first time many people find it difficult to get the lengths of lines and the sizes of angles right. This is because it is natural to try and draw what you know about something rather than what your eyes actually see.

Imagine drawing a table that is four feet long and two feet wide. From above it will appear as in figure **1** in the diagram *right*. If you sit in front of the same table at a slight

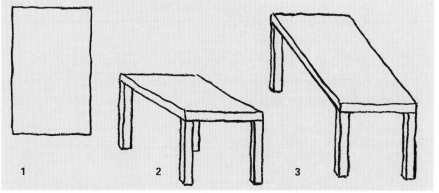

angle to it, and a few feet away from it, then it will resemble figure **2**. However, most beginners will try to draw the table as in **3**, because they know the table to be longer than it is wide.

The problems illustrated by the above example are easily overcome once you let your eye tell you what to draw, and on the following page we show you a few simple exercises that will help you to recognise and draw the different angles and perspectives to be found in our project drawing of a kitchen.

Above: This drawing by Horace Walpole (1717-1797) of his house in Strawberry Hill, Twickenham, demonstrates an effective use of linear perspective and the foreshortening effect it has on objects such as the table on the left of the foreground. Our project drawing for this lesson, *left*, of a kitchen is essentially an exercise in drawing an interior scene in perspective.

When drawing an interior, the lines coming straight towards you are shortened because of the foreshortening effect of perspective. However, horizontal lines that remain the same distance from your eye don't change. The following exercises will help you to see what happens to various lines and angles, and so enable you to draw objects in perspective. For the sake of clarity, some of the examples have been slightly simplified.

Table
In this example the table is gradually foreshortened as the angle of view changes. Notice how line **a** gradually becomes shorter while line **b** remains the same.

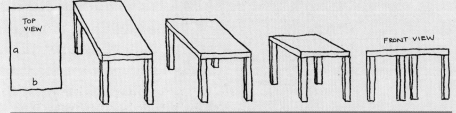

Book on table
Practise drawing the effects of foreshortening by putting a large book near the corner of a table and drawing it from different angles.

Line **a** is foreshortened and so will probably be shorter in relation to line **b** than you think it is. Look at the angle between line **a** and the horizontal. This may also be smaller than you think. Another thing to bear in mind in this example is the distance between the front of the book and the edge of the table, **c**. Again, this may be shorter than you expect at first glance. When you have begun to understand how to draw a single object, try the same exercise with a number of books or other objects, *right*.

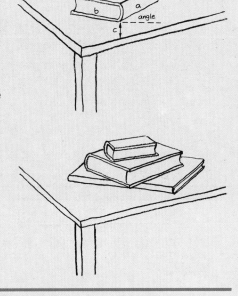

Getting the angle right
A simple way of training your eye to get angles right is to shut one eye and half shut the other. Without opening your eyes, hold your paper up horizontal and close to your subject. Transfer the angle

of the line you wish to draw on to your paper as shown *below left*.

Next open your eyes and lower your paper to a comfortable drawing position. Then draw a line parallel to the dotted line, in the centre of the page where you want to draw your object, as shown *below*.

With practice you will be able to draw these angles without aid.

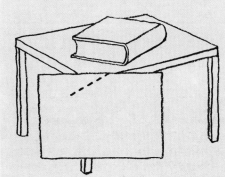

Drawing a tiled floor

1 Draw the lines of tiles coming towards you. Make sure that the distances between them are equal in the foreground.

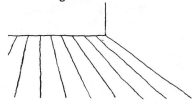

2 Gauge the depth of the tiles in the row nearest to you by eye, then draw two parallel lines horizontally across the first set of lines, as shown.

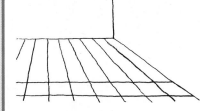

3 Draw a diagonal line starting from the lefthand corner of one of the tiles in the row and extending it across the page to the righthand corner.

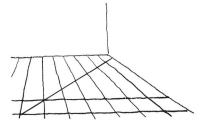

4 Where the diagonal intersects the other lines, draw horizontal parallel lines. You will find that you have a tiled floor with perfect foreshortened perspective!

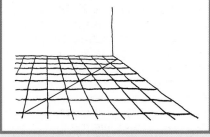

IN THE KITCHEN

M A T E R I A L S

HB and 2B pencils
pad of cartridge paper
ruler
eraser
fixative spray

Our drawing of a kitchen, with its built-in units and tiled floor, is a wonderful subject for practising perspective drawing. This project is designed to show you how to put the practical tips on the previous pages on the foreshortening of objects into context.

1 Using an HB pencil, lightly draw in the kitchen table, using your knowledge of foreshortening. Using the receding lines of the table, establish its vanishing point (see page 192). Construct guide lines to this vanishing point so that you can draw in the kitchen units and floorboards. All objects have 2 VPs, right and left, so you will need to establish the righthand VP as well (not shown here). Now draw in the main outlines using the VP lines to get the angles right. Draw the verticals and the chair.

2 Carefully rub out your perspective lines and begin to draw in the cupboards, door panels and drawers using a 2B pencil. Sketch in the outlines of objects such as the bowl sitting on the work surface, the saucepans hanging under the cupboard and the window blind over the window on the right. Keep looking at your kitchen through half-closed eyes to make sure you have the distances and angles right.

3 When you are satisfied with the look of all the objects and angles, consider where the light source is coming from. In our picture it is mainly from the window on the right. Note how the light falls on the various surfaces and gently shade in all the areas where the light casts subdued shadows.

4 The darkest areas of the kitchen are those not exposed to light. Using a firmer hand, shade in the sides of the cupboards and edges of the saucepans and onions. Pay particular attention to the subtle way in which the light casts longer shadows down the side of the cupboards to the right. Shade in the black and white floor tiles and shape the blind over the window, leaving parts white to depict any areas of reflected light.

5 Finally, stand back and take an overall look at your finished drawing. Lift out any areas of shading that appear too black using an eraser. Sharpen up the outlines of knobs and handles, then spray the whole drawing with fixative spray to prevent it smudging.

When you have completed your drawing of a kitchen you will begin to see that drawing in perspective is easier than it looks. As you become familiar with looking at objects in this way, you will be able to produce drawings in perfect perspective without the need for guide lines.

DRAWING A GROUP

On pages 199–204 we introduced you to life drawing and concentrated on a static, seated figure. In this lesson we move on to drawing groups, and give you practical tips on how to capture the dynamic of a group, with all its character and vitality.

Learning to draw groups of human figures is not an easy task, but it is extremely rewarding and will open your eyes afresh to the innumerable types of faces, expressions and movements of people around you.

An excellent way of understanding how figures can come together to produce a moving design or still harmony is by drawing copies of other people's paintings. Rembrandt, Stanley Spencer and Breughel all painted human figures in various types of pose. Contemporary group paintings often appear 'cropped', as if the painting was a perfect representation of the artist's original sketch. The groups of figures look natural, unposed and spontaneous. However, many artists produce finished works from several sketches made during repeated visits to a particular bar or theatre auditorium, and they strive to balance the lights and darks in their paintings to produce harmonious or dramatic effects.

Drawing a series of sketches and then bringing them together to form one image

is a very useful way for the beginner to approach drawing groups. You could get friends or family to pose for you, but it is far more rewarding to venture outside, and drawing strangers rather than people you know is easier at first.

The best places to start are where you feel inconspicuous and comfortable enough to spend time drawing the people around you: the corner of a café or restaurant; in a parked car among crowds of people; under an umbrella on the beach; in a railway station. If you feel shy, conceal your sketchbook behind a newspaper!

On the following page we show you examples of group drawings and give you tips on the important elements to look out for when sketching outdoor groups.

Above: This drawing is a workshop study for 'Burning of the Borgo' by Raphael (1483-1520). Raphael was a Renaissance painter whose main interest was the family group. Here we see how his characters, although looking in different directions, are held together as a group by their close proximity, and by the way the folds of their clothes appear to touch and merge. Our project drawing, *left*, takes a pavement café scene as its subject, and its success depends largely on the overall shape formed by the figures.

Drawing a large group can appear impossible — how to draw this chaos in which every element moves constantly, *below right*. You will only be able to draw marks and lines at first. However, after a little practice you will be able to remember more and more, and your memory will guide your hand. Try to absorb as much as possible of what is going on in front of you, then draw until you can't remember any more, rather than endlessly bobbing your head up and down.

Make fast gestural sketches (see *below*) of the movement and poses around you. Forget about recognisable features such as clothing and facial details, and concentrate on the outlines. Above all, keep your hand moving; let it jump from figure to figure so that you capture the moment with a few lines of movement.

Give your eye a little time to overcome its panic; to calm down until the hand dares to make its first marks! After a while you will be less concerned with being conspicuous and more concerned with how to capture certain elements and features.

AT THE BEACH

The beach is a perfect place to watch people playing, sunbathing, or just standing in the shallows. Use a marking pen or pen and ink, and add a light wash to turn your 'sketch' into a 'drawing'.

Work around the form of your group, and look carefully before you draw a line. See what kind of line works with the pose. If the person moves and you need a particular feature, wait for a while — they may return to their original pose. Human beings naturally 'group' themselves, so you don't need to pose them yourself.

GESTURES

Initially, drawing groups of people is very daunting, and you need to practise with small groups of two or three people at first. Most famous 'group' paintings were compiled in the artist's studio from many sketches done outdoors.

Be aware of the gestures and poses of the people you draw. Watch how the body moves, bends, turns, runs and sits. Draw gestures quickly as a moving line on your page — two seconds of drawing time can capture a fleeting pose.

Watch out for the direction of the lines of the pose, **1**, and respond to the line of the figure, the tilt of the head and the bend of the waist, **2**. Note and draw the lines of action that flow through the figures, and across them, and look for the axis of the spine and head — you are creating a form of calligraphy.

The gestural drawing *left* was based on the boys pictured *below*.

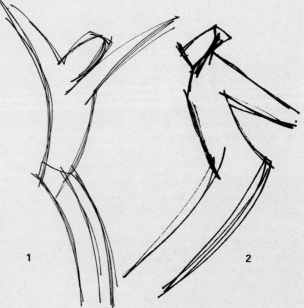

1

2

PAVEMENT CAFE

The relaxed atmosphere of a pavement café creates an ideal place in which to sit and sketch. In our project drawing we have chosen a group of friends meeting for a drink and a chat. The standing figure is essential to our composition, and when drawing a similar group from life you must work quickly—no group will remain exactly as you want it for very long.

1 Working as quickly as possible and keeping the pencil moving freely, sketch in the central seated figure. Start with the head and move down the body using a strong, fluid line. Don't worry about detail at this stage, just try to capture the pose of the figure.

M A T E R I A L S

NOT surface watercolour pad
2B pencil
putty rubber
fixative spray

2 Once the outline has been completed, draw in the chair on which the figure is sitting, then add the folds and creases in his jacket and trousers and lightly sketch in the edge of the table top.

3 Next sketch in the standing figure, starting from the head, as in step 1. Note his position in relation to the first figure, and the overall shape their outlines form. Part of the standing figure's back will be obscured by the seated figure on the left of the group, so only draw what you can see.

4 Still working quickly, sketch in the seated figure on the left. Keep the pencil moving fluidly across the picture, and return to the previously drawn figures to make slight alterations or corrections as necessary.

5 Now draw the man smoking his cigarette on the right of the group. Notice how the composition of the group is balanced by this man and his position in relation to the standing figure, who is looking over and out of the picture.

6 Now that your group composition is complete you can begin to fill in the details. Draw in the folded café umbrellas and shade in the shadows cast under the table.

7 Draw in the café sign then, using cross-hatching and a firmer hand, draw in the darkened windows behind the group. This effect 'throws' the figures forward and creates depth. Add more detailing on clothing and hair.

8 Finally work across the whole picture, solidifying the figures by adding shading to the drapes of the coats and the legs under the table. When you are satisfied with the result, spray your picture with fixative to prevent it smudging.

When you have finished your drawing you will begin to see how groups are not merely a collection of individuals — a group composition interacts as a whole. Try to apply this harmony when composing your own group drawings.

USING REFERENCES

When faced with a clean piece of paper and the urge to draw, your mind may sometimes go blank — where to start? At times like this a stock of reference material can save the day and fire your imagination, whether you are copying an idea from a photograph, for example, or simply using an existing image for original inspiration.

Using reference material to provide subject matter for your drawings not only jogs your imagination, it can also provide useful guidelines for composition, colour and tonality.

Inspiration can come from many sources, but perhaps the most useful tool of the 20th century is the camera. Snapshots are really a form of sketchbook, and provide a wealth of information about places you have visited, people you have met, family, friends, interesting lighting effects and odd juxtapositions of objects. Photographic reference material can also be used selectively — you can base a drawing on part of an image, invert it, reverse it or modify it.

Similarly magazines, advertisements and slides can be used as reference material. If you want a particular outline you can project a slide on to a wall and trace the projected image on to tracing paper. Other sources are books, videos — where a frame can be 'frozen' and copied — or even photographs taken off a television screen. Frozen action shots enable you to see exactly what is going on and so allow you to re-produce the image at your leisure.

Build up your own collection of reference books and files of cuttings from magazines, as well as keeping a sketchbook or any jottings done on the back of envelopes or scraps of paper. Libraries are also excellent places to hunt for reference material.

The beauty of drawing from an existing image, and particularly a photograph, is that you can enlarge or reduce it and modify parts as you go. However, keep an open mind and also draw inspiration from poetry, your favourite novel or a song. These more abstract references can provide you with images that are uniquely your own.

Above left: This sepia drawing of Wightwick Manor was done by its architect Edmund Hodgkinson two years after its construction in 1887. A photograph would be a good starting point for drawing such a detailed building — our drawing of Bodiam Castle *below* was based on one.

Once you have chosen your reference material you need to put it to use. Here we show you how to transfer a photographic image to cartridge paper, and explain how a simple grid system can be used to enlarge, reduce or modify the picture.

TRACING

Using lightweight tracing paper — approximately 60gsm is the most suitable — carefully trace off your image. Put a piece of carbon paper or grey graphite paper on top of the cartridge paper and lay your tracing on top. Attach the tracing and carbon paper to the cartridge paper with a strip of masking tape to prevent them moving while you transfer the image (*below*). Now draw over the lines of the traced image using a hard pencil or pointed instrument.

If you don't want to use carbon paper, scribble over the back of the tracing with a soft pencil, then turn the tracing over and attach it to the cartridge paper with masking tape. Go over the image with a hard pencil or pointed instrument.

Alternatively, tape your reference to a window or light box and hold a piece of cartridge paper over the top. The strong backlighting will enable you to see the image through the cartridge paper. You can then draw it straight on to the paper without needing to use carbon paper.

ENLARGING AND REDUCING

More often than not the reference material will be the wrong size and has to be enlarged or reduced.

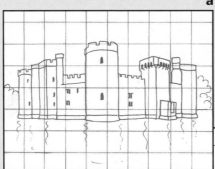

A simple way of doing this is to draw a grid of squares on a piece of tracing paper. This is then laid over the reference image (**a**). A grid using the same number of squares is then drawn on the cartridge paper, the size of the squares being reduced or enlarged depending on how big you want your finished drawing to be. For example, if you want to double the size of the reference image and the grid squares are $\frac{1}{2}$inch, then the second grid should be double the size — the squares being 1 inch.

When both grids are complete, look at the reference and draw the parts of the image that fall within a particular square into the corresponding square of the larger grid (**b**). Do this with all the squares and you will end up with a drawing double the size of the reference image. You can then rub out the guidelines. To save yourself the trouble of having to rub out the lines you can do the second grid and drawing on tracing paper and then transfer the image (as explained under Tracing, *left*).

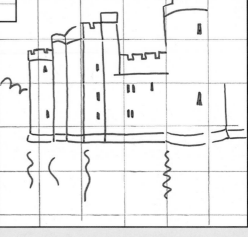

This method of 'squaring up' can also be used to enlarge or reduce an image to a specific percentage (**c**).

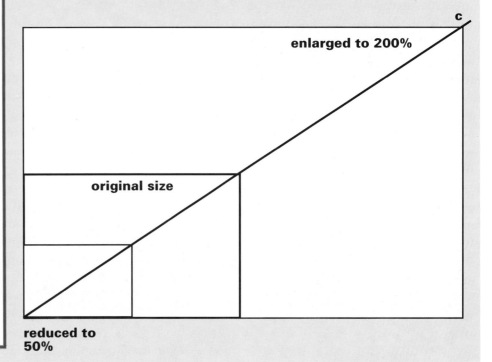

enlarged to 200%

original size

reduced to 50%

BODIAM CASTLE

The subject of this lesson's drawing project is Bodiam Castle. A photograph was used as reference material, but certain characteristics have been altered to make a more interesting composition. If you are using your own photograph don't feel that you have to make an exact copy. Any changes you make will enhance the originality of your drawing — reference material is simply a spur to your own creativity.

MATERIALS

reference photograph
A3 cartridge pad
A3 lightweight (60gsm) tracing paper
carbon paper
masking tape
pencils: HB, 6H, 4B
putty rubber

1 Tape the reference photograph to the cartridge pad and lay your tracing paper over the top. Using the HB pencil, lightly trace the outline of the castle and indicate areas of shadow on the masonry. Simple vertical lines indicate the reflections in the water. Don't worry about the finer details at this stage — it's not necessary to slavishly copy the original and anything superfluous should be omitted.

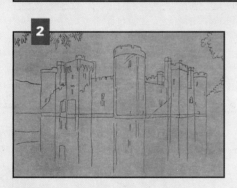

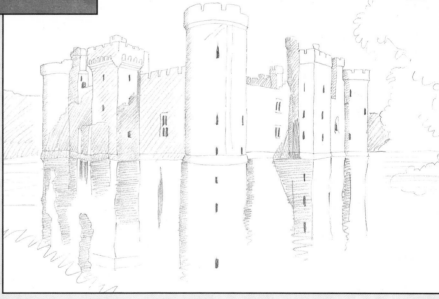

2 Tape the tracing to a piece of cartridge paper using a small piece of masking tape, then slip a piece of carbon paper in between the tracing and the cartridge paper, carbon side down. Using a 6H pencil and gentle pressure, go over all the lines of the tracing to transfer it to the cartridge paper.

3 Remove the masking tape, tracing and carbon paper to reveal the sketch on the cartridge paper. To make the composition more dramatic you can amend parts of the castle. Gently rub out the top of the central tower, the square parapet to the left and the adjoining wall, then re-draw them, making them slightly taller than the original. Give the parapets a larger overhang to make them a focal point on the lefthand side of the drawing. If you prefer, do these alterations on the tracing paper at step 2 to avoid any smudges — alternatively you could leave them out altogether.

Using an HB pencil, go over the whole outline to strengthen the lines. Refer to the original reference picture and, using a 4B pencil, start to depict areas of shadow with soft, hatched lines, using horizontal lines to portray ripples on the water.

4 With the 4B pencil, add more detail to the parapet of the square-topped tower on the left, and sketch its reflection in the water. Draw light, horizontal lines across the walls of the castle to indicate the layers of masonry. As you draw these lines, pay attention to the perspective and draw the horizontals accordingly — the central tower should stand forward, so slightly angle the horizontals of the walls to the left and right so that they appear to recede. Strengthen the three-dimensional quality of the drawing by adding more shading to areas of the castle that are in shadow.

5 Using the 4B pencil, begin filling in the masonry detail. Vary the pressure of the lines to depict the weatherbeaten stonework, and darken random areas to express a sense of irregularity. If some lines appear too dominant, tone them down by gently rubbing them with a putty rubber. Strengthen the tones in the water of the moat, and use soft, vertical strokes to depict the blurred effect of the water rippling over the reflected windows.

6 Still using the 4B pencil, work over the whole building to strengthen the tones and create a stronger sensation of sunlight. Draw in smaller details such as weeds, algae and cracks in the stonework, then add horizontal swirls and sharp lines to suggest plants and ripples on the water.

Using spontaneous strokes, shading and strong black marks, describe the various vegetation in the foreground, and finish off your drawing by using the side of the pencil to softly shade the sky behind the castle. Leave white areas to suggest the clouds.

> **Compare your finished drawing with your reference image. While it should resemble the original, it will have a spontaneity and 'personality' of its own. The three-dimensional quality achievable in a drawing is often more apparent than in a photograph, and any alterations you have made will only serve to enhance this effect.**

SPHERES AND ELLIPSES

The world is full of rounded objects which, at first glance, may appear too daunting to draw. However, if you simplify complex structures into geometrical shapes you will find that drawing rounded forms is easier than it seems, and in this lesson we show you how to 'see' objects in terms of cylinders, circles and cones.

Perfect mathematical shapes do not exist in the natural world. Nevertheless, to get a sense of the shape and form of a rounded object in order to be able to draw it, it is sometimes helpful to break the object down into shapes such as cylinders, cones and spheres.

When drawing a still life containing cylindrical shapes such as bottles, vases and tins, remember that they are three-dimensional objects and draw them as if they were transparent in order to get a sense of the shape. The most important thing to be aware of is how the ellipse (the oval shape formed by the changing perspective of a circle) alters according to your eye level. The top and base of a cylinder are circular, but when viewed from the side at different angles these circles are seen as ellipses, and the depth of each ellipse changes with the angle of view.

When drawing an elliptical shape, draw the whole shape, even if some of it will not be visible in your finished drawing. By doing this you will be sure to get the perspective right. You can then erase or paint over the parts that will be hidden in the final picture. Use light pressure, allowing the pencil point to glide across the surface of the paper. Lines drawn with too much pressure often

look awkward and uneven, and unwanted lines are difficult to erase. Always use a flowing, continuous stroke for this kind of shape, moving your hand 'from the shoulder' rather than from the wrist in order to have maximum fluidity of movement. Once you have perfected this action you will be well on the way to mastering the exercises given in this lesson.

A still life of everyday objects, such as this collection of kitchenware, *above left*, by Antony Dufont, is full of cylindrical, conical and elliptical forms. Even the jug is based on a cylinder. Our project drawing, *below*, concentrates on drawing these shapes in perspective.

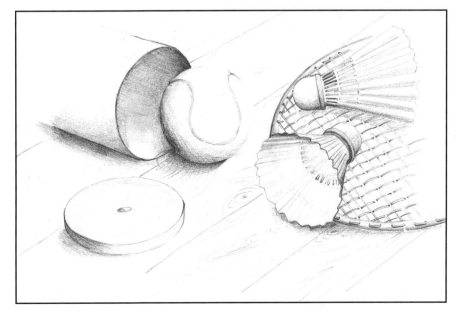

On this page we show you a few simple exercises that will help you to draw circles, cylinders and cones in perspective. You can then start to combine these shapes (either whole or in part) to create recognisable drawings of everyday objects — anything from bottles and glasses to shuttlecocks and tennis balls, as in this lesson's project drawing.

To understand the way in which the shape of a flat circle alters when viewed from different angles, hold a glass in front of you and look straight down on it. You will see that the top edge forms a perfect circle. As you gently tip the glass away from you the circle becomes distorted and 'flattened', **1**. This shape is called an ellipse.

A common mistake is to make the ellipse too pointed. As you practise example **1**, make sure that the opposite ends of your ellipses are rounded, **2**.

To begin drawing cylindrical shapes (solid forms derived from circles), draw a square or rectangle and draw an ellipse at each end, **3**. Vary the width of the ellipses to get a sense of how they change according to the 'height' or 'depth' of your eye level.

Set up your own cylindrical objects (such as an aerosol can and a tumbler of water) and draw them as if they were transparent so that the tops and bottoms can be compared. In example **4** the can on the left has been drawn with an identical ellipse top and bottom. This is impossible unless you look directly down on to an object, and the perspective is therefore wrong. The can in the centre shows how the top ellipse should be shallower. Note how, in the tumbler of water on the right, there is an additional ellipse drawn for the water line.

Objects such as vases, jugs and bottles are cylindrical forms. Note that the elliptical curves become deeper as they fall below eye level, **5**.

Your viewpoint determines the shape of the base. A bottle starts off as a cylindrical form, **6**, the 'depth' of the base again being determined by the angle of view.

A circle, cylinder or cone can be superimposed over a drawing in order to see how the parts relate to each other, and to assess their overall shape. Circles and cones can be used when drawing from life to help describe the shape of a human face, **7**, or a flower, **8**.

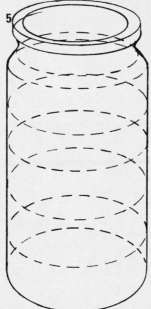

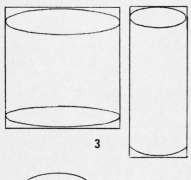

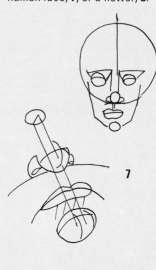

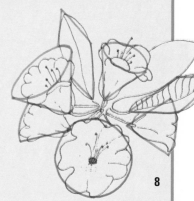

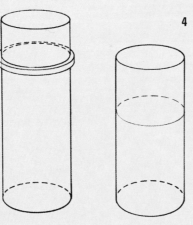

LIGHT AND SHADE

Note the direction of the light source and reflected light. Spherical objects should be shaded and modelled according to the way the light falls on them. In the drawing of the sphere, *right,* the light falls from above and left. Some of the light hits the wall on the right and bounces off it to lighten the righthand side of the sphere, which is furthest from the light source.

SHUTTLECOCKS AND TENNIS BALL

Our project drawing for this lesson is a simple still life of shuttlecocks, tennis ball and racket. To simplify the subject, this attractive composition can be seen purely in terms of circles, ellipses and cones connected by a few straight lines — even the wood graining on the floorboards is comprised of ellipses!

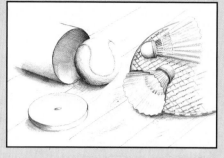

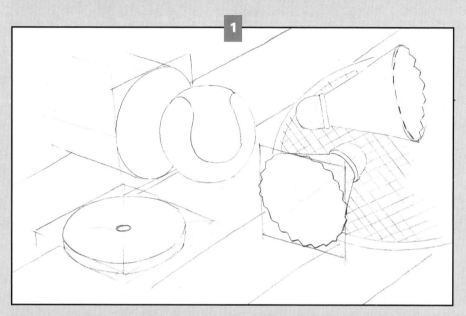

1

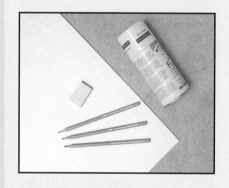

2

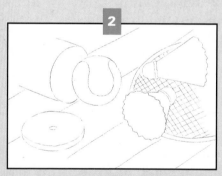

M A T E R I A L S

cartridge paper
HB, 2B and 6B pencils
eraser
fixative

1 To draw the tennis-ball container, lid and foreground shuttlecock in perspective, think of them in terms of geometric shapes and for each one lightly sketch a square in perspective using the HB pencil. Draw lines diagonally across each 'square' from corner to corner, then mark a point halfway along the edges of the squares. Join the points on the edges of the squares in a gentle curve to form an ellipse.

Make the shuttlecock ellipse jagged to depict its fluted edge.

Sketch in the outlines of the remaining objects, remembering to show the whole of each elliptical shape even if you cannot see it — for example the base of each shuttlecock and the fluted end of the rear shuttlecock. These lines will be erased later. Sketch in the floorboards and racket strings using flowing freehand strokes.

2 Erase the guidelines and any parts of the drawing that are hidden — such as the ellipses at the base of each shuttlecock. Still using the HB pencil, strengthen the outlines of the shuttlecocks and the lid of the tennis-ball container.

3 Using the 2B pencil, add details such as the line of the plastic 'feathers' on the shuttlecocks and the seam on the tennis ball. Begin to model form by lightly shading areas in shadow. In our composition the light source is coming from top right, so the shadows will fall to the left.

3

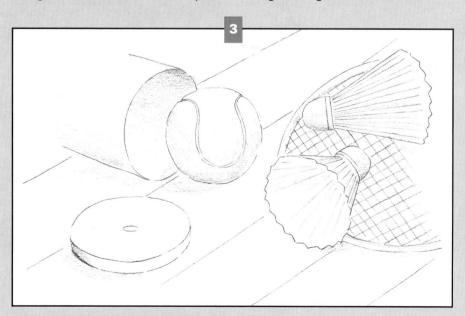

4 Switch to the 6B pencil and, using gentle pressure, strengthen areas in deepest shadow, such as the top inner edge of the ball container, the lower edge of the tennis ball and the inner edge of the foreground shuttlecock. Using short, overlapping strokes, build up a basket-weave texture to represent the strings of the racket.

Start to sketch the grain on the floorboards. Make a small dot to represent the 'heart' of the wood grain, then draw loose elliptical shapes of increasing size around this to create a 'rippling' effect.

5 Complete the floorboards, then go over the whole drawing with the 6B pencil, strengthening the shading to model form. Complete the detailing on the shuttlecocks, using shading to accentuate the fluted edges. Using your finger, slightly smudge the inside of the tennis ball container to blend the pencil strokes, then spray the finished drawing with fixative to protect it.

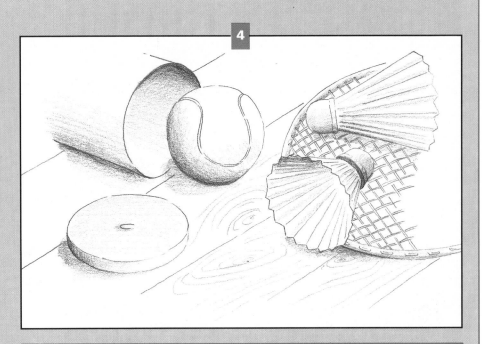

When you have completed this drawing you will see that what began as a fairly technical drawing of geometric shapes has become a well-modelled drawing of attractive forms. Once you have mastered the perspective of ellipses, drawing rounded shapes should pose you no problem. Try setting up your own still life of everyday objects — you'll be surprised by the number of objects that are based on the shapes of cylinder, circle and cone.

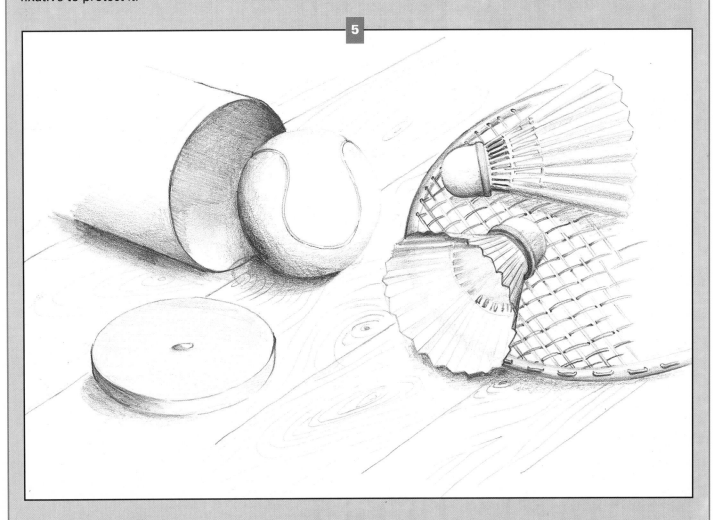

METAL AND GLASS

Metal and glass objects present the artist with a number of special problems. Both have shiny and reflective surfaces, which give rise to a complicated pattern of reflections and tones. In this lesson we show you how to capture the translucence of glass and the solid appearance of metal.

The key to the successful depiction of glass and metal objects is gentle gradation of tone. Both surfaces are hard and smooth, so when using pencil as the drawing medium it is important to avoid any abrupt changes in the direction of the shading, and to use cross-hatching sparingly otherwise the texture will become too dense and lose its essential reflective quality.

Not only is glass usually transparent, but it also reflects the objects around it — often creating beautiful patterns. These surface patterns can be convincingly built up by blending a wide range of grey tones together; the reflected patterns also help to indicate the form and volume of glass and metal objects. Because of the peculiar way light is refracted through curved glass many, often fascinating, distortions will also occur. However, it is important to be selective about these aspects, as too much visual information can lead to a confused drawing. Remember too that the white of the paper will always play an important part in the modelling of form, and the best depictions of shiny, reflective surfaces are often achieved by

'lifting out' and blending the pencil marks with a putty rubber.

Reflections of life
On the following page we show you some examples of still-life compositions featuring glass and metal objects. However, if you prefer to draw an urban scene there is a wealth of material to be found — such as car bodywork and windows, glass or 'mirror'-clad office blocks, and shop fronts.

This type of drawing can take you some time, and because the constantly changing light may affect the reflections minute-by-minute, it can often be a good idea to take a photograph of such a scene and use it as reference material at a later date.

In this still life by Beryl Underwood, *above left*, gentle gradations of tone have been used to build up the transparent glass surface of the wine carafe and the liquid within. Cross-hatching has been used sparingly to depict more solid forms such as the frying-pan handle, and we use these techniques in our still life for this lesson's drawing project *below*.

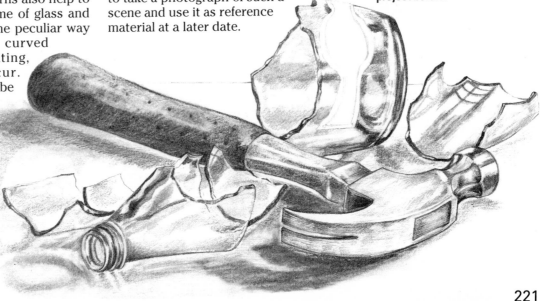

The best way to get to grips with drawing metal and glass surfaces is simply to experiment and practise. However, on this page we show you a few examples of different objects and give you tips on how to achieve various effects. You will need several pencils — as a rule of thumb, 6B is ideal for heavy, dark tones; 2B for medium tones; and HB for the initial sketched outline.

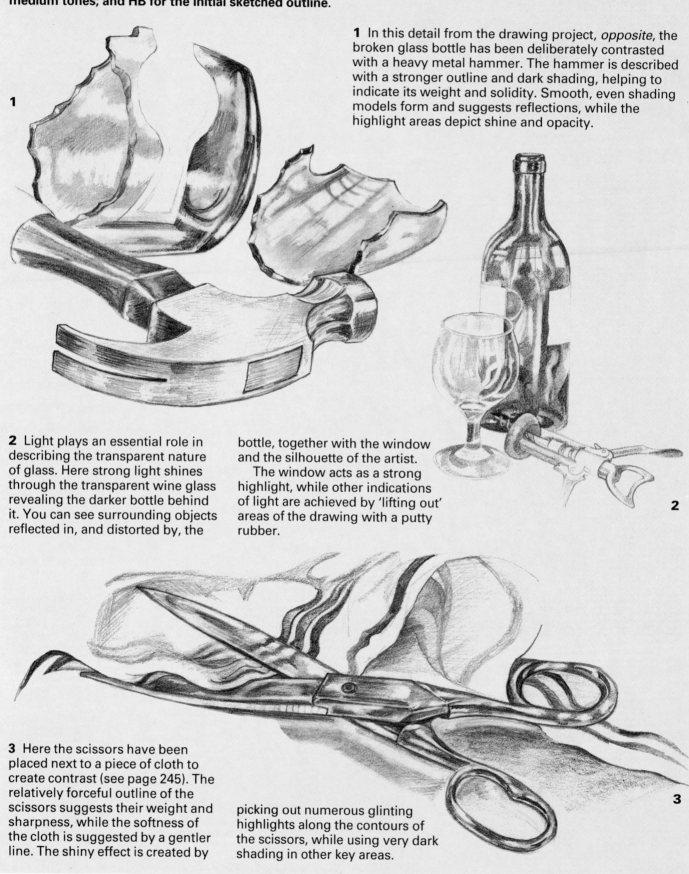

1 In this detail from the drawing project, *opposite*, the broken glass bottle has been deliberately contrasted with a heavy metal hammer. The hammer is described with a stronger outline and dark shading, helping to indicate its weight and solidity. Smooth, even shading models form and suggests reflections, while the highlight areas depict shine and opacity.

2 Light plays an essential role in describing the transparent nature of glass. Here strong light shines through the transparent wine glass revealing the darker bottle behind it. You can see surrounding objects reflected in, and distorted by, the bottle, together with the window and the silhouette of the artist.

The window acts as a strong highlight, while other indications of light are achieved by 'lifting out' areas of the drawing with a putty rubber.

3 Here the scissors have been placed next to a piece of cloth to create contrast (see page 245). The relatively forceful outline of the scissors suggests their weight and sharpness, while the softness of the cloth is suggested by a gentler line. The shiny effect is created by picking out numerous glinting highlights along the contours of the scissors, while using very dark shading in other key areas.

BREAKING GLASS

The subject of this lesson's project drawing is a still life composition of a broken bottle and the hammer that broke it! Shiny metal and glass are similar in that they both reflect light and the objects around them. However, glass is also translucent and in this drawing we show you how to use different weights of pencil to describe the qualities of both surfaces.

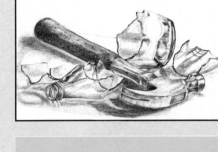

MATERIALS

white cartridge paper
HB, 2B, 3B, 6B pencils
scalpel blade
putty rubber
fixative

1

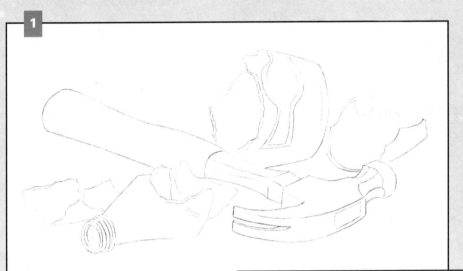

1 Using the HB pencil, lightly sketch the outline of the basic shapes. The head of the hammer, base of the hammer handle and top and bottom of the broken bottle can be seen in terms of cylinders, cones and ellipses (see page 218) and this will help you to draw the objects in perspective.

2

3

2 Look at the way the light falls on the objects then, still using the HB pencil, begin to shade in some of the darker areas of the composition. Combine light, evenly-hatched strokes in one direction with areas of heavier cross-hatching in different directions to begin to model form.

3 Continue building the shading using the 2B pencil. Block in the dark handle of the hammer with strokes in different directions. Indicate some of the reflections on the glass, and strengthen the darker areas of the hammer head.

4 Using the 3B pencil, begin to draw in the shadows cast by the objects. This will create a solid plane on which the objects can 'sit'. With a sharp 6B pencil, re-work the edges of the broken bottle, darkening and re-defining them.

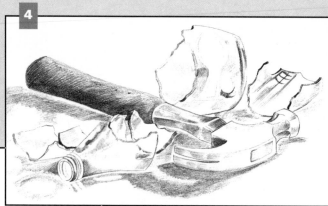

5 Use the 6B pencil to darken the cast shadows and build up the dark tones in the composition — pay particular attention to the modelling of the hammer head and handle as these are the most solid forms. Now, using the putty rubber, gently smudge the shading on the broken glass so that the pencil lines merge and create a translucent quality.

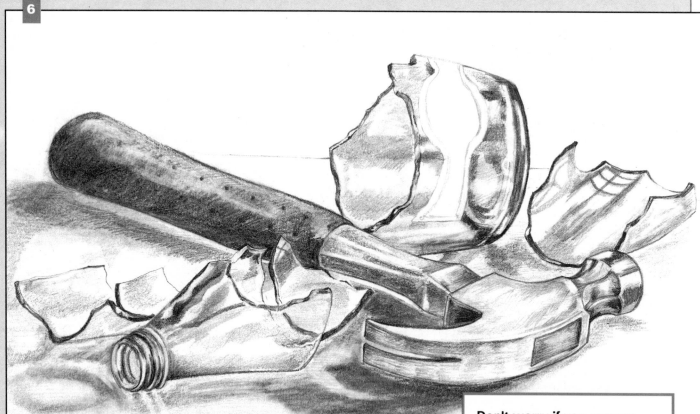

6 Go over the whole drawing, strengthening the tones with different weights of shading. To create the highlights, 'lift out' areas of shading on the bottle and hammer using bold strokes of the putty rubber. Finally, use the 6B pencil to strengthen the darker tones in order to create contrast. When the drawing is finished, spray it with a light mist of fixative to prevent it smudging.

Don't worry if you remove too much of the pencil shading when you are using the putty rubber to create the highlights. This is easily corrected by re-working the area with pencil.

DRAWING A CAR

The bodywork of a car is constructed almost entirely of shiny, curved surfaces in metal, glass and chrome, all adding up to a medley of reflections and highlights that can be very confusing for an untrained eye. In this lesson we give you some practical tips and techniques to help you draw realistic-looking vehicles.

Drawing a car is an exercise which presents the artist with a complex set of problems. When light strikes a metallic surface it can often create a misleading impression of the shape and contours of an object. A concave shape can sometimes appear convex, and perspective can often appear distorted. In addition to this, the gleaming paint used to protect and decorate the car acts as a mirror, reflecting images of the immediate surroundings. So before attempting to draw a car you need to be fully aware of the delicate interplay between light and reflection, which combine to give the effect of solidity.

For your first attempt, don't be over-ambitious in your choice of car. An over-elaborate design will result in your drawing looking fussy and unnecessarily intricate. Visit a library, look in a specialist car magazine or take a series of photographs of cars in the street until you find a subject that you feel comfortable with.

If possible, draw from 'life'. Your own car, if you have one, would be ideal, if only because you probably know it very well. If

you do have to draw from a photograph, make sure that it is larger than your intended drawing.

The bodywork of a car is mechanically produced. Its delicate curves are the result of years of design and planning by a team of experts. To reproduce these lines with a sure hand, you will need to practise drawing circles and curves freehand until you feel confident. Above all, don't be afraid to make mistakes! A few sweeps of an eraser will allow you ample opportunity to get the drawing right.

This pencil drawing of the Monaco Grand Prix, *above*, by F. Gordon Crosby, demonstrates how the skilful representation of light and shade produces both realistic-looking cars and an illusion of speed and movement. Our project for this lesson, *below*, uses coloured pencils to create the various reflective and tonal qualities that are vital in making a car drawing realistic.

To sort out the jumble of tones and reflections that make up a car, there is nothing to beat careful observation. Study your subject minutely from different angles, and make plenty of sketches. Below are some explanations and exercises to help you understand some of the problems before you start on the drawing project.

1 It is best to draw your car from the front or side. From any other angle details such as wheels and headlights will appear as elipses and be difficult to draw accurately. If you look at a car head on in daylight, you will see it is lit by light from three main sources. The brightest light, from the sky above, will hit the upper surfaces, making them the lightest. Light from the horizon (eye level) is less bright, and will light the sides of the car. The ground will reflect light from the first two sources on to the lower parts of the car. It is as well to keep these three light sources in mind when you are drawing.

2 shows how these three light sources will show their effect on the paintwork of the car, and **3** shows how they produce reflections in a round chrome object, such as a convex hub-cap.

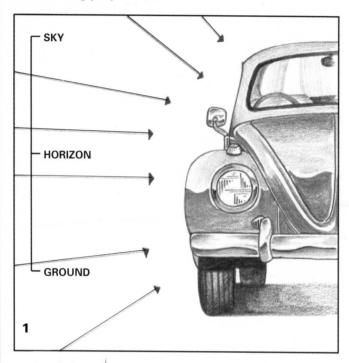

1

SKY

HORIZON

GROUND

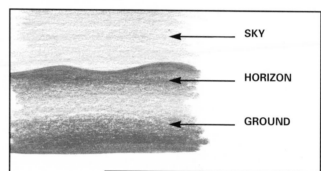

SKY

HORIZON

GROUND

2

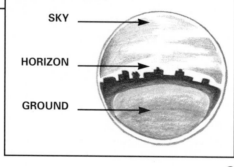

SKY

HORIZON

GROUND

3

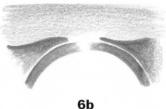

4

4 To help you reproduce these effects, practise using coloured pencil to draw parallel lines of different thickness. Note that light pressure creates a light tone, heavier pressure darker tones.

5 Create solid areas of tone by using varying pressure. Then create a graded tone, and finally the gradations of reflected light as seen on a car (as in **2**).

6(a) This is a soft tone with a dark tone (a shadow) over the top.
(b) These are the shapes and reflections seen on a wheel arch of a car. The white area in the centre is a reflection of the sun. **(c)** On a convex side panel you get a highlight that looks like the sun setting on the horizon.

7 A tyre. Draw the outline with an HB pencil. Fill in for the solid dark areas, and fade out into the areas that are lit by sunlight. Where the tyre touches the ground a highlight is usually produced. On cars that have wheels set into the bodywork there are no highlights as the tyres are in shadow.

5

6a

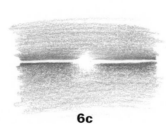

6b   **6c**

7

SHINY RED BEETLE

Our drawing project of a Beetle car is essentially an essay on what happens when light strikes curved, shiny and reflective surfaces. If you can get that right, the car will practically draw itself.

PROJECT

MATERIALS

HB pencil
4B pencil
putty eraser
set of coloured pencils
A3 cartridge paper (420 x 297mm)
board or drawing board
masking tape
ruler

1 Using a soft 4B pencil, sketch the main outlines of the car. Don't press too hard with the pencil as these lines are merely a guide.

2 Now begin to add more detail, such as windows, wheels and tyres. Sketch in the background. Then go over all the pencil lines lightly with an eraser, leaving them faint but still visible to the eye.

HELPFUL HINTS

If you have trouble drawing circles, you can buy a circle template from any artist's shop.

It is a good idea to have two pencils of the same colour. Sharpen one to a fine point to use for detail, and shape the other to a long, flattened point to use for shading.

Keep a piece of tracing paper handy to place over the drawing area where your hand is resting, to avoid smudging.

3 Now you can start to add colour to your drawing. Study the finished project drawing carefully and note where the main highlights are. Leave these areas white, and start to shade in the light and medium tones on the bodywork using a crimson pencil. Use ivory black to shade in the pale tone round the tyres and under the car, and increase the intensity for the darker shadows. Use a very pale tone of golden brown in the background.

4 The dark uneven line on the side of the car is caused by reflections. Increase the intensity of the colour to its darkest tone at the edge of this line. Shade in the other areas of dark tone at the base of the wheel arches, the rear and front ends of the bodywork, and the other dark patches you can see on the drawing.

5 Using a sharp HB pencil, draw in the detailing round the windows, windscreen, door, etc. Add more to the background, using terracotta for the door and window surrounds, and very pale shading in spectrum blue for the glass. Intensify the shading on the road under the car.

6 Now put in the fine detail. Using blue and black pencils sharpened to a fine point, draw in the reflections on the metal hub caps and bumpers, and the car windows. Add more detail and tone to the background, but do not overdo this as you don't want it to distract from the car. Run the eraser lightly over the windows in the background so that the shading on them is very faint. You can also use the eraser to lift colour off the car to increase the highlights.

As you can see, a car is a complicated piece of machinery, especially when you try to draw it. Keep looking and sketching, and when you can see every car as a collection of tones, highlights and reflections you will be well on the way to becoming an accomplished car artist!

USING COLOURED PENCILS

We have already used a range of coloured pencils and some shading techniques in our drawing of a car on pages 225–8. Now we show you how to use coloured pencils to achieve a much broader range of effects from soft, light-toned sketches to strongly delineated drawings that are rich in colour and tonal quality.

In many respects coloured pencils can be used like graphite pencils — shading and cross-hatching techniques being used to build tone and form. However, the obvious major difference is colour, and the semi-opaque quality of coloured pencils makes their handling similar to watercolours.

Because of this 'transparent' quality, two or more colours can be overlaid to create a different colour — if you shade yellow over blue you will get green. By varying the pressure of the strokes and the distances between hatched lines, an infinite range of shade and tone can be produced using only a few original colours, and different paper surfaces will also affect the end result.

Coloured pencil is a practical medium which allows for a spontaneity and directness often denied by watercolour and oils. When doing quick sketches or drawing outdoors they provide immediate, exciting and controllable results with the minimum of equipment, and by experimenting you will discover ways of making marks and combining colours to create complex and pleasing results.

Another advantage of coloured pencils is the way in which they can be combined with other media. For example, they are useful for adding definition and texture to watercolour sketches or, when used in a linear way, to form the foundation of a pastel drawing. They can also be combined with water-soluble crayons or brushed over with a solvent such as turpentine to create a 'painterly' effect.

However, for your first attempt at using coloured pencils it is a good idea to select a colourful, interesting, yet simple subject using just a few colours and paper with a medium-grained surface. This will enable you to use the materials to their best advantage and discover the wide range of effects you can achieve with them.

This illustration, *above left*, of a place setting with a plate of mussels, French bread and a glass of wine was drawn by Madeleine David using a fairly limited range of coloured pencils. Tone and form have been built up with shading and hatching — techniques used in our project drawing of a plate of cakes, *below*.

One of the most exciting aspects of using coloured pencils is their capacity to be mixed and blended to produce a broad colour spectrum. Here we demonstrate some of the optical mixing effects produced by using overlaid shading and hatching techniques, a limited range of colours, and varying the degree of pressure.

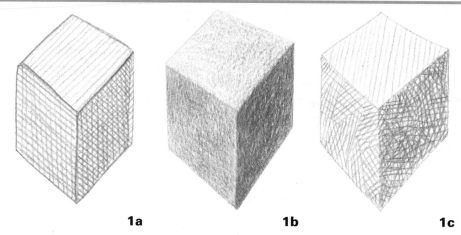

1a

1b

1c

1a The top of the cube is hatched with evenly-spaced parallel lines. These are cross-hatched on the left, then a set of diagonal lines are overlaid on the right to build up areas of tone. In this sample the hatching is evenly-spaced.

1b A soft effect is achieved on top of the cube by block shading the area using gentle pressure. Adding

another layer increases the tone on the left, and a third layer, using more pressure, achieves greater depth of tone on the right.

1c In this sample the cross-hatching on the sides is loose and

less controlled, with lines drawn in different directions.

2a The above samples were all done in one colour. The introduction of other colours creates greater tonal variation. Here the top of the cube is evenly hatched in red and blue. Notice how the texture changes with the addition of blue diagonals on the left, and how the addition of red diagonals on the right appears to alter the tone.

2b Here the primary colours red, blue and yellow are hatched to create an even colour change. Notice how green appears where the blue and yellow overlap.

2c Areas of hatching in different directions results in a more lively tone and colour.

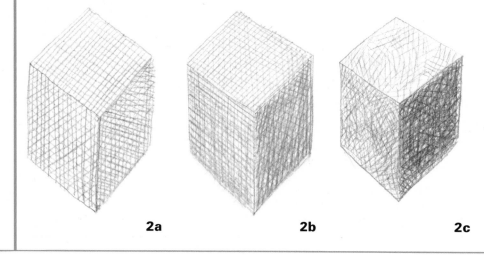

2a

2b

2c

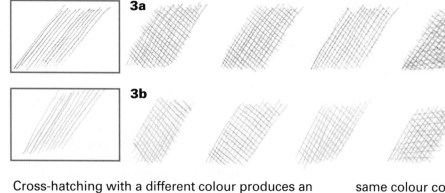

3a

3b

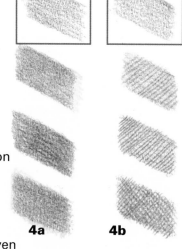

Cross-hatching with a different colour produces an illusion of colour mixing where the lines cross. The above samples show the effect of different colour combinations using blue as the constant in **3a** and red in **3b**. Further subtlety in shade and tone can be introduced, depending on when a colour is overlayed. For example, where blue, red and yellow are all used together in **3a** (with blue as the constant and red and yellow being overlayed) the tone is darker, while the

same colour combination in **3b** (with red as the constant and blue and yellow being overlaid) results in a lighter tone.

Colours can also be mixed using smooth, even shading, **4a**. Cross-hatching in a different colour serves to enhance a plain, shaded background, **4b**.

4a

4b

A PLATE OF CAKES

A plate of fancy cakes is an appealing subject for a drawing in coloured pencil — their pastel colours have an immediate attraction, while the geometric shapes and simple decoration of the cakes form an uncluttered composition that leaves you free to concentrate on building shade, texture and tone.

M A T E R I A L S

cartridge paper
set of coloured pencils
eraser

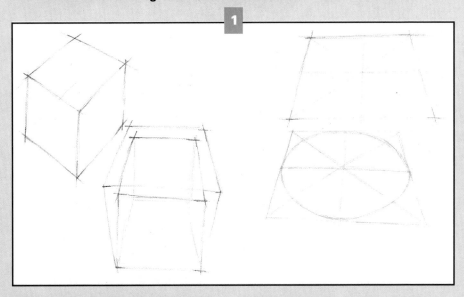

1 It is a good idea to start this drawing by thinking of your composition as a group of simple geometric shapes — the cakes are cubes, while the plate is a distorted circle. When a circular object is seen in perspective its shape becomes elliptical. Practise this by drawing a square in perspective. Draw lines diagonally across the square from corner to corner. Draw a horizontal and a vertical line where the two diagonals meet. To draw the ellipse, simply 'join up' with a curved line the points where the horizontal and vertical lines meet the edges of the square.

2 Using a pale grey coloured pencil, lightly outline the shapes of the cakes on the plate. Make sure that you have the

proportions and perspective right, then re-define key elements such as the edges of the paper cake cases using gentle pressure to make a sharper, darker line.

3 Using colours that most closely match those of your cakes, start to 'fill in' your drawing, using light, feathery strokes and gentle pressure. Gently shade the cakes with softly hatched strokes so that the general effect is of warm colour. Use a darker shade of each original colour to gently cross-hatch areas of shadow and build tone. Use a combination of open lines to suggest areas of general tone (such as the plate and surrounding table top), and tighter, more solid shading to define edges and blocks of colour.

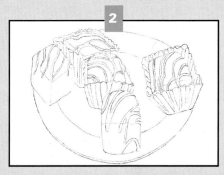

4 Using dark brown and blue-grey, emphasise the piped icing on top of the cakes with single lines. Draw single lines of grey and purple around the fluting of the cake cases, and create a soft, smudgy effect using grey, light blue and purple to suggest the paper folds. Overlay areas of soft smudgy shading in pink and yellow, as appropriate, to depict the colour of each cake showing through the paper cases.

5 Begin to model a three-dimensional quality by cross-hatching combinations of colour on each cake, paying attention to the direction of the light. For the yellow cakes, gently cross-hatch in pale pink and pale orange to create tonal contrast. Use the same cross-hatching technique on the remaining cakes, using pale purple, pale blue and pale orange for the pink cakes, and purple and dark brown for the brown cake. Make the hatching and shading quite dense around the edges of the piping to portray cast shadows, and to highlight the modelling.

6 Strengthen the cast shadows on the plate by building up hatched layers of yellow, pink and blue. More intense, dark blue cross-hatching will denote the shadow beneath the plate. Finally, stand back from your drawing and look at the overall effect. If necessary, strengthen any areas of tone or colour with blues or darker shades of the original colour.

In coloured pencil drawing, as in watercolour painting, white is not often applied as a colour. Leave areas of the paper untouched where white is required. As coloured pencils (unlike pastels) don't smudge easily, there is no need to spray your finished drawing with fixative.

DRAMA AND LIGHT

In previous lessons we have seen how coloured pencil marks can be overlaid to build colour, tone and texture. Here we concentrate specifically on blending colours to depict the effects of light — a technique that can create surprisingly dramatic results, as we show by putting the spotlight on a ballerina in this lesson's project drawing.

Light is an essential component in any drawing — an awareness of light helps to create volume and space, and adds dramatic effect. A subject lit from the side with a strong light will cast a shadow, and although these shadows may appear to be negative areas at first, in drawing terms they are equally as important as light because the effect of light is created by strong contrast. In coloured pencil drawing the shadows are also composed of colour, and serve to define the plane and surface upon which a subject rests, as well as describing the volume of the form.

Modelling form

Flat areas of colour do not suggest shape. It is the interplay of light and shade that helps to create an illusion of form. This is particularly apparent if the light source is very strong.

Colour is also affected by reflected light. A child's drawing of a face will usually be coloured in with a pink crayon. But skin colour is composed of many different colours — just as a white china cup, for instance, may appear to have pink or blue lights in it. This effect is created by the reflection of other colours around the object, as well as the way in which light plays on the surface. Similarly in a coloured pencil drawing of skin tones the light creates areas of greens, purples and blues, particularly when seen in artificial light.

The subtle quality of coloured pencils make them ideal for portraying a wide variety of light effects. By the careful observation of light, shade and colour, and by the exaggeration and blending of the colours you see, it is possible to model

convincing three-dimensional forms.

On the following page we show you a few examples of how to use coloured pencils to depict light and form. The colours can be used dry and cross-hatched to build up a rich network of infinitely variable colour combinations. Alternatively, water-soluble coloured pencils can be used. In this case the paper should be light, as this produces the highlight areas.

In this coloured-pencil drawing by Beryl Underwood, *above*, the figure is illuminated by a strong light from the left. Skin texture and tone have been built up with cross-hatching, and the effects of light have been captured in colour. Similar techniques are used in this lesson's project drawing of a ballerina, *right*.

On this page we show you how to depict the effects of light on various objects by combining colour, texture and tone. We also show you how to build up some of the colour effects you will need to capture the glowing quality of our ballerina in the project drawing, *opposite*. Use coloured pencils that will give strong colour, and good-quality cartridge paper or watercolour paper. The latter is particularly suitable for enhancing the transparency of colours, and is the best paper to use with water-soluble pencils.

1 Overlaying colours is a good way to use coloured pencils. The colours can be made to glow, as in this drawing of an egg — the complementary colours of orange and purple playing off each other to give the effect of light bouncing off the surface. To create a sense of light you need strong contrasts, but note that even in the deepest shadow there is still colour.

1

2 By gradually overlaying pale colours such as yellow with darker colours such as indigo, blue or violet, it is possible to depict a cylindrical form strongly lit from one side.

1

2

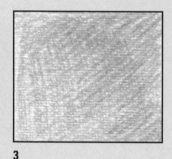

3

4

5

COLOUR EFFECTS

1 Cross-hatching colours produces a subtle effect which is useful for areas in shadow. Here diagonal lines of magenta have been closely cross-hatched with turquoise and overlaid with cross-hatching in orange chrome.

2 Undulating lines in one direction create a wavy pattern that suggests movement, the areas of white paper creating highlights. This effect is particularly useful for rippling water effects or to suggest the movement of a flowing skirt. By changing the

colour of some of the lines you can suggest the movement of light across an object.

3 Flesh colours in shadow are a mixture of colours, depending on the light source. In artificial light flesh colours in shadow contain green, blue and purple, while in natural light the colours will be warmer. Draw broken, diagonal lines of sienna natural and overlay lines of ivory and turquoise in different directions. Now introduce flecks of magenta and light blue to produce a muted flesh tone.

4 This is a detail of the ballerina's skirt from the

project drawing opposite. Draw an undulating line to represent the edge of the skirt using cobalt blue. Add touches of violet and turquoise to depict the folds of the skirt. Fill in the background with cross-hatching in ultramarine. If you are using water-soluble coloured pencils you can add extra light effects by brushing over the violet and turquoise with a wet brush. This creates a translucent effect.

5 Cross-hatching in cobalt blue and turquoise using different pressures will produce a textural effect that is useful for backgrounds. Here

the colour has been worked densely in the centre of the example, while the white paper shows through towards the bottom, producing highlights. Again, if you use water-soluble coloured pencils you can create further interest by blending the denser colour with a wet brush.

STAR STRUCK

The subject of our project drawing for this lesson is a ballerina basking in the glory of the spotlight. Tone and texture are built by cross-hatching to model form, while the effects of light are created through the use of colour and the white of the paper. We have used water-soluble pencils, but ordinary coloured pencils will work just as well.

MATERIALS

cream watercolour paper
set of coloured pencils (dry or water-soluble) to include the following colours or nearest equivalents: magenta, light blue, cobalt blue, burnt umber, ultramarine, flesh pink, violet, moss green, turquoise, sienna natural, golden ochre, lime green, ivory
paintbrush, size 4
water jar and water

1 Sketch the outline of the figure in colour, using the sienna natural or equivalent brown crayon for the head and torso, and burnt umber for the hair strands. Outline the ballet shoes in magenta and lightly sketch in the outline of the skirt using cobalt blue.

2 Consider the structure of the figure and the shape of the muscles. Note how the light falls on the figure, then begin to build up the skin tone on the arms and neck with cross-hatching in ivory and sienna natural. Make the direction of the lines follow the form of the body. Using similar techniques, begin to model the form of the torso and legs with shading in ivory, sienna natural, cobalt blue and turquoise. Strengthen the lines on the hair and shade the shoes with flesh pink.

3 The light is coming from the righthand side of the figure. Using downward strokes, add turquoise shading to the face, arms and legs to depict the areas of the body that are in soft shadow. Using cross-hatching, build the shape of the torso, modelling the breasts, rib-cage and waist of the ballerina with soft shading in violet, ultramarine and cobalt blue, following the direction of the light. Erase the sketched outline of the skirt, and indicate its frilly edge with light blue and turquoise.

4 Where the thigh of the left leg is turned away from the light source it is darkest — add violet shading to this area. Begin to develop the background by blending ultramarine, cobalt blue and turquoise in light shading and cross-hatching, overlaying the colours to form intense, dark areas around the skirt on the lefthand side, and just above the edge of the stage between the ballerina's legs. If you are using water-soluble pencils you can disperse the pigment slightly with a wet brush to blur the background. Add touches of golden ochre and lime green to the inside of the left arm to indicate reflected light.

When you have successfully completed this drawing you will see how easy it is — through the use of a few coloured pencil strokes — to capture the full drama of a figure caught in the glare of the spotlight.

5 To produce the effect of light travelling through a net skirt, draw bold green lines in the direction of the material — note how few lines are needed to depict a full white skirt against the light. Add touches of violet to the folds, and work lightly with turquoise at the base of the skirt.

Darken the hair with burnt umber, then draw the facial features in lightly. Add more gentle shading to the neck, arm and shoes. Strengthen the flesh tones on the face and arms using the colours as described on page 234 (see Colour effects, **3**). Finally, reinforce the shadows behind the feet. This enhances the impression of a strong light source moving across the floor, and defines the ground plane to support the upright figure.

DRAWING ANIMALS

Animals are wonderful subjects to draw, offering an extraordinary variety of form, texture, movement and mannerism, but the fact that they are almost always on the move can be rather daunting. We give you some tips on how to get the best out of your animal models.

When you first start trying to draw an animal, you may find it very disconcerting if your 'sitter' keeps moving about. Start with your own pet if you have one, and sketch it at rest to begin with, so that you have time to study its form at your leisure.

Pet shops are another source of subjects — you can draw them quickly on a small sketchbook while watching them through the window. Go to a zoo and spend your first visit just familiarising yourself with the different species. Make some quick sketches, or take some photographs to work from at home. You can go back to the zoo at a later stage to draw a chosen animal in more detail, or to record a variety of patterns and textures.

Try the effects of different media — some are more successful than others in capturing the softness of fur and hair. Conté crayon is good for fur (we use it in the project for this lesson), while pen and ink are suitable for black and white zebras and the stripes of tigers. You can also use smudged charcoal for fur and hair with harder Conté crayon for the main outlines.

Capturing the flow

Line drawings are a good way to get the feel of the underlying structure of an animal's body and how the different parts fit together. When you are drawing a moving animal, concentrate more on capturing the direction of movement rather than delineating form. Look at the changing angles of the body and ignore the details. A series of very simple outlines at this stage will be invaluable later when you want to draw a complete picture.

The pastel drawing *above* by Neil Forster successfully conveys the impression of young dogs at play. The focus of attention is on the dogs' heads, which are finished in detail, while their bodies are only scantily outlined. There is a great sense of movement in the drawing, and a feeling of the affection between the animals. Soft pastels have been used to convey the velvety texture of the dogs' coats.

Our drawing project for this lesson, *below*, uses Conté crayons to portray the fluffy coats of two ginger kittens.

GETTING STARTED

Line drawing is useful for your initial sketches when speed is the all-important factor. Using a pencil, draw the main outline and contours of your subject. Don't worry if your drawings look rather crude at first. You are training your hand and eye and, with practice, you will develop a photographic memory of your subject and be able to remember a particular pose long enough to add more detail.

All animals can be seen as simple geometric shapes, **1**, so look carefully at your subject to see how it can be simplified into ovals, circles and triangles. Use these shapes to get the parts in proportion and to establish how they connect. Keep these shapes in mind when drawing the animal in any pose, **2**. When you are happy with this basic sketch, you can blend the different shapes by softening the outlines and adding minimal detail, **3**.

Animals on the move

When an animal is moving, watch it carefully to see if you can detect a pattern in its movement. Make a quick sketch of each phase of the movement, noting the position of the legs and the changing angles of the head and tail. You can use brush and ink to make a series of free flowing sketches to show each phase of movement, **4**. Then as the animal continues to move, you can add more detail to each sketch.

If you want to indicate the contours of the body as well as the outline, **5**, use a fine brush and ink, or pen and ink. These are wonderful for conveying the suppleness of an animal's body and the shape of the muscles. Again, keep detail to a minimum for the best results.

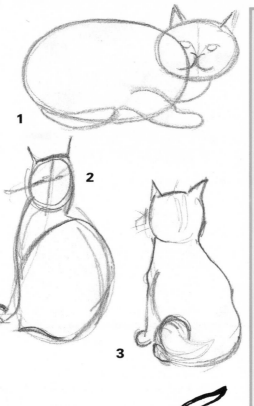

UNDERSTANDING ANATOMY

If you know a little about the underlying structure of an animal's body you will find it easier to get the various parts of the body to link up convincingly. The fluid, curving shape of a cat's skeleton *below* shows the set of the head and tail, and the length of the legs in relation to the body.

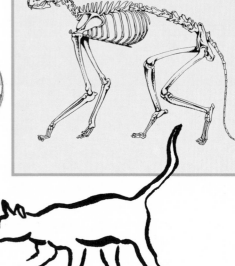

DRAWING FUR

The texture of an animal's coat varies in different areas of its body. Experiment with a variety of marks for short, tough hairs, long, silky hair and soft fur. Build up short hairs, **6**, in soft pencil strokes in the direction they lie. Give shape and form by adding darker areas for shadow. For long hair, **7**, use different grades of pencil to provide variety of line and tone.

JASPER AND CARROT

M A T E R I A L S

buff-coloured cartridge paper
Conté crayons in sanguine, black, white
and sepia
pencil eraser
fixative

Our two ginger kittens made delightful models for our drawing project. Because they were so lively, it was necessary to sketch them at play over a period of days to gather enough information to make this drawing. We chose Conté crayon as the drawing medium to give the effect of their fluffy coats.

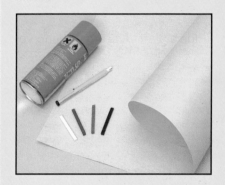

1 Using the tip of the sanguine crayon, roughly sketch the outline shape of your subject. Try to visualise the grouping in terms of ovals, circles and triangles, and lightly sketch guidelines for the positioning of the mouth, nose, eyes and ears. When you are satisfied with the proportions, sketch in the features.

2 Now using the side of the sanguine crayon, block in areas of colour to give an overall body shape. Press a little harder in places where there is cast shadow, such as the inner ears and behind the head, and also to emphasise areas such as 'cheeks'. Gently rub the drawing with your (clean) fingers to blend the strokes. Use the pencil rubber to highlight areas that are to remain the colour of the paper, such as around the eyes and the top of the flanks where the light is reflected. The advantage of using a buff coloured paper is that you will be able to achieve greater tonal effect when you come to use the white crayon.

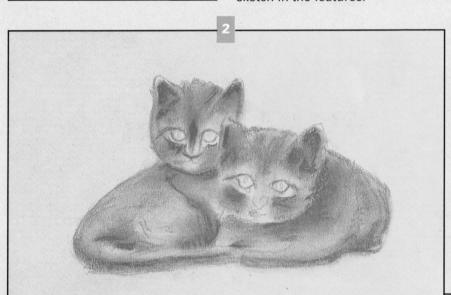

3 Use the tip of the crayons to define the detailing. Use the black crayon to define the eyes, cheeks and body contours, and to shade around the underside of the kittens to give a feeling of depth and create a slightly three-dimensional effect. Use light strokes of sanguine to delineate the direction of the fur on face and body, and add sepia for tonal contrast. Gently smudge the colours together with your fingertips to soften the effect and blend the strokes.

4 Now using the tip of the white crayon, highlight the tips of the fur, paying attention to the way the light falls on it and the direction in which it lies. Shade all round the grouping to create a feeling of space and project the drawing off the page.

5 Using the fingertips, blend the white highlights to achieve a soft, furry texture, adding a few more soft white strokes for definition where necessary. Use the very tip of the white crayon and 'suggest' the whiskers with light, swift strokes. Don't overdo the whiskers or they will look unrealistic. Finally, blend the background using your fingertips and spray the whole drawing with fixative.

4

5

This is a sophisticated drawing and you will have learned a good deal from it about the problems of drawing animals. You will gain more confidence as you continue to sketch your pets.

USING CONTE CRAYONS

We used a limited range of Conté crayons in our drawing of kittens on pages 239–40. Now we take a closer look at how to use an extended range of these versatile crayons which are marvellous for portraying the subtle colours and surface textures found in nature.

Conté crayons come in short, square sticks. They are made of compressed pigment, which gives a strong, intense colour. Originally available only in black, white and reddish browns, Conté crayons can today be obtained in a range of bright, seductive colours.

Like chalks and pastels, Conté needs to be worked on a soft ground paper such as watercolour or Ingres paper, which will retain the particles of pigment.

Working with coloured Conté is an exciting challenge. Colour, depth and form are built up in layers by cross-hatching, or by smudging the Conté with a 'stump', bristle, or simply with a finger. Work on an easel which slopes slightly forward so that the dust can fall away, and apply the colour freely, using plenty of crayon.

On the page overleaf we show you various techniques for using Conté crayons to build up layers of colour.

Light and colour
When you are drawing the project for this lesson, bear in mind that colour is affected by light. A landscape seen in a clear grey light will contain some very different colours compared to when it is seen in a warm golden light. As the light changes, so do the colours of the objects and their shadows. Even when drawing a still life it's important to keep the light consistent so that the colours remain the same. Remember, too, that light bounces off surfaces and reflects on objects. A red object, for example, will reflect some green light if it is near a green object.

Conté crayons are just one of a range of colour sticks (that includes chalks and pastels) that are wonderful for portraying delicate and luminous effects. The detail *below* from 'Still life with fruit' by Neil Forster shows how you can achieve the effect of transparency in these media, while our project *above* captures the varied colours and textures of vegetables.

You can achieve many different and interesting effects using Conté crayons. They can be applied quite freely using plenty of crayon, smudging for a smooth, soft effect and pulling out details with hard, fine lines. Experiment with the crayons to get a feel of their qualities. Here are some of the most useful techniques you are likely to need when drawing with Conté crayons.

1 Form a new tone by smudging two colours together, here a light and medium green, by applying both colours liberally and allowing them to overlap. This technique is useful for creating a base colour, or a smooth texture.

2 For more control, use a stump for smudging the Conté. This is a small fibre stick shaped to a point, which you can use to blend colours, soften outlines or highlight areas. When the end gets dirty, sharpen it with a knife.

3 When one colour is seen against another, its character changes. Experiment by laying a two-tone base and hatching, ie making diagonal strokes in the same direction, in a third colour on top.

4 Use two tones of green, and apply the Conté in short, thick strokes. This creates a dense green texture which, seen from a distance, becomes a mid-tone green.

5 Use two contrasting colours, here blue and green. Smudge the blue to form the body colour, and then work over the surface lightly with green, so that the Conté catches the surface of the paper.

6 The technique shown in **5** can also be used to build up several layers of different colours.

7 For a rich effect you can build up an intense network of texture by using hatching strokes (diagonal lines applied in the same direction) in several colours.

8 A broken colour effect is achieved by pushing the end of the stick flat on to the paper and twisting so the crayon crumbles slightly. This can be used for creating highlights.

9 Cross hatching, ie diagonal lines in two directions, is useful for building a rich colour tone. Several layers of colour can be used, changing the tone as they build up.

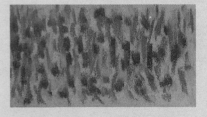

10 Dashes of different colours will create rich, varied textures.

11 By using dashes following an underlying structure, the colour can create a lively surface, increasing the sense of rhythm in a drawing.

12 Dots of different colours animate the surface texture and, depending on the size of dot, blend optically when seen from a distance.

TOO GOOD TO EAT

This project of colourful vegetables shows you how to put the exercises on the previous pages into practice. Our Conté crayon still life uses a variety of colours and techniques to create a vibrant picture from a group of mundane greengroceries.

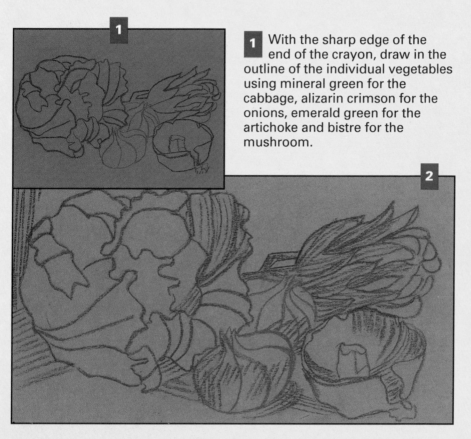

1 With the sharp edge of the end of the crayon, draw in the outline of the individual vegetables using mineral green for the cabbage, alizarin crimson for the onions, emerald green for the artichoke and bistre for the mushroom.

M A T E R I A L S

sheet of sandstone-coloured Canford cover paper, or bronze Ingres paper
box of 48 assorted Conté crayons to include the following colours: white 2B (2456), bistre (1), sanguine (7), black 2B (2460), Naples yellow (47), Indian yellow (37), scarlet (28), purple (19), flesh (48), madder (38), cyclamen (41), alizarin crimson (66), Persian violet (55), lilac (26), violet (5), Prussian blue (22), dark ultramarine (46), cobalt blue (69), ultramarine (10), Payne's grey (53), cold green (73), Prussian green (43), emerald green (34), mineral green (30), light green (8), lime (50), leaf green (76), burnt umber (82), sepia grey (42), burnt sienna (23)
fixative spray

2 Using the end of the Prussian blue crayon, apply it in lines to denote the shadows cast on the vegetables and work surface.

The lines should follow the contour of the shapes so that the structure of each vegetable is defined.

3 Using the same colours you used to draw the outlines, begin to build up the colour of each vegetable with light strokes of shading. Blend the blue shading into the base of the cabbage, smudging it lightly with clean fingertips. For the darker areas of the cabbage use a mixture of emerald green, mineral green and cold green smudged together. Use lime and grey green for the lighter areas. Give definition to the outer leaves of the artichoke and cabbage and the side of the mushroom with black crayon, and begin to sketch in the light areas of the mushroom with flesh, Naples yellow and white.

4 Add more touches of white to the mushroom, and begin to build up the artichoke with lines of dark ultramarine, emerald green and mineral green. Add little touches of yellow to highlight the tips of the artichoke. Now start to shape the onions so that they begin to take on a three-dimensional form. Use strokes and hatching of cyclamen, madder and alizarin crimson to build up the shape, smudging to blend.

5 Consider the direction of the light on your still life, and model the forms of what you

actually see using cross-hatching and dabs of Naples yellow and flesh for the lighter areas. Build up layers of lines for darker areas using dark ultramarine, bistre and sepia grey, and add more layers of smudged colour to the cabbage and onions to build and define.

Now you need to begin to relate your still life to its background. Use strokes of light green tones in the foreground and a mixture of mineral green and emerald green in the background and blend them with your fingers.

6 Continue adding layers of colour to form a rich, velvety surface. Use yellows, pale greens and white to highlight, and black to define, where necessary. Careful observation of how the light falls on the vegetables will tell you all you need to know! When you have finished your drawing, spray it with fixative spray.

In your final drawing you should notice a distinct difference between the surface textures. The layering of Conté colours produces this effect, as well as creating a sense of volume, space and light.

USING CONTRASTS

On pages 209–12 we considered the importance of composition in a drawing and showed you how to group different elements together in a meaningful and pleasing way. In this lesson we look at ways of creating additional visual interest by using contrasts of texture, shape and tone.

Contrast is vital in a drawing or painting. No matter how exciting the colour or image, if there is no contrast of texture, shape or tone then the picture will be visually unconvincing.

When you watch a classic black-and-white film from the forties you are usually unaware that it is a monochromatic picture. Light and shade, a sparkle of brightness here, a mist of gloom elsewhere, combine through contrast to provide a palette in your mind's eye.

This phenomenon is equally true of a black-and-white still life, provided the composition of your image is correct. Composition is an art, and if the picture catches the eye of the viewer and holds the attention, then colour becomes of secondary consideration.

Shapes are much more important — curves, angles, cylinders, cones and spheres. Textures created by hatching, cross-hatching, overlaying and shading add visual interest and depth to a drawing; tone matters — items which are all made of the same material tend to react to light in the same way, regardless of shape, so select objects with different tonal qualities. Lighting can be used to enhance a composition, but don't let it distract.

Ideally a complete composition should be at once harmonious, yet diverse. You might expect a fish to bed down with a lemon, but it would look out of place with a book — unless you intend your drawing to have a surreal element.

On the following page we show you a few examples of compositions that have been set up to illustrate the effective use of contrasting textures, shapes and tones. Practise them in pencil, or use Conté crayons as we have done in our project drawing for this lesson.

This pastel drawing by Lucy Willis, *above left*, entitled 'Shoes and milk bottle' is an example of a mundane subject made interesting by the juxtaposition of contrasting shapes and tones within the composition. The rounded, reflective milk bottle stands solid and familiar beside the randomly placed shoes — their different textures and tones making up a harmonious still life. The wooden window frame and metal chain-link fence outside add additional areas of contrast.

This drawing would have been just as effective in black and white, and in our drawing project for this lesson, *left*, we show you how to portray contrasting objects using Conté crayons in black, white and grey.

TEXTURE, SHAPE AND TONE

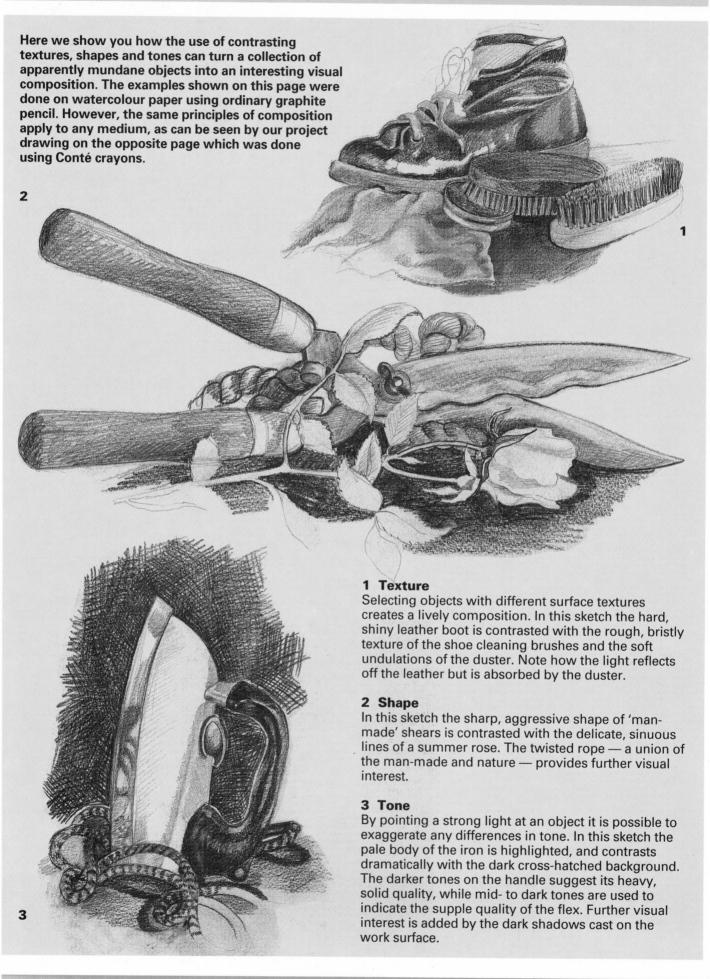

Here we show you how the use of contrasting textures, shapes and tones can turn a collection of apparently mundane objects into an interesting visual composition. The examples shown on this page were done on watercolour paper using ordinary graphite pencil. However, the same principles of composition apply to any medium, as can be seen by our project drawing on the opposite page which was done using Conté crayons.

1 Texture
Selecting objects with different surface textures creates a lively composition. In this sketch the hard, shiny leather boot is contrasted with the rough, bristly texture of the shoe cleaning brushes and the soft undulations of the duster. Note how the light reflects off the leather but is absorbed by the duster.

2 Shape
In this sketch the sharp, aggressive shape of 'man-made' shears is contrasted with the delicate, sinuous lines of a summer rose. The twisted rope — a union of the man-made and nature — provides further visual interest.

3 Tone
By pointing a strong light at an object it is possible to exaggerate any differences in tone. In this sketch the pale body of the iron is highlighted, and contrasts dramatically with the dark cross-hatched background. The darker tones on the handle suggest its heavy, solid quality, while mid- to dark tones are used to indicate the supple quality of the flex. Further visual interest is added by the dark shadows cast on the work surface.

NIGHT THOUGHTS

Our drawing project for this lesson is an atmospheric still-life arrangement of books, lamp and quill pen reminiscent of Dickensian times. It is drawn in Conté crayon using just three basic colours, and demonstrates how — by the juxtaposition of interesting shapes, tones and textures — a monochromatic drawing can be just as vital and evocative as a full-colour composition.

1 Using the blue grey Conté crayon, lightly draw in the outline of the books, lamp fitting and lamp base. Change to the light grey crayon and use it to draw in the outline of the candle, glass bulb and quill pen.

MATERIALS

white watercolour paper
Conté crayons in the following colours: white 2B (2456), white B (2456), black B (2460), black 2B (2460), brown grey (81), blue grey (72), dark grey (33), light grey (20), sepia grey (42), black (09)
paper drawing 'tortillon' for fine blending
Rowney perfix colourless fixative
fixative spray diffuser

2 In a still life such as this the light source comes from the lamp itself. Consider how the shadows fall, then shade in the darkest cast shadows on the lamp base and books using the dark grey crayon and gentle pressure. Using the same colour, begin to shade in the shadows cast on the table, then work over this shading with the black 2B crayon. Add a little black to the top, righthand edge of the bottom book.

3 Using a combination of black 2B and dark grey, block in the background, blending it with your fingers until it is opaque. Use a paper drawing 'tortillon' to blend the crayon around more fiddly areas such as the lamp handle. Leave the area to the right of the bottom book dark grey to create contrast where the light hits the back wall. Using blue grey and light grey, block in the foreground of the composition, smudging and blending the crayons together as before. Add a little brown grey crayon around the quill pen to help lift it from its background.

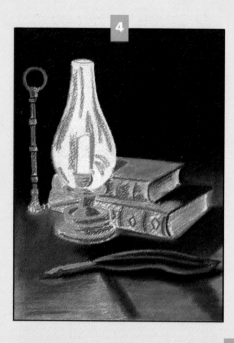

4 Go over the outline of the books in sepia grey, then block shade the covers in light grey. Begin to pick out the pattern details on the spines of the books using the dark grey crayon.

Now start to define the lamp. Use light grey to indicate the lighter metal parts of the lamp base, and shade blue grey in firm, short strokes to depict the darker shadows on the glass bulb. With the light grey crayon, highlight the nib and feathers of the quill pen, using strokes of black B for the darker tones on the feathers.

5 Work over the whole drawing with sepia grey and black, building detail on the books and emphasising the darker areas. Pay particular attention to the base of the lamp and its handle.

White is now introduced into the drawing for the first time. Using white 2B and white B in bold, sweeping strokes, follow the form of the glass bulb, then shade in the candle. Balance the strong white highlights with equally strong bands of blue grey and brown grey. Using black 2B and dark grey, work over the quill and strengthen the shadows on the table.

6 Use black and dark grey to define the handle of the lamp, then pick out highlights in white. Using white and light grey, suggest further texture on the book covers, and blend the colours together in swirling movements to create pattern on the spine of the uppermost book. Build up more layers of black, white and light grey detail on the quill pen.

Finally, work over the glass bulb, blending the crayons with your fingertips to create a soft look of diffused light. Add further strokes of white to portray the flame of the candle and any reflections in the glass, then spray the entire drawing with fixative to prevent smudging.

From this drawing you will appreciate how effective the use of strong contrasts — light, shape and texture — can be. When you have completed this monochromatic drawing you might like to try the same composition again, this time using another colour such as yellow for the diffused candlelight.

PEN AND INK

We have already introduced you to pencil drawing, and by now you will have acquired quite a repertoire of pencil techniques. In this lesson we move on to the rewarding medium of pen and ink, and show you how to use this technique to produce highly professional-looking results.

For many centuries artists used reed pens (cut from a reed, cane or bamboo), or quill pens (cut from the flight feathers of a goose or swan) for their drawings. While these pens can still be used today, it is the flexible metal drawing pens that became available in the early 19th century that now provide one of the most effective drawing tools for the artist. There are, of course, a whole host of other pens — fountain pens, felt-tip pens, marker pens and ballpoint pens — which can all be used with varying degrees of success, and which have the advantage of a ready supply of ink. Rapid developments in technology mean that new products are constantly becoming available, and it is worth making regular visits to your local art shop to investigate. You can also improvise — a twig or matchstick dipped in ink can create some exciting effects.

The mark that you make with your pen will depend greatly on the ink and type of paper that you select. In general it is safe to say that in order to achieve a fluid line with the pen, the paper should have a fairly smooth surface, so a good quality cartridge paper, or NOT-pressed watercolour paper would be a good choice for most pens. A technical drawing pen requires paper with a smoother surface, and a reed pen would look most effective on paper with a rougher surface.

The right ink
Black indian ink is a good choice for flexible drawing pens; broad calligraphic pens (to which you attach a reservoir to hold a greater quantity of ink) require a non-waterproof ink to achieve good ink flow. Fountain pens must be filled with fountain pen ink — drawing ink will clog them up. Coloured drawing inks are available, but as they are not completely light fast they tend to fade if exposed to direct sunlight. If you are a real purist, you could grind up your own ink on an inkstone using Chinese stick ink and a little water.

Rhythmic lines
Be responsive to your pen and aim to create rhythmic lines. Textures and tones are built up with lines, dots and dashes (see examples overleaf), but remember to keep an eye on the overall drawing and to create areas of light and dark, allowing the paper to say as much as the ink. A single sensitive pen line with nuances of light and dark can describe the volume of a form just as well as highly worked areas of tones.

Pen and ink drawing is a highly versatile line technique. The drawing *above* of 'A wooded road' by Rembrandt (1606-69) uses a reed pen and brown ink to render a serene and peaceful scene. This is in marked contrast to drawings by Vincent Van Gogh (1853-90) who also used a reed pen to produce frenzied textures created with abrupt lines, crosses, dots and dashes. Working a little later than Van Gogh, Henri Gaudier-Brzeska (1891-1915) used a flexible metal nib to produce drawings with great economy of line to suggest the nature of his subjects. Today technical artists in engineering and architect's offices use the controlled line of a technical drawing pen to make clear explanatory drawings. In our project for this lesson, *left*, we show you how to use a flexible steel nib and black indian ink to produce a pleasing drawing of a Norman church.

TYPES OF LINE

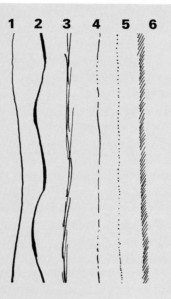

The flexibility of drawing pens allows for great freedom and variety in the type of line that can be achieved, *right*.

You can produce a flowing line to which increasing pressure is applied to strengthen the line (**1**); a line where pace and pressure are used to create variety (**2**); a line built up from a series of short strokes (**3**); a line created by a series of dots, dashes and short strokes (**4**); a line made with dots (**5**); a line built up from short, hatched strokes (**6**).

TYPES OF PEN

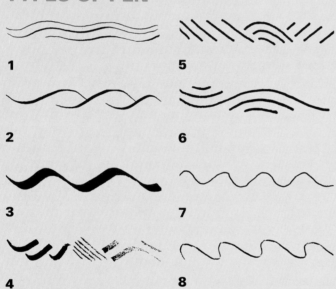

The pens shown *right* make the marks shown *above*.

Some nibs have to be fitted into a pen holder and then dipped in ink. These include: (**1**) mapping pens, which produce a fine line (they are very small and require a special holder); (**2**) flexible drawing nibs, available in a wide variety, which produce sensitive lines that can be varied with pressure; (**3**) calligraphic square-edged pens, which produce a contrast of thick and thin strokes; and (**4**) reed pens, which can be cut from a piece of bamboo and which produce a softer line than steel nibs.

Pens with a built-in supply of ink include: (**5**) fountain pens, which though handy, often have little flexibility; (**6**) fibre-tipped pens and marker pens, available in a wide range, with permanent and non-permanent ink; (**7**) technical drawing pens, which produce a controlled, even line — they need to be held upright for good ink flow and can be used very freely; and (**8**) ballpoint pens, which can produce a surprisingly sensitive line.

TEXTURES AND TONES

Drawing pens can be used to create effective tones and textures, *above*. A gradual build-up of hatched tones can be used to express increasingly dark areas of a drawing (**1-4**). A right-handed person will usually hatch from top right to bottom left (while a left-hander will hatch from top left to bottom right). Areas of texture can be built up with a more complex and random method using short, straight lines (**5**) or curved lines (**6**). Stippling is achieved by building up a mosaic of tiny dots; by varying the density of the dots you can achieve areas of different tonal values to suggest light and shade (**7**). An area of larger dots or dashes drawn quickly (**8**) creates a more vigorous texture.

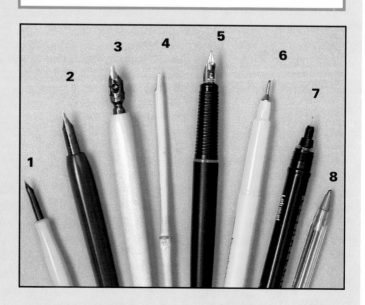

NORMAN CHURCH

This drawing of a Norman church and churchyard is done with a fine steel drawing nib and black ink. The special appeal of this kind of pen and ink drawing lies in its essential simplicity — it suggests the scene with an economy of line and the minimum of detail.

drawing or cartridge paper with a smooth, non-absorbent surface
fine steel drawing nib and holder
black indian drawing ink
2B pencil and eraser
tissues

1

1 Draw up the main outlines of the composition in pencil, using the eraser and re-drawing where necessary. Take plenty of time over this, as it is important to get the main outlines drawn in fairly accurately at the pencil stage. Once you start drawing in ink it is much harder to correct any errors.

2

2 Now start drawing over your pencil lines in ink. This is where you discover how important it is to have a steady hand that draws a sure line. Practise using the pen first on scrap paper until you feel confident you can draw a clean, steady line.

3

3 When stage 2 is completely dry you can rub out the pencil marks. Now start to draw in some of the details such as the fence, the details of the windows and buttress, and the tombstones.

4 Add more detail — the foreground bushes, the brickwork of the wall and some of the roof tiling. Only a selection of details are drawn in — too much would be overwhelming.

5 Finally a selection of textures are drawn in. These include the texture of the roof tiles and the dots on the end wall indicating the patina of ageing.

In this kind of drawing selection is all important. Most of the detailing is concentrated in the foreground and the trees in the background are kept quite simple. This helps to focus attention on the main subject — the church.

COMPOSITION

The selection of subject matter, the way it is arranged, and the viewpoint from which it is seen are all part of the composition process and vital to the success of a drawing or painting. We show you the basics of composition and some of the classic rules.

Whatever the subject of a drawing — landscape, interior, still life, figure drawing or portrait — you should think first about its composition. This means deciding on the underlying structure before you start to draw.

Why is composition important? It is not enough simply to draw what you see. If you do, your drawing may appear banal and uninteresting. The essence of a successful drawing is that it communicates the vision of the artist — the excitement that impelled him or her to draw that particular subject in that particular way. And composition is a vital part of that vision.

One of the first decisions you need to make concerns format. This in itself can affect the mood of the drawing. A horizontal or 'landscape' format suggests calm and serenity, and is appropriate for seascapes and landscapes. A vertical or 'portrait' format can be dynamic.

Imposing order

Composition proper involves arranging the elements in the picture so that they relate to each other in a meaningful way, and also create a pleasing and satisfying image as a whole. It is up to you to impose order and coherence on your subject. With an interior still life or figure drawing, you can actually arrange the components to your liking. With an outdoor scene, it is a question of selecting one particular view.

Decide which are the most important elements in your composition, and try to create links between them. Is there a balance between light and dark areas, between detailed and less defined areas?

Structuring a drawing becomes easier with practice. It's a good idea to study the classic composition rules overleaf and see how you might apply them to your own work. They will show you that an underlying geometric structure leads to a strong and well-balanced composition.

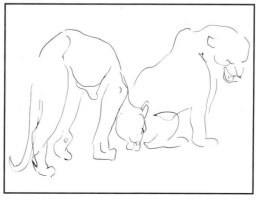

In his drawing for the frontispiece of *An evil motherhood, above,* Aubrey Beardsley demonstrates his mastery of pen and ink line drawing while the composition focuses firmly on the figure in the chair. Successful composition also contributes to the powerful impact of Henri Gaudier-Brzeska's simple line drawing of 'Lionesses', *left.*

CHOOSING A VIEWPOINT

Many beginners tend to choose the first view they see of a subject. But you should consider your subject from many viewpoints. Move around it and look at it from above, from the side, from behind, from afar and close to. Ask yourself what aspect of the scene interested you in the first place? Should you include the outlying environment or move in closer?

Using a viewfinder (see below) will help to isolate a view. It is always a good idea to make a few thumbnail sketches in your sketchbook. As a result, your initial idea of what was the best viewpoint may change completely.

A general view of a landscape scene from a distance.

A closer view of the same scene from a different angle.

A close-up of the church from a high level with the mountains behind gives a completely different 'feel' to the picture.

Moving in very close to the subject reveals the designs and patterns of nature:

Red cabbage

Snail shell

Bark of a tree

MAKING AND USING A VIEWFINDER

An invaluable aid in choosing your viewpoint and the format of your image is a viewfinder. A piece of card with a rectangular hole cut in it (**1**), or two 'L' shaped pieces of card which overlap and provide various aperture sizes (**2**) will do.

Use your viewfinder to move into and away from your subject (**3**). Hold up your viewfinder, look at your subject and simultaneously draw in the main shapes roughly to see your composition on paper. Do this from different distances

and viewpoints before choosing the best result. You will be surprised at how this device can alter your initial idea for your composition. Take plenty of time getting to know your subject before starting to draw.

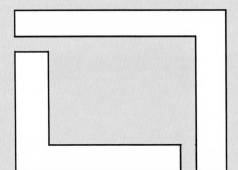

1　　　　**2**

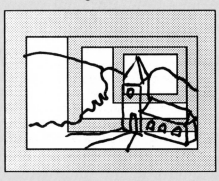

3

CLASSIC COMPOSITION SCHEMES

Renaissance artists often composed their pictures according to rules that relied heavily on underlying geometry. Some examples of classic composition schemes are shown below.

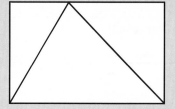  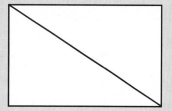 

A scheme based on a triangle within a rectangle, much used in the Renaissance, provides a clear focal point.

A scheme in which the rectangle is bisected by a diagonal, creating dynamic movement across the picture area. It was often used by Rembrandt.

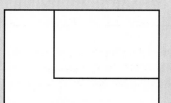  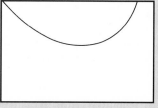 

A scheme in which a rectangle is divided into two unequal parts, which has much in common with the Golden Section (see below).

A scheme in which a curve bisects a rectangle.

GOLDEN SECTION

The Golden Section is an academic principle of composition that was invented by the Roman architect and painter Vitruvius while working on the wall paintings at Pompeii. He studied the organisation of shapes and space and the best location of the main subject.

The easiest method of composition was to put the main subject in the middle (**1**), but Vitruvius wanted to break this symmetry and began looking at how far to one side he could place the main object or point of interest without losing symmetry or balance within the picture area (**2**). Vitruvius worked out the solution and established the Golden Section or Golden Mean, whereby a straight line is divided into two unequal parts so that the ratio of the smaller part to the greater is the same as that of the greater to the whole. Mathematically this is difficult to calculate, but an approximation is 8:13 (**3**). Vitruvius found that to calculate the Golden Section you should multiply the length by 0.618.

An easier rule of thumb is to think of thirds. Divide your picture plane into thirds along its height and length (**4**). The points where your lines cross are known as 'golden points', and these are the points where you can place the main element of your picture. Matisse used the Golden Section or thirds method in many of his still life compositions.

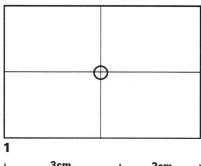

1

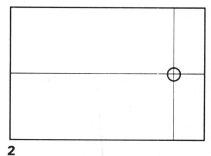

2

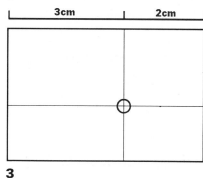

3

4

PROJECT

DOMESTIC INTERIOR

MATERIALS

Edding 1800 black fibre tip pen size 0.5
good quality cartridge paper with a
smooth, non-absorbent surface
HB pencil
eraser

For our second pen and ink project we have chosen a line drawing of a corner of a living room done with a fibre tip pen. You can either follow our drawing, or draw a corner of your own room, composing the picture following the principles of composition we have outlined. An underlying structure will give a feeling of unity and harmony to what may appear to be an essentially simple drawing.

1 Look at our picture (or your own composition) carefully, and draw in, in pencil, all the lines you intend to draw in ink.

2 When you are satisfied with your pencil drawing, start drawing over the pencil lines carefully with the fibre tip pen.

3 When you have completed the ink drawing, leave until completely dry. Rub out the pencil lines.

This kind of drawing relies on a strong line uncluttered by too much detail. Its very simplicity is the essence of its distinctive style.

HATCHING AND CROSS-HATCHING

In previous lessons we have shown you how to produce pen and ink drawings with an economy of line and the minimum of detail. In this lesson we move on to create more complex and sophisticated drawings by using simple hatching and cross-hatching techniques.

Hatching and cross-hatching in pen and ink are techniques that enable a rich and variable range of tones to be built up by the artist. Although at first glance the effects may appear to be quite complicated, cross-hatching techniques can be broken down into logical steps.

Our drawing project is an old timbered building, and this subject provides a wealth of shapes which are ideal for cross-hatching purposes. If you are going to pick a subject for yourself, choose a view straight-on, avoiding too much perspective, and one that contains simple patches of tone.

You can use any good quality paper for this sort of drawing as long as it has a smooth surface. If you use a watercolour paper the surface will produce a slightly softer drawing because the lines will break slightly as the pen tip jumps across the tiny hollows in the surface.

For cross-hatching, your choice of pen is important. The nib should move easily forwards as well as backwards, and for our drawing project we have used a Rotring art pen with a fine drawing tip. This type of pen uses standard ink cartridges so choose the black, water-soluble kind. If you prefer you can buy empty cartridges and fill them with black Indian ink, which is not water soluble when dry. Ordinary fountain pens can be used, but in most cases the nib will only work if drawn backwards or sideways. For cross-hatching it is essential that the nib works when pushed forwards. Ballpoints and stilo-tipped pens are suitable, but the line produced can often look too mechanical, while fibre-tipped pens may become worn and produce clumsy lines.

On the following pages we give you a few exercises to help you train your hand in the movements required for cross-hatching, a technique that will enhance any pencil or pen and ink drawing.

The drawing *above*, entitled 'Cox's Livery Stables, Cambridge, 1920' by Henry Rushbury (1889-1968), uses pen and ink hatching and cross-hatching combined with a wash to create a range of tones and textures. In our project drawing of Dragon Hall, *left*, we use a wider variety of hatching techniques to describe the many textures of the different materials used in this half-timbered building.

The samples of cross-hatching given here are designed to give your hand and eye vital practice — although the exercises are relatively simple, complete control of the pen is essential. The samples will also reveal whether your paper and pen are suitable for the technique before you embark on our drawing project for this lesson.

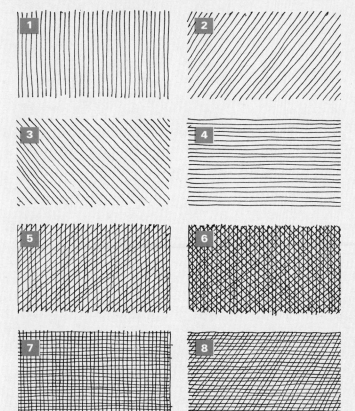

1 Holding the pen vertically, and starting from the top, draw a series of evenly-spaced vertical parallel lines.

2 Here the lines are again parallel, but this time they are angled at about 45º to the vertical. The pen starts drawing at top left and ends at bottom right.

3 Mirror-image of **2**. Both samples will vary according to whether the artist is right or lefthanded.

4 Simple horizontal parallel lines. These lines are important where a predominant horizontal characteristic is obvious, whether on land or sea. The pen can be held at 45º to the paper, or vertically.

5 Samples **1-4** are the basic lines. Here the cross-hatching begins. Vertical lines as in **1** are

cross-hatched with lines as in **2**. The spacing should be as regular as possible, but don't use a ruler as this produces uncomfortably artificial tones.

6 Here samples **1**, **2** and **3** come together in a three-part texture. Notice how the tone darkens where the lines wobble and come together. Similarly, as the lines part the tone lightens.

7 This texture, using lines **1** and **4**, may seem the most obvious to draw, yet the resulting quality is most insistent and the squares seem to describe a texture rather then a tone. However, as soon as a diagonal is introduced the tone reads in a more gentle way.

8 Here the horizontal and diagonal produce a more gentle texture but a similar tone to that found in **7**.

9 Here the first stage involves vertical lines, but the second stage involves lines at only 10º or 20º from the vertical. This finer variation in direction increases the tonal quality and reduces the obvious texture.

10 If the two sets of lines of **9** are repeated, a third line will both darken and enrich the tonal value of the whole area.

11 Sample **9** and the addition of the lines added in **10** have a fourth set laid over them at about 35º from the vertical.

12 Here a fifth line is added at about 35º from the vertical as in **11**, but this time in the opposite direction. The texture of the white spaces becomes finer as the number of lines in the cross-hatching increases.

13 All the previous examples involved complete lines. Here

the lines consist of dashes; the diagonal set creates a hit-and-miss relationship with the vertical set, and the white spaces produce texture.

14 Here the lines are made in short batches in different directions. By overlapping the batches a tonal ripple runs through the sample. This technique is suitable for herringbone brickwork, but in another context could represent a grassy field.

15 A variation on **14** involves rows of short marks in the same direction.

16 Here each direction of line is drawn from left to right. Eight different directions are superimposed, each starting one-eighth of the total area further to the right. The result is a fine gradation of tone, useful for modelling form.

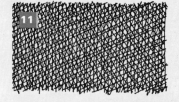

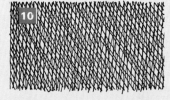

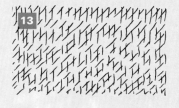

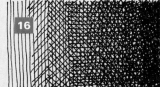

DRAGON HALL

The subject of our drawing project for this lesson is Dragon Hall in Norwich. Its timber-frame construction provides a pattern of textures ideal for an exercise in cross-hatching. The final result is a composition of timeless appeal.

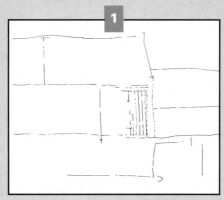

1 Look at the proportions of the building carefully, then sketch in the ridge of the roof, the gutter line, the line where the bottom of the first floor overhangs the street and the main ground line where the building meets the pavement. Draw in the main vertical wall where the lower part of the building meets the main building. Don't worry if your lines aren't completely straight — the beauty of an old building is that it is often crooked, so any wobbliness in your lines won't matter at all.

Next, indicate the position of the main vertical beams, starting from the wall where the different levels meet. Draw vertical lines to indicate the position of the drainpipe and the vertical of the tiles as you look at the roof of the building (the other lines of tiles will be drawn slightly sloping because of the effects of perspective).

M A T E R I A L S

cartridge paper
Rotring art pen with a fine (F) tip
black, water-soluble ink cartridges

2 Draw in the remaining verticals, windows and doors, adding details such as window panes and the chimney stack as you go. Notice how the tiles of the roof slope away from the first vertical drawn. The roof of the smaller building will slope even further over on the righthand side. In a building of this sort there is a clear logic in the spacing of beams and plaster infills, but don't make the drawing mechanical by assuming that all the beams and spaces are equal — there will be variations and bends in the timber.

3 The darkest and richest tones will be the windows. Begin the cross-hatching by filling in each pane with a fine set of vertical lines. Note how this immediately begins to bring your drawing to life. Next, draw short runs of vertical lines down the beams and along the tarred base of the building. Start to bring out the passageway between the two parts of the building in the same way. Begin to indicate the individual roof tiles using wavy lines and areas of vertical hatching. Don't use straight horizontals or the roof will look unrealistic.

4 Add a second range of lines to the window panes, and begin to cross-hatch other areas. Some of the line directions may lie in the structural direction of the object — as with the beams — but some may ignore structure and simply be applied to increase tonal depth. Hatch lines following the perspective direction of the passageway, and develop parts of the roof, diagonally hatching across patches of tiles. Indicate the brickwork on the end wall with single lines, and add tone to the brickwork between the beams.

5 Develop the cross-hatching on areas in shadow such as the side of the chimney, under the gutter and windows and under overhanging beams. Suggest curtains in the windows of the lower building by darkening the middle part of the window. The infill between the beams on the lower part of the building is made of herringbone brickwork and suggested by zig-zag hatching. Finally, develop the roof, and strengthen any edges or tones which appear too gentle.

> Working with pen is close work, so stand back from your drawing to see the effect — overall the whole building must be convincing as a complete structure. Remember to preserve some untouched areas of white paper, for other areas will look richer by contrast.

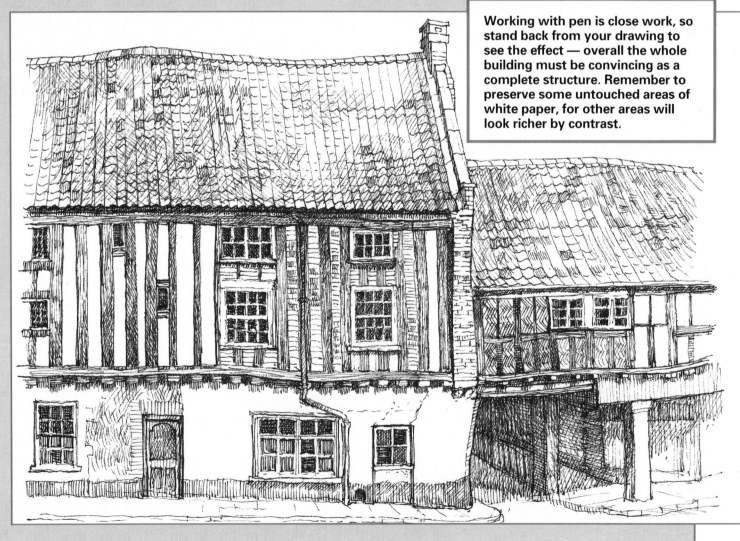

PASTELS

Pastels are a wonderful medium offering a wide range of colours and tremendous scope for experimenting. In this lesson we show you how to combine pastels to produce interesting textural effects, and use some of these techniques in an attractive drawing of tulips.

I f you look at the pastel works of Degas, you will see how he loved to experiment with different techniques. He used dark colours over light colours, and light colours over dark with equal ease. This versatility of pastels can be a great help to the beginner. Whereas over-working paint can damage the paper, mistakes or a change of plan are easy to put right with pastel. That doesn't mean that pastel work itself is easy — it takes patience and practice to arrive at the the results you are aiming for.

The right pastel

There are two types of pastel — the original crumbly chalky pastels and the more recent oil pastels. Oil pastels are quite different from the chalky ones; they are less subtle and harder to blend. In this lesson we are dealing with chalk pastels only. These can be divided into three grades — hard, medium and soft. The darker colours tend to be hard and the paler colours soft. Each grade has its advantages, and we have used all three in our project drawing of tulips. Hard pastels are good for sharp outlines and picking out detail, while soft pastels are useful for large areas of blended colour. Medium pastels are particularly suited to highlighting, shading and textural work. But there are no set rules — the best way of finding out the different uses of each type of pastel is by experimenting yourself.

Soft pastels are messy and make a lot of dust. Pin your paper to a drawing board held in an upright position, to avoid smudging your colours, and cover the floor to protect it. You'll have to remove the paper wrapping on your pastels to get full use from each stick, and this means your fingers will also get dusty as you work. Keep a damp cloth or tissues handy to wipe your fingers between different pastels or you could ruin the clarity of your colours.

The bright, clear colours of late summer flowers are vividly portrayed in this pastel drawing of 'Blue vase and yellow flowers' by Kay Gallwey, *above*. We also use pastels for our project drawing of tulips, *left*.

Think big when working with pastels. They are ideal for working on a grand scale, so use a large sheet of paper for practising these basic techniques that will give you an indication of what you can achieve with pastels.

1 Blending

Blending produces the soft, subtle tones that are unique to pastels. Shade different colours next to each other, interlacing some of the strokes so they merge. Then gently blend with your fingertips. This is the best method of blending as the pressure can be controlled very precisely. Use a torchon for fine detail.

2 Side of stick

It is easier to use the side of the stick to cover large areas. This produces an interesting texture especially on a roughly finished watercolour paper. You can use one colour on top of another and then either leave them, or blend or partially blend them.

3 Blending and using the side of stick

You can use these techniques together for a textured effect over an area of lightly blended colour. Either use the side of a dark stick over pale blended pastel or pale pastel over a dark area.

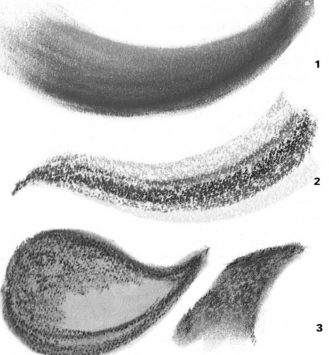

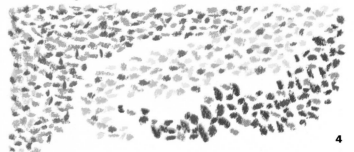

MATERIALS

Pastels

Pastels come in an enormous range of colours and sizes. As they are expensive it's sensible to choose just the colours you need for your first picture. You can build up your collection as you progress.

Paper

Good quality paper is essential for pastel drawing. Try Ingres paper which has a faint linear pattern and comes in a variety of subtle colours. Canson is also good and has a slightly mottled finish. Rough pressed watercolour paper is ideal for a textured finish and can be obtained in one or two pastel shades as well as white. You can use coloured paper to enhance the picture but a pastel drawing can also look very striking on a white background.

Putty rubber

A very soft rubber which removes colour.

Tissues

Useful for blending thin layers of pastel and also for removing unwanted layers of overworked pastel.

Torchon

A torchon looks like a paper pencil. It is used for blending, and is particularly useful for areas of fine detail. You can make your own by rolling a piece of paper very tightly and securing it with glue.

Fixative

Spray finished work to prevent smudging. Even after fixing you need to handle your drawing with care.

4 Pointillism

This was originally an extreme form of Impressionism but is also suitable for pastels. The colours are not mixed on the paper but placed next to each other in small dots. When you look at the picture from a distance, your eye blends the dots or points to form one colour. Look at the works of the French painter Seurat to get an idea of the effect of pointillism.

5 Line build up

This is a similar technique to pointillism, but uses lines instead of dots to create one colour. Using lines of complementary or contrasting colours close together gives attractive results.

TULIP SONATA

The unique soft, matt quality of pastels is particularly suitable for natural subjects such as these tulips. Use a large sheet of paper to give you space for long, flowing strokes to convey the sinuous natural contours of the leaves, stems and petals. Working on a large scale will also make blending the colours easier.

1 Draw out the composition carefully in pencil.

2 Go over the outline of the flowers in dark red. A soft pastel was used here for its rough, textured line. Outline the leaves and stems in pale green hard pastel and draw the stamen of the central tulip in hard white.

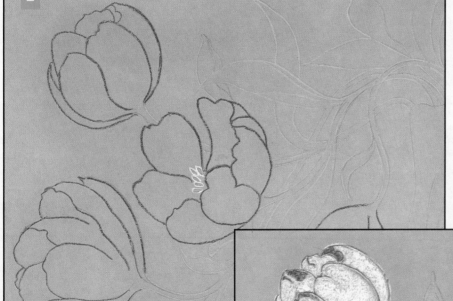

3 Roughly fill in the tulip petals with dark red and soft white. Break the pastels and then use the side of the stick for filling in. The darker colours are a lot stronger than the light colours so use less of the red. Fill in all of the stems and most of the leaves with medium pale green.

M A T E R I A L S

Grey-green Ingres paper 23.5 x 18 inches
soft pastels in white, dark red, dark green, turquoise, yellow ochre and pale yellow
hard pastels in white and pale green
medium pastel in pale green
pencil and eraser
tissues and fixative

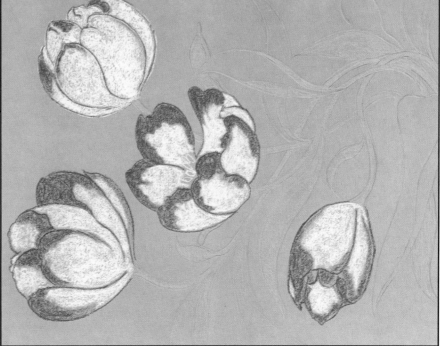

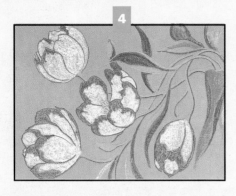

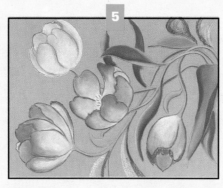

colour or refine the texture. If you get too much build up of pastel, remove it with a tissue to reveal the base colour and start again.

4 Add dark green to the leaves and the underside of the stems, yellow and ochre to the leaf on the far right and turquoise to the centre of the leaf in front of it. If you wish you can add a little turquoise to the centre of the other leaves.

5 Now start blending with your fingertips. Take the strokes in the direction of the growth of the petal or leaf, and leave some parts unblended or only partially blended, as with the leaves *top right* and *bottom centre*. More pastel can be added to change the

6 All that blending will have smudged a lot of your textured outlines so draw them in again. Use the side of a soft, dark pastel to add texture and depth where it is needed, for example in the flower centres. Use the side or end of a white or pale yellow pastel for highlights on the tops of leaves, stems and petals. Colour the stamen with yellow and ochre. When you are happy with the result, spray lightly with fixative to help stop the pastel smudging.

When using pastels, remember to work on a large scale as it's difficult to blend colour in a small area. Draw your tulips boldly and freely — your completed drawing will make an attractive wall decoration.

SKETCHING OUTDOORS

Pastel is a versatile medium for outdoor sketching, giving you a range of marks from fine lines to grainy masses of colour which can be used to match the variety of textures and colours to be found in the natural landscape.

Unlike paints, pastels have to be mixed on the paper and, while it is possible to achieve subtle colorations by interweaving and overlaying colours, it often pays to take a bolder, broadly impressionistic approach. Sometimes you will need to exaggerate colour relationships in order to clarify your drawing and obtain effective contrasts of light and shade — but if the tones are carefully judged they will appear to be correctly balanced overall.

Colours for landscape work

For outdoor sketching you need to choose pastels in a colour range that takes into account the predominance of greens in the landscape. However, greens in nature vary widely, and your pastel selection will only represent relative values (yellow-green, blue-green, grey-green) rather than precise equivalents. Further variation can be achieved using other pure hues to enhance or modify the impression. For example, in order to depict the highlights of a grassy field in full sunlight the best effect might be produced by using touches of pure yellow.

Complementary colours are useful for subtle tones and to bring life to shaded areas, so include red and violet in your selection to balance the greens. Earth colours, including yellow ochre, burnt sienna and burnt umber, are also natural choices for a 'landscape palette'. You may need black to develop the density of branches and foliage in full shade, but use it sparingly or it will deaden, rather than darken, other colours.

As the sky may occupy more than half your picture you need blue and white, but re-creating the complexity of light will also require colours from grey to purple and gold, pale orange and pink. On the following page we describe various ways of portraying trees and skies — inevitably the main features of many outdoor sketches.

This attractive impression of a 'Greenhouse at Norton Conyers' by Lesley Fotherby, *above*, is an excellent example of how a few bold strokes of pastel can suggest the wild beauty of nature in an overgrown garden. This drawing was done on grey paper, large areas of which show through to enhance the loosely applied areas of colour.

In our project drawing for this lesson, *left*, we show you how to achieve a wide variety of tones and textures using a relatively limited palette of colours.

SKY STUDIES

When sketching outdoors it is a good idea to make quick studies of the sky. Pick your colours carefully — cobalt blue has a relatively warm quality which enhances summer skies, while cerulean blue is colder. Note how colours change — pale blue can appear quite intense until juxtaposed with a stronger colour which can make it seem almost white.

1

2

3

4

1 In reality fluffy white clouds have well-defined edges and distinctive shapes. However, hard edges look unnatural in a drawing, so use your pastels to create a solid impression. Here strong white highlights are blended with subtle grey and mauve shading.

2 Individual clouds over a lighter sky-cover are depicted using warm and cool blue pastels, together with white and touches of mauve, all applied in the same direction. This sample is on white paper which gives the sky a lighter quality.

3 Heavily applied and lightly hatched pink, purple and grey tints suggest a threatening, stormy sky — and the intensity of hue and tone provides contrast with the greens of the landscape.

4 A rising or setting sun lights the sky directly above the horizon. Pale orange-yellow blends into blue to suggest the clear quality of sunrise. Sunset colours are more pink or golden. Mid-beige paper shows through the blue, adding to the effect.

TREE STUDIES

There is an overwhelming mass of detail in a single tree, but individual elements are less obvious from a distance. Start by defining the general shapes and patterns of branches and foliage, then use pastel marks to create texture and tone, as in these samples.

1

2

3

4

1 Different greens have been applied to define the shape and colour of the foliage. Don't work your sketch too densely or you will lose any definition of form. Blocking in patches of sky helps to open up a shape that has become too solid and indistinct.

2 With a mass of trees standing together, try to identify clear differences of colour, shape and texture.

3 An unusual silhouette can form an interesting focal point for a composition. Use bold, crisp strokes to delineate tree trunks and branches.

4 Trees on the horizon should be seen as a series of simple shapes. Blue tints subtly merge with darker greens to enhance the sense of distance, and the pale 'halo' effect around them suggests backlighting.

RUIN IN THE WOODS

The subject of our drawing project for this lesson is a ruined archway in the woods. Soft pastels are the ideal medium for this type of drawing because of their rich, vibrant colours and subtle blending qualities. It will be helpful to practise the tree studies on the previous page before starting this drawing.

1 Using the sepia grey pastel, outline the ruined archway and draw in the trunk of the tree on the left. Change to the red earth pastel and outline the trees to the right of the archway and the two overlapping trees on the left. Switch to the olive green and outline the undergrowth in the left foreground, and one side of the remaining tree to the left of the archway. Then outline the foliage on the right with emerald green and use the same colour to complete the olive green tree.

M A T E R I A L S

Bockingford watercolour pad
Rowney Artists' Soft Pastels: lizard green (tint 5) and sap green (tint 1 and tint 5)
set of 24 Conté Soft Pastels to include the following: light blue (29), scarlet (28), golden ochre (63), Prussian green (43), emerald green (34), mineral green (30), light green (08), olive green (16), red earth (31), natural umber (54), blue grey (72), sepia grey (42), light grey (20) and white (13)
fixative spray

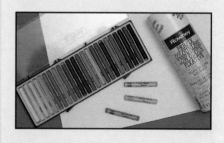

2 Using light blue, shade in the area where the sky is visible behind the trees on the left, then work over this with white. Now block in the background foliage using sap green tint 1 and gently smudge it with your fingertips to soften the edges. Add a few darker marks on top of this using the side of sap green tint 5, then using the pastel in the same way, add hints of golden ochre where the foliage meets the sky.

Very lightly shade in the foreground using light green worked on top of lizard green tint 5.

3 Begin working on the archway by covering the whole arch in light grey. Build up the colour in several layers. Create the effect of brickwork and the dark shadows under the arch using sepia grey, then indicate further shadows by using a combination of Prussian green and blue grey. Using Prussian green, emerald green and a little red earth, suggest the ivy and other creepers using a series of dots and tiny dashes. Block in the tree on the left with sepia grey and the remaining trees with red earth, leaving some of the white paper showing through.

4 Continue building up layers of colour on the tree trunks and branches, first using Prussian green, then hatching with sepia grey and emerald green. Establish the direction of the light by putting sap green tint 1 on the righthand side of the trees. With sap green tint 5 and a few strokes of emerald green, indicate the paler tones of distant trees through the archway.

Increase the amount of foliage on the archway by adding dots of olive green, emerald green and mineral green. Work on the foreground next, using light green to highlight areas of foliage and mineral green to define leaves and plants.

5 Intensify the highlights on the trees using overlaid sap green tint 1 and a little lizard green tint 5. Gently blend the greens with your fingertips. Now begin to depict the canopy of leaves using stippled strokes and dots of mineral green, olive green and light green.

Return to the foreground and, using a combination of emerald green and mineral green, start to re-define the ferns and build up the shadows and darker plants. Introduce lizard green tint 5 to highlight some of the leaves, and suggest a few red berries in the right foreground using scarlet.

6 Work over the drawing as a whole to strengthen tones and textures and create depth. Add a few light strokes of natural umber to the brickwork of the arch then, using sap green tint 1 and a few tiny dots of lizard green tint 5, highlight the ivy and other creepers.

Using a similarly loose technique, add bright highlights of lizard green tint 5 to the tree foliage and undergrowth, gently smudging and blending as you go. Finally, pull out some of the stronger leaf shapes among the trees — particularly on the branches of the tree in the right foreground — and in the foreground using emerald green and Prussian green. When you are satisfied with the result, spray lightly with fixative.

You can see from this drawing how it is possible to achieve a rich intensity of colour by using different layers of pastel. A convincing impression of a natural scene has been depicted by overlaying different greens and highlighting with natural earth colours and peacock hues such as emerald green and Prussian blue.

NATURAL SURFACES

In previous lessons we have shown you how to use Conté crayons and pastels to produce soft, luxurious effects. Oil pastels are another variation on the dry pastel and chalk range, and in this lesson we show you how to get the best out of them, and how to portray dry, crumbly surfaces such as sand and cliffs.

Oil pastels are made from a mixture of pigment, wax and animal fat. Because they are wax-based they have certain characteristics in common with wax crayons, but they contain more pigment and become quite soft and malleable in warm temperatures.

Because of their creamy, oily texture, oil pastels produce rich colours which react with paper of different tone and texture to produce a variety of results. Any good quality paper is suitable, but a cool, grey colour provides an ideal neutral base — white paper tends to show through oil pastels, leaving white 'spots' which 'jump' and destroy the tonal unity of a drawing. Natural textures such as dry, crumbly cliff faces and sandy beaches are best depicted on sugar paper, or any paper with quite a rough, absorbent surface, as this will produce a looser texture — only the raised parts of the paper collecting the colour.

As with most artist's materials, each manufacturer has their own particular range of colours, so it is a good idea to stick to a set of pastels from one maker. Some manufacturers will use more pigment in their oil pastels than others, so the tonal effect of a drawing will alter if you switch between brands. A set of 24 oil pastels will provide you with a good range of colours.

Oil pastels can be blended and mixed directly on your drawing surface and, unlike dry pastels and chalks, don't need to be fixed — although you should take care not to rub them too hard. On the following pages we show you samples of application techniques and, in this lesson's project drawing, how to portray a rugged coastline.

In this drawing entitled 'Seascape' by W. Innes, *above left*, oil pastels are used to depict a whole range of natural surfaces by overlaying and blending colours to produce different tones and textures. Our project drawing of cliffs, *below*, uses the same techniques.

Oil pastels can be applied and blended straight on to the paper, as shown in the exercises on this page. Samples 1-8 demonstrate simple three-colour effects produced using two colours, while samples 9-16 introduce a wider range of colours and techniques. These exercises were all produced on a heavy weight grey sugar paper using the colours and techniques that you will need for this lesson's project drawing.

1 In this sample dark purple is applied to form a solid patch (left). Because of its texture, some of the paper still shows through. White is applied in the same way (right) and then worked back over the purple to produce an entirely different purple (centre), rather than just a paler version of the original.

2 Dark purple is applied as in **1**, but this time it is paired with Indian red. The area of overlap has a darker tone.

3 Brown and white produce a pinker combination. When you want a gentle colour, start with a stronger version and overwork it with a paler pastel. This changes a dark tone to a mid-tone. Here white has softened the dark brown considerably.

4 The brown is as in sample **3** but a pale salmon colour has been substituted for the white. The mixed result is similar to **3**, only slightly warmer.

5 Blue and yellow combine to make green, and the particular type of green depends on the two starting colours.

6 In this sample the blue is the same as in **5** but this time it is combined with an orange/ochre to make a warmer green. As you select colours, think whether you need them to be cool (blue) or warm (towards the orange/red side) and mix them accordingly.

7 Not all combinations need to be obvious or harsh. Here soft cerulean blue is paired with grey. Because the tones are similar, the gradation is gentle.

8 The two blues here combine to form a variation of both, working together to form a gentle gradation from one to the other without producing a third colour, as in the previous samples. This characteristic of oil pastels is invaluable when drawing skies.

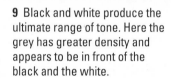

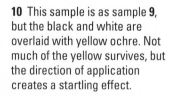

9 Black and white produce the ultimate range of tone. Here the grey has greater density and appears to be in front of the black and the white.

10 This sample is as sample **9**, but the black and white are overlaid with yellow ochre. Not much of the yellow survives, but the direction of application creates a startling effect.

11 Here a solid patch of lemon yellow is overworked with a few loose marks of green, and both are then overworked with lemon yellow. The overlaid yellow mixes the first two colours together to produce an apple green that appears to stand out in front of them.

12 Yellow is applied as in **11**, but here random strokes of Indian red are applied using different pressures. Overlaid lemon yellow again creates an advancing effect. This is useful for modelling form.

13 Here a soft turquoise blue provides the bed for two paler blues producing a gently varied soft blue. Lines of purple are then drawn across it and 'float' in the blue void. Pale blue is then drawn across these lines, blurring them and taking the colour on through them. Oil pastels pick up some of the colour they pass over — here traces of white have been picked up at the bottom of the mark — and these trace elements add life to a drawing.

14 In this sample three blues are laid in patches with jabs of Indian red floating across them.

15 Soft salmon is cross-hatched in several colours to produce tone and texture.

16 Here the same background is overworked with blue and yellow cross-hatching. The variegated green base acts as a texture over which more complex shapes can be drawn.

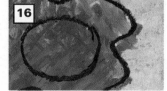

RUGGED CLIFFS

This rugged coastline of crumbling cliffs and sandy beaches — with its strongly contrasting forms and tones — provides an ideal subject for oil pastel drawing. Their rich colours and bold lines perfectly capture the textures of nature, and if you are drawing from life oil pastels have the added advantage of being sandproof!

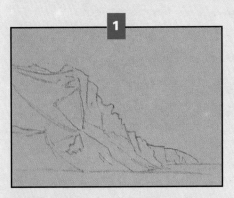

COLOUR KEY

1	2	3
4	5	6
7	8	9
10	11	12
13	14	15

1 purple	9 strong blue
2 dark brown	10 olive green
3 white	11 Indian red
4 golden yellow	12 pale grey
5 cerulean blue	13 black
6 blue	14 lemon yellow
7 pale turquoise	15 green
8 salmon pink	

M A T E R I A L S

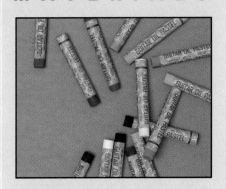

heavy weight grey sugar paper
set of oil pastels with colours
equivalent to those used here (see
colour chart, *left*)

1 Using the top, angled edge of the purple pastel, lightly draw the outline of all the main shapes. With a subject such as crumbling cliffs you don't need to worry about being too precise — it is the general shape that is important.

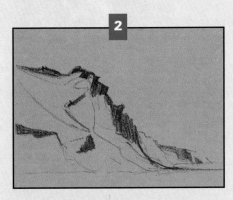

2 Lightly apply dark brown to the areas of the cliffs that appear to be in deepest shadow, and carry the shadow of the highest part of the cliff down on to the beach.

3 Look at the clouds and see how they are positioned in relation to the cliffs — if you are drawing from life, catch them as they move towards you otherwise an arrangement that suits your composition will pass out of sight too quickly. In this case draw a white outline diagonally from the top of the cliffs and shade in the lightest areas. Also shade white patches on the lightest areas of the cliff and the beach. Soften some of the lower clouds with golden

yellow, and use the same colour to shade areas of sliding sand on the sloping part of the cliff. Now begin to develop the sky, using gentle

shading in cerulean blue for the lower part, and blue and pale turquoise to develop the stronger upper areas.

4 You can now begin to block shade the remaining parts of the outline. Use salmon pink on the upper left cliffs and foreground beach, then use strong blue to define the main areas where the cliffs are in shadow — the far right, middle and bottom left foreground. Next use olive green for the grass at the top left and down the face of the cliffs on the far right. Use Indian red to strengthen areas where the rocks can be seen through the grass. Darken the crevices with purple, and run this down on to the beach.

Start to overlay white on lighter areas, and develop the clouds and sky with pale grey. Don't worry if your drawing looks rather crude at this stage; these are the basic layers over which you will blend other colours to model form.

5 Re-work the landslip area on the left and the sunlit areas on the cliffs on the far right using salmon pink. Use white to increase any pale tones and Indian red to warm the shaded areas. Lemon yellow in the foreground and on the distant cliffs modifies the light, while purple strengthens the cliffs and strong blue is added to deepen the upper sky.

Modify the olive green applied at Step 4 with touches of green, then add Indian red hatching on the rocks in the foreground and centre. Use black to re-define the original outline, deepen the tone of the areas in shade and to form the rocks on the beach in the foreground. Continue working over the drawing until you are satisfied with the result.

Your completed drawing is built up from many overlaid colours. Each layer covers more of the paper and builds a creamy texture, and it is the contrast between the smooth areas and the parts where the paper shows through that gives the drawing its natural vitality.

PATTERNS OF LANDSCAPE

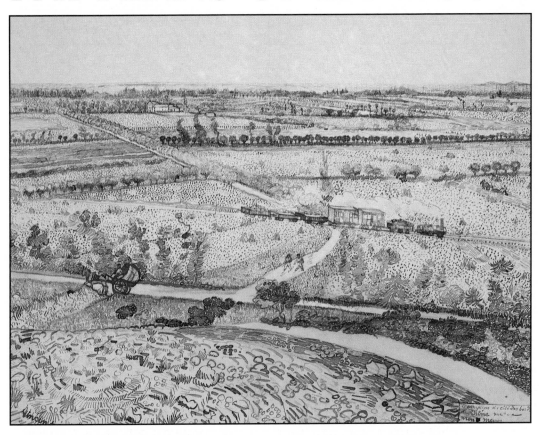

This pen-and-ink drawing entitled 'The countryside on the banks of the Rhône' by Vincent Van Gogh (1853-1890), *left*, shows how, from a bird's eye view, an arable landscape is transformed into a clearly-defined pattern of fields and hedges. This patchwork effect is broken only by the sweep of the river and the rise of the hill in the foreground. This view of the countryside is enhanced by Van Gogh's gentle modelling of nature's textures achieved through dots, dashes and lines drawn using subtle brown tones.

When you look down from the window of an aeroplane and see the countryside spread out beneath you, you will often see that fields, mountains and rivers take on a different aspect, and formal geometric patterns emerge. In this lesson we show you how to use the natural patterns of a mountain range to create an interesting 'structural' composition.

Rocks and mountains have underlying structural systems. Over millions of years rock faces become weathered and the overall shape frequently echoes the planes or strata found in one hand-size piece of rock. When you look at a mountain range you will see that there is a rhythm to the ridges and, although jagged and uneven, the planes are usually at right angles to one another. When drawing the structural pattern of a mountainous landscape — as in our project drawing, *right* — geometric shapes will form the basis of the drawing. By emphasising the way the light falls on the surface of rocks and creates shadows in crevices, you will be able to build up a three-dimensional 'map' of the landscape.

The amount of textural detail you include will vary, depending on how close you are to the mountains. At first glance a mountain range appears like a wall — and trees become areas of flat colour. It is the tonal areas that create form and indicate earth formations — texture is not important.

Colour plays a vital role. It gives a graphic landscape a sense of perspective and is a useful device for delineating the line where foreground meets background. Aerial perspective is particularly apparent when looking at a mountain range from a distance, and this can be depicted by using cool blues in the background and stronger colours in the foreground.

In nature light effects often change too quickly to capture. However, if the framework of shapes is drawn quickly with pencil or pen-and-ink, the development of colour can be added later. Our project drawing of the Alps combines a pen-and-ink structural drawing made on the spot with the effects of colour added from memory.

Our project drawing, *below*, is a view of the Alps done using a combination of pen-and-ink line drawing and gouache paint. As with Van Gogh's landscape, *above left*, geometric patterns, texture and tone combine in a satisfying composition of a natural landscape.

On this page we show you how to build pattern and tone using simple colours within a pen-and-ink framework. In a drawing showing the patterns of a landscape, areas of colour need to be bold and smooth. Gouache paints are ideal for this — similar to watercolours, gouache paints contain added glycerine, making them thicker and more soluble. This quality makes them suitable for flat, uniform areas of opaque colour.

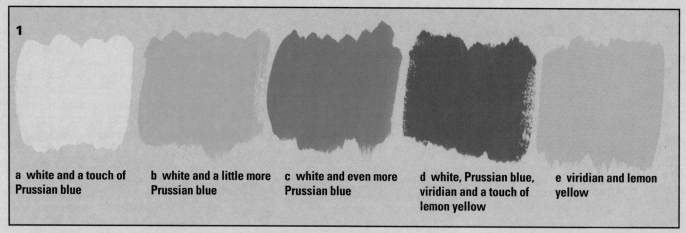

1

a white and a touch of Prussian blue

b white and a little more Prussian blue

c white and even more Prussian blue

d white, Prussian blue, viridian and a touch of lemon yellow

e viridian and lemon yellow

1 The samples **a-e** *above* are the colour mixes used in this lesson's drawing project. Note how there is not only a colour change, but also a tonal change. Samples **a-d** have a progressively darker tone, while **e** has a tonal value similar to **b**.

2 In this example the paint is applied in a similar way to the way you would use coloured pencil or pastel. The marks made retain the ground paper as a texture.

3 The relationship between line and colour is important, for the

2

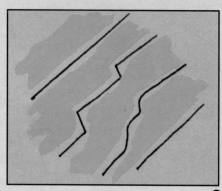

3

line should remain as a dominant part of the whole structure. Stop

the paint well short of the pen line, and leave the edge uneven.

EXPERIMENTING WITH COLOUR

In many compositions the initial colour scheme may not always be the most successful. Experimenting with colour can create surprising changes in the mood and atmosphere of a

picture. The line elements may be exactly the same, but the colour can be varied. Here, a range of oranges brings a warm glow to the whole scene, **1**.

Using blues with a dramatic change of tone in the sky, **2**, can evoke night time — the land lit by the moon — or storm clouds.

A single colour and white (monochrome) can be very effective when dealing with tone. In this example, **3**, the white seems to suggest snow on the uppermost rock faces.

The colour possibilities are endless, yet they all stem from a single pen-and-ink line drawing.

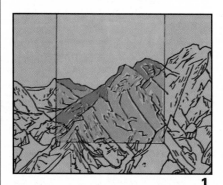

1

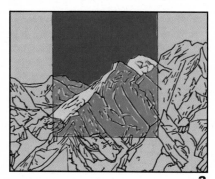

2

3

ALPINE LANDSCAPE

The natural landscape has always been a source of inspiration for the artist. In our project drawing for this lesson we take a new look at this traditional subject, concentrating on the patterns formed by the structure of a mountain range in order to create a pleasing — almost abstract — composition.

1 Using pen-and-ink, draw the outline of the mountain peaks and the pattern formed by the fields in the foreground. Try and maintain a rhythm in the ridges, making the 'direction' of the rocky outcrops either 45⁰ to the vertical or at right angles to each other. Keep the shapes in the foreground simple, gradually fragmenting them towards the background.

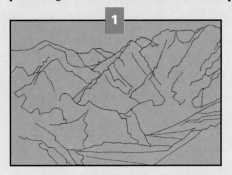

M A T E R I A L S

heavyweight grey sugar paper
Rotring art pen with a fine (F) tip
Rotring ink cartridges
designer's gouache paints: white,
Prussian blue, lemon yellow, viridian
watercolour paintbrush, size 6
palette
water jar and water
tissues

2 Individual areas of the mountain can now be developed. Use short, directional lines, following the lines of the rock strata. Keep the foreground areas simple, as in step 1, adding more detail to the broken, jagged rocks on the sides of the furthermost mountain ridges.

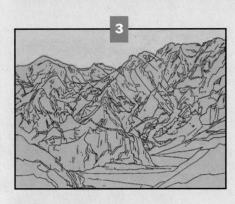

3 Mix a pale blue to match colour sample **a** on the opposite page using white and Prussian blue. Paint this colour over the sky area but don't take it right up to the line of the mountain top — leave a slight gap where sky and mountain meet.

4 Using white and a little more Prussian blue, mix a slightly stronger blue to match sample **b** on the opposite page. Lay this colour over areas of the mountain in bright, but not full, light. Leave areas of grey paper showing through to create texture. This will add considerably to the overall look of the complicated rocky surface.

5 Mix the darkest blue to match sample **c** on page 274 by adding a little more Prussian blue to the paint mix used in step 4. Keeping the brushstrokes loose and the texture broken, paint in the parts of the mountain that fall in shadow, following the direction of the pen-and-ink lines.

6 Paint in groups of 'trees' in the foreground and middle distance using the dark green mixed from white, Prussian blue, viridian and lemon yellow as in sample **d**. Apply the paint in vertical strokes, overworking the marks but leaving parts of the paper showing through here and there.

7 The pale green is mixed from viridian and lemon yellow — as in sample **e**. Use this to paint flat blocks of colour in the foreground fields and valley bottom. With the pale blue paint mix used in step 3 and broken brushstrokes, paint in the rock faces that are in brightest light. Leave the picture to dry.

Using pen-and-ink, draw lines to strengthen the main ridges where the central focus of the composition lies. Finally, add short, vertical ink lines to the green tree areas to indicate slight texture.

When you have completed your picture stand back and look at it from a slight distance. You will be surprised at the amount of information it is possible to convey by 'mapping-out' the pattern of the landscape using the minimum of detail and colour.

INDEX